MURDER ON THE HOME FRONT

MURDER ON THE HOME FRONT

A True Story of Morgues, Murderers and Mystery in the Blitz

Molly Lefebure

ISIS
LARGE PRINT
Oxford

First published in Great Britain 1954
by
Heinemann Books

Published in Large Print 2014 by ISIS Publishing Ltd.,
7 Centremead, Osney Mead, Oxford OX2 0ES
by arrangement with
Little, Brown Book Group
an Hachette UK Company

CIP data is available for this title from the British Library

ISBN 978–0–7531–5346–8 (hb)
ISBN 978–0–7531–5347–5 (pb)

Printed and bound in Great Britain by
T. J. International Ltd., Padstow, Cornwall

CONTENTS

ACKNOWLEDGMENTS

The author wishes especially to thank Dr Keith Simpson for generously allowing her access to his records.

FOREWORD

by Keith Simpson

Few young journalists can have had the remarkable experience that befell Molly Lefebure on her translation from "crime and news" reporter on a London newspaper to a job then quite unique — private secretary to a pathologist engaged in scientific crime detection in and around the Metropolis. These were the days when Spilsbury was fading and the "Yard" team for crime investigation was plainly due for a reshuffle: a war of chaos was on overhead and the perpetual war against the underworld of crime had nevertheless to be maintained below.

Miss Lefebure, with her delightful flow of interest in people and things, in humour and pathos, in crime and its personalities, discourses here, with both purpose and an engaging restraint, on the colourful days that flowed by so ceaselessly; on people and on strange happenings — stranger indeed than fiction. She did a remarkable job remarkably well, and the following pages bear no small testimony to her intense interest in her singular occupation.

Guy's Hospital,
London.

CHAPTER
ONE

A Good Job for Corpses

The murdered baby had been discovered in a small suitcase. Dr Keith Simpson, Home Office pathologist doing the post-mortem on the child, wanted it photographed in the suitcase exactly as it had been found. So he asked the Southwark mortuary keeper, West, and his secretary, myself, to take the case, complete with baby, round to Guy's Hospital to be photographed.

The case with its pathetic contents was quite heavy, so West carried it while I tripped along beside him. The journey from Southwark mortuary to Guy's was a short one across a desolate bomb-site. As we were walking across here West suddenly began to grin and chortle, as if at a marvellous joke. I asked him what it was and he replied he'd like to see a copper stop us and ask to see what we had in the case.

The notion appalled me. We should certainly look a very desperate couple; a suitcase with a murdered baby in it! Luckily, however, nobody stopped us. (It would have been interesting, of course, to have seen the expression on the face of an eager war-reserve constable, say, had he asked to inspect our bag. P.C. 49 would have been dull entertainment in comparison.)

West and I often joke about this adventure now when we talk over old times; those years when I worked with Keith Simpson in London's public mortuaries on a non-stop round of post-mortems, investigating murders, suicides, manslaughters, infanticides, accidents, criminal abortions, and those multitudinous cases that West calls "straight 'uns".

Besides the non-stop post-mortems were the coroners' courts, the police courts, magistrates' courts, assize courts, the Old Bailey. Frequent visits to Scotland Yard. The work in prisons, hospitals, asylums. The never-ending exploration of London; the alleys and filthy courtyards and tenements of Limehouse, Rotherhithe, Poplar, Shoreditch, Bethnal Green, Whitechapel, Stratford-by-Bow, the amazing no man's land of the suburbs, the ever fascinating backwaters of Kensington, Fulham, Walham Green, Streatham, Battersea, Wandsworth, East Ham, Walthamstow. The West End, a complete and intriguing contrast, plushy, well-washed, but with its sordid secrets in Chelsea, Westminster, Marylebone.

The journeys into the country on murder cases with the bodies in ditches, the bodies in spinneys and copses, the bodies among the cabbages and in squalid cottages, the bodies in pubs and on country cricket pitches, the bodies in select little villas and in old tin barns.

Those endless bodies, anything from ten to twenty-eight in a day, five and sometimes six days a week. All the public mortuaries from Portsmouth to Paddington. Five years of mortuaries, prying into the secrets of thousands, literally thousands, of bodies, each with a tale to tell.

There are people who say corpses don't talk, but indeed they do. They talk of easy lives in pleasant homes, of hard dirty lives in rooms where lice crawl up and down the walls and the ceiling drips, like a decaying skin, in clammy stinking drops to the floor. They talk of hopes that were not fulfilled, joys that ended in sorrow, of tragedy, broken hearts, stupidity, cruelty, depravity, perversion, crime of every kind, and of goodness, devotion, motherhood, sacrifice, every kind of love, everything you have ever thought or heard of and a great many things you would never have imagined in your wildest moments.

There they all are on the p.m. table: the coster's wife who killed herself because her husband sold his pony, the one creature in the world she had ever really loved and been loved by. There is the baby whose mother left it to starve while she had a good time hitting the hay with American soldiers. The little girl whose new party dress caught fire. The old gentleman who lived in Leytonstone sixty years and never departed once from his wife, his job as a railway clerk, his bowls club and the interminable straight and narrow. The soldier who came home on leave to find his wife in bed with another man and gassed himself. The sailor who came home from sea to find his wife in bed with another man and shot her. The old lady who put her head in the gas-oven because she was certain the wireless had given her cancer. The airman who baled out and his parachute didn't open. The bright young thing who didn't want a baby. The tart who picked up a killer for a client. The pansy who couldn't face life any more. The treasurer who embezzled the funds, the typist who discovered she was married to a bigamist. Yes, there they all are.

And my goodness, how they talk! Everything about them talks. The way they look, the way they died, where they died, why they died. In the mortuary, under the skilled hands of Dr Simpson, they yielded up their secrets, talking of everything from natural death to murder.

While sitting beside him at her little table, typing away for dear life, was Miss Lefebure, typing the post-mortem reports which the pathologist dictated as he worked. And in the courts there she was too, taking shorthand notes. There she was in the hospitals, the prisons, at the scenes of crimes. Carrying her notebook and the little buff envelopes into which she popped the hairs and the fibres, the buttons and the cigarette-butts, and all the other small but vital things that are found on or near the bodies and on which a five-day trial at the Old Bailey may ultimately hinge.

"A horrible job. I'd never allow a daughter of mine to do it," declared one of my father's friends.

"A fas-cin-ating job, darling. How I'd adore it!" gasped a girl who worked at the Board of Trade.

"You've a nasty, morbid, unfeminine streak in you, I'm afraid," wrote a boy friend.

"You'll never regret going to work in the mortuaries, Miss Molly," said a coroner's officer of my acquaintance. "You'll find there's never a dull moment with the bodies around. It's a real good job for corpses, seeing as how you're interested in corpses."

But whoever they were, and however they reacted to the job, they all asked me the same question, "How did you get the job?"

I was working as a reporter on a chain of East London suburban weeklies and it was the first year of World War Two. I had earlier taken a secretarial course, to attain good shorthand, and I had studied journalism at London University. Now I was a junior reporter, struggling in the throes of an existence only to be advocated to those training for the Olympic Marathon, or doing penance for some appalling crime. I walked on an average twelve miles a day, at a conservative estimate, worked from eight-thirty in the morning till ten-thirty at night, seven days a week, starting at a pound a week. In my case I was ambitious to be a writer and any person nursing such a lunatic and unwholesome aim in life should be subjected to every chastisement possible, to drive the devil out, as it were.

So for nearly two years I toiled and sweated round the eastern suburbs, covering everything from Boy Scout meetings to the blitz. The assignments I most enjoyed were the court ones: Coroner's Court and Stratford Police Court. The fascination of these places was for me never-ending.

The Coroner's Court was Walthamstow, where Dr P. B. Skeels, then Coroner for Metropolitan Essex, sat twice weekly. Dr Skeels — who unhappily died recently

— was the first coroner I ever met; I came to know him well, and became very fond of him.

Scarlet like a turkey-cock when angry, genial as the sun when in a sociable mood, interested in everything and everybody, energetic, enthusiastic, uncompromising, he was affectionately and loyally regarded by his coroner's officers, who amongst themselves called him "Papa Squeals". He was undoubtedly Victorian, but in the best sense of the term, and everyone who knew him esteemed him. He was scrupulous to a degree, honest, with much dignity when he appeared in court, beautiful manners and strong moral convictions. He applied his high standards to himself as strictly as he applied them to others. He hated thoughtless, indolent people who brought about the death of others, not through vice or malice, but casual couldn't-care-lessness. Such people made him so very angry he would sit in his big chair, scarlet in the face, quite unable to speak for a second or two and indeed nearly choking. I recall a mother who had lightheartedly placed her baby in an iron bath of scalding water. With her Dr Skeels was the image of wrath indeed. But with another mother whose baby had accidentally suffocated in its cot he was all sympathy and kindness and went off into a detailed discourse on why a baby's pillow must be hard, advocating that favourite of his, the hay pillow.

He detested half-liars. A man was once giving evidence upon his alcoholic father, trying hard to avoid making any mention of whisky. "He was addicted to a nightly beverage," explained the devoted son. "Do you by any chance mean whisky?" rapped Dr Skeels. "His favourite beverage," murmured the son. "You would describe whisky as a beverage?" "Yes." "Ah-ah. And your father partook of this . . . ah . . . this . . . er . . . beverage to an excess?" The edge to Dr Skeels' voice was deadly.

Dr Skeels quite often lingered in court after the morning's hearing to chat with the reporters — a courteous gesture which we all appreciated, for too many people treat reporters like bits of something the cat has brought in. On one of these occasions he began talking about Dr Keith Simpson, the young Home Office pathologist who often gave medical evidence at the court. Dr Skeels told us that Dr Simpson had a brilliant career ahead of him, that he was already spoken of as Spilsbury's successor, and was worth watching, "For you should, as pressmen, know who are the up and coming men and he is certainly one of them."

Now I had already for some time been eyeing Dr Simpson with great interest. He certainly looked remarkable; there was a something of genius about him, a hint of lightning flashes and thunderbolts. I frequently mused upon his unique but intriguing occupation, wondering whether cutting up bodies all day long had any effects upon the cutter-upper, so to speak, and I also wondered what it was like in a mortuary and wished I could go in one and view a post-mortem, for I felt I should like to know what I looked like inside.

It was at this point that Dr Simpson came up to me, tapped me on the shoulder and asked me for my secretarial services.

This little scene took place in Walthamstow cemetery — a suitable spot — and quite flabbergasted me, for I had never until then exchanged a word with Dr Simpson, indeed never dreamt he had noted my existence. Yet now he came up to me, said he wanted a word with me, and asked me if I had ever thought of doing secretarial work. I gooped at him.

He went on to assure me he thought I had the qualifications necessary for a medical secretary. I looked him coldly in the eye and turned the offer politely, but firmly, down. I remembered only too well the horror of secretarial work and secretarial young ladies I had developed at secretarial college. Dr Simpson gave me a phone number to ring in case I changed my mind, but I don't think he really expected to hear from me again.

By three that afternoon I had changed my mind.

I had, for one thing, mentioned the offer of this job to a fellow reporter and she had been astounded I had refused it. "You must be crazy. You're interested in crime, you're always saying you'd like to be a crime reporter. Dr Simpson is one of the big crime experts. With him you'd learn masses about crime. It sounds a wonderful job to me."

"But would I ever be any good as a secretary?"

"Oh, you could hold down a secretarial job if you tried."

The other thing that tempted me of course was curiosity. To discover what goes on in mortuaries.

So at twelve p.m. I was offered the job, by three p.m. that same day I had accepted it. Next morning I gave my editor a fortnight's notice and Dr Simpson lent me a book on forensic medicine, with many illustrations of cut-throats, drowners, hangings, shootings, poisonings and the like. Each night, for the next fortnight, after I had finished writing copy for the newspaper I settled down with forensic medicine before I went to bed.

CHAPTER
TWO

My First Day in the Mortuaries

It turned out that no secretary, good, bad, or indifferent, had ever set foot in a mortuary before. I took this pioneer step one early spring day in nineteen-forty-one, and the mortuary was Southwark.

Southwark mortuary stands in St George's churchyard, on the site of the old Marshalsea prison, at the end of the Borough, London's most flavoursome thoroughfare. I travelled there by taxi, and the driver was a bit distant when I asked for Southwark mortuary and said he had no idea where it was. He knew St George's Church, though, so at the church he deposited me. I crossed the churchyard, pulled at the mortuary bell, which clanged and tolled a doleful, old-time ditty, and was quickly ushered through the front door, across the courtyard, through a doorway marked, "Private. Doctors only", into the post-mortem room where Dr Simpson was at work examining two bodies.

He was garbed in a white p.m. (post-mortem) gown, a rubber apron, rubber gloves and white rubber galoshes and was armed with a very large knife, which he brandished genially at me as he bade me good-morning. He then introduced me to a small, quick, dark man who was swabbing the interior of one of the bodies with a sponge. This was West, the mortuary keeper, a celebrated personality, and destined to become one of my greatest friends. But that first morning, eyeing me rather speculatively across the bodies, West merely gave me a polite bow. He has told me since that he was waiting for me to scream, or faint, or throw a fit, but I didn't. "There were two dirty, stinking bodies on that table and I thought, 'Here comes a young woman to work where no woman's ever worked before, and what'll she do?' But you came in smiling, and went on smiling."

Now the truth was that I had been aching to see inside a mortuary, and watch a post-mortem, for a long time, so that I was only too delighted to have at last achieved my ambition, and was much too pleased and excited to think about fainting.

Dr Simpson did two p.ms. at Southwark that morning, and on that first occasion I merely watched him. He explained that in the future I would have to sit close by with the typewriter and type a report which he would dictate to me as he dissected.

The two bodies lay on gleaming white porcelain tables, each body with the head propped on a small wooden block, and Keith Simpson dissected the organs on a small wooden mobile table. West swabbed the bodies, handed instruments, washed and tidied things up as the work progressed. Everything in that white place was very clean. There was a mingled odour of bodies and disinfectant, which at first I found unpleasant, but to which I gradually became acclimatised. The thing about post-mortems which I most disliked in those early days was the sound of a saw raspingly opening a skull.

Post-mortem work in the hands of an expert is amazingly clean, absolutely fascinating, quite devoid of horror. I was lucky to see only experts at work at the beginning; later I occasionally saw students at Guy's trying their hands at the job, and over their efforts I draw a veil. Luckily by that time I was quite hardened. But, of course, everybody has to make a first attempt, whether it be at performing a post-mortem or, shall we say, bathing a baby. There always has to be a start.

On that first day with Dr Simpson I saw post-mortems at Southwark, Hammersmith, Poplar, Leyton and Walthamstow. The cases were all non-inquest, simple cases, "B" cases, the coroners' officers call them. In all, I saw eight post-mortems that first day. They were far too interesting to make me feel ill. Nevertheless it was a strange day. Besides the p.ms. we attended two inquests at Hammersmith, and at lunch-time we went to Guy's Hospital, where Dr Simpson had his headquarters.

The now famous Department of Forensic Medicine at Guy's had not at that time come into being, but Dr Simpson, who was Assistant Curator to the Gordon Museum at Guy's, had already an embryo forensic medicine department in the Museum. It was in the Curator's office that we did all our filing, report writing, correspondence and so forth, amidst a gleaming array of specimen jars in which floated grotesque babies, slashed wrists, ruptured hearts, stomach ulcers, lung cancers, bowel tumours, cerebral aneurisms and the like. Here, too, we generally took afternoon tea, with the one and only Ireland, the Museum assistant.

Yes, that first day on my new job seemed strange, and I arrived back at my digs that evening feeling pretty tired. But very pleased with myself, because I had been in mortuaries, and watched post-mortems, and, moreover, not felt ill.

My landlady was waiting for me, all agog. "Did you see any of those dreadful post-mortems?" she asked.

"Yes, eight."

"Eight? Never!"

And making noises of disapproval she went to fetch my dinner, the centrepiece of which was a dish of chops.

When she brought in those chops I realised, with a jerk, that I must either eat them, resolutely, or become a vegetarian for life.

Somehow or other, I ate them.

"Well, dear," said my landlady, popping in presently to see how I was getting on, "would you like another chop?"

I said no, thank you.

"Oh, I hope this awful job isn't going to affect your appetite."

I replied firmly that I had no intention of letting it do anything of the sort, but I felt I had eaten enough chops for the evening. And turned my attention, with relief, to stewed fruit and junket . . .

CHAPTER
THREE

Life in the Mortuaries

The world of coroners, courts and mortuaries in those days was very definitely overshadowed by a Great Man; a modest, unassuming Great Man, but Great, for all that. He, of course, was Sir Bernard Spilsbury.

I was introduced to Sir Bernard at Hackney Coroner's Court, about a fortnight after I had started work with Keith Simpson. "Spilsbury" had become such a legend it was difficult to believe there really was a man, Spilsbury. I had always visualised him as a slight, somewhat mysterious person, slinking from shadow to shadow, carrying a bag of autopsy instruments. When I met him he was certainly carrying the celebrated bag, but there the likeness between the imagined and the actual Spilsbury abruptly ended.

Sir Bernard Spilsbury looked, more than anything else in the world, like a prosperous gentleman farmer. Very tall — though stooping slightly in his later years — powerful, with broad shoulders and a very ruddy, open, earnest face, you would have said he was an expert on dairy herds, or sugar-beet crops, or agricultural fertilisers, but you would not have suspected that he was Sir Bernard Spilsbury. He was reserved, modest and courteous in manner, very serious, very intent on his work. Indeed, he appeared to exist for nothing but his work. And above everything was his complete integrity.

His handwriting was the most astonishing I have ever seen. He wrote his p.m. reports by hand, and the writing was like some hieroglyphic which professors despairingly pore over. I once sat next to him at the Old Bailey; while waiting to give evidence he took two notebooks from his famous bag and proceeded to copy notes from one book into the other. These notes were written in green ink and each completed page was a bewildering sight. He sat there very quietly and absorbedly writing, waiting to give evidence which would probably prove to be the vital evidence of the trial, yet, when I sat down beside him, humble secretary that I was, he had a "Good-afternoon" and a charming smile for me.

He always gave evidence in a quiet voice, with marvellous clarity, and his evidence carried enormous weight with the juries.

I never saw him do a p.m. — I wish I had. He did not like to have people in the mortuary while he worked, excepting those persons who absolutely had to be there.

He was accorded a vast respect. For a mortuary keeper to announce, "I've got Sir Bernard coming here to do a p.m. this afternoon," was the equivalent of saying that King Solomon was due to appear in all his might and glory. Not that Sir Bernard was the least ostentatious. Very far from it. Nevertheless, he carried an aura with him; an aura which had been thrust upon him, one sensed. I think that so far as he was concerned he might have been perfectly content to have spent his life poring over a microscope examining unsensational slides. But Fate had arranged things differently. He became a front-page figure of exceptional proportions.

Once I went to St Bartholomew's Hospital, where Dr Simpson was to do a post-mortem. St Bartholomew's is London's oldest hospital and the autopsy instruments the attendant proffered Dr Simpson looked as if they might very well have been used by St Bartholomew himself. Dr Simpson politely refused them. "I always carry my own instruments," he explained. Said the attendant, "Sir Bernard Spilsbury *always* uses these." "Nevertheless," replied Dr Simpson, gently but firmly, "I prefer to use my own." "But," said the dazed attendant, "Sir Bernard Spilsbury always uses these!"

There was a gleam in Dr Simpson's eye as he again expressed polite preference for his own instruments. The attendant was literally dumbfounded. He simply could not believe it. It was as though a trumpeter from another land had visited the royal court of ancient Egypt in its heyday and refused the proffered use of Tutankhamen's trumpet.

Despite these adulations Sir Bernard was a deeply modest man; a quiet, withheld man, withheld not in pride but in natural reticence.

It was said, and was probably true, that nobody ever really succeeded in getting to know him. Everyone looked forward to the day when he would publish his memoirs, but he never kept systematic personal notes of his work; he was not, one suspects, very much inclined to reminisce to the world at large, and so the memoirs never appeared. When he died he carried innumerable thrilling stories with him.

For it is not just the inside knowledge of the facts of the big, front-page murders which make a pathologist's work so intensely interesting, it is also the astonishing, infinitely varied, little incidents of day-to-day life in the mortuaries. You could spend a hundred years in London's mortuaries and never be bored.

One morning, for example, walking into Hammersmith mortuary, I was drawn up short by the sight of an enormous hairy man lying on the p.m. table, the nearest human thing I have ever seen to a gorilla, clasping between huge Neanderthal hands folded on his huge Neanderthal chest a dimity posy of snowdrops. I stood staring, and MacKay, the mortuary keeper, came up to me.

"Former British Fascist, Miss Lefebure. Used to be a P.T. instructor to the Hitler Youth Movement in Germany. Looks the type, doesn't he?"

"But why is he cuddling that dear little bunch of snowdrops, MacKay?"

"Special request of a relative, Miss Lefebure," said MacKay, drily.

"My, my, my," I murmured. A lot of my time in those early days was spent in murmuring "My, my, my".

Laughable things occur frequently in the mortuaries; but the laughter they provoke is of the internal, wry sort; grotesques, like details from a Bosch.

A day or two after the Fascist and the snowdrops I was at Poplar mortuary. As I walked past the huge refrigerator where the bodies were kept I saw two undertakers, splendid in their black coats and top-hats (they had come direct from a funeral), tussling to remove a very stout matron from one of the metal refrigerator trays.

"Blimey," said one of the undertakers, "she's frozen to it, mate. We'll never get her off."

They stood the tray up on end, against the wall, in the hope the plump matron would slide off, but there she remained, stuck to her tray, up against the wall, like some unique mural decoration.

"She's stuck orright. What'll we do? Can't wait for her to thaw."

"Chip her off," responded the other.

So they borrowed two chisels, and chipped her off. Tinkle-tinkle went the ice while, as they had no notion I was listening, for I had disappeared into the doctor's office, they made appropriate but unprintable comments about the plump matron . . .

Episode three, which showed me how strange some of my duties were to be, concerned a pair of new gloves I bought one day on my way to work, and the slashed wrist and hand of a suicide, a young window-cleaner with a broken heart who had cut his throat and wrists. The wrist wounds were especially fine ones, from the pathologist's point of view, and Keith Simpson asked the Coroner for permission to remove a hand and wrist to place in the Gordon Museum. So the hand was removed. Then came a problem.

"What can we carry it back to Guy's in?"

Dr Simpson's gaze roamed around the mortuary and fell on my table.

"Miss Lefebure, what about that nice little bag your new gloves are in? Might I borrow that?"

"But of course, please do."

So the new gloves went in my pocket, and I tripped out of the mortuary bearing the hand in the pretty little candy-striped paper carrier-bag which a chic shop-assistant had given me barely an hour ago. What would she, poor creature, have said?

CHAPTER
FOUR

My First Murder

The telephone bell was ringing all the time we worked, with messages from Coroners' officers. "Three cases at Hackney, one a suspected food poisoning." "Two at Walthamstow, one an old woman fell out of bed, the other an infanticide." "A suicide at Wandsworth, cut-throat." "Two straight cases and a drowner at Southwark." And so it went on. And then one day in June the Leyton Coroner's officer (P.C. Goodwin, since retired), was explaining over the phone, rather breathlessly, that he had a murder, a shooting by a soldier, who had already given himself up. "It is a murder, but it isn't a real good murder," explained the excellent man. "I'm sorry it isn't a real good 'un. You haven't had a real good 'un yet, have you, Miss Molly?" (Because of the difficulty of the name Lefebure, they all called me Miss Molly.)

Goodwin had a definite notion of what a murder should be. "Not much of a murder, sir, just a husband run a sword through his wife," he observed on another occasion. But Goodwin had definite notions on a variety of subjects. He was very talkative, even for a police constable. He also had a nice disregard for convention.

Once, I remember, at Whipps Cross Hospital, he disappeared from the p.m. room into the adjoining chapel, a small room with a bier and prie-dieu, used as a viewing room. Goodwin was in there for some five or ten minutes, then he bobbed back to us, beaming. "Guess what I've just been doing, Dr Simpson." "I've no idea, Goodwin." "Just eaten half a dozen oysters," said Goodwin.

But to return to Leyton, where I saw my first murder victim — the victim of a murder that was just a shooting, as Goodwin said. Indeed, he was right. A young soldier, a deserter, had wandered around for a week, "waiting for a chance to kill somebody," as he scrawled in his pocket diary, and had finally selected, completely at random, an elderly man who was picking vegetables on his allotment. Having shot the man, the soldier gave himself up.

Not a big, front-page case at all. I had to wait till the following September before a "proper" murder came our way, a "good 'un". Then it was the Surrey police, phoning us to say they had "a sticky job at Weybridge".

So to Weybridge we drove, to a nice, pretty little house called "The Nook", the home of an old lady who had retired to Surrey for rest and quiet. Through the flower-filled front garden, dozy in the September sunshine, we walked, into a hall where the furniture lay overturned and fragments of smashed glass were scattered everywhere on the carpets. Up the stairs, past many paintings of tranquil religious subjects, into a bedroom, the most disordered room I have ever seen.

The bed was piled with tossed clothes, coverlets, a pink wool shawl, jewel cases, scarves, trinkets. The dressing-table was a-scatter with little oddments — all the drawers were pulled open. A piece of material was jammed in the wardrobe door. On the floor was a jumble of an elderly lady's straw hats, a red brooch, watch-chains, a pink eiderdown quilt on which rested a bottle of brandy and a bottle of lotion, and an upturned oil-stove with a bloodstained petticoat round it. Another bottle of brandy was on the bedside table. Meanwhile, unaware of the disturbance, a little clock stood placidly ticking on the mantelpiece, staring calmly at nothing with its small, round face . . .

Lying in the midst of this confusion, between the upturned stove and a small, overturned table, half on the eiderdown and half on the carpet, clad only in a pink cotton nightgown, was an old white-headed woman, flat on her back, her arms flung out, her right hand still grasping a tumbler with a drain of brandy in it. She had a black eye and a dark trickle of blood ran from her nose and the corner of her mouth.

Around her now milled several detectives, powdering the furniture surfaces for fingerprints, while two Scotland Yard photographers, who had somehow managed to squeeze into the room with their apparatus, were taking flashlights. Dr Simpson, Supt T. Roberts of the Surrey County Constabulary, and myself squeezed ourselves in too. We were joined by the Weybridge pathologist, the late Dr Eric Gardner, and he and Dr Simpson began collecting clues.

Some hair, a cigarette-end, the broken handle of a comb, some bloodstained cotton-wool, were handed to me and I put them in little buff envelopes, to which I fastened descriptive labels. Nothing was touched by hand; forceps were used for picking up these things and placing them in the envelopes. Dr Simpson also took scrapings from under the old lady's fingernails, for such scrapings may provide such important information as hairs, clothing fibres, often from the murderer. He also took measurements of the room, the body, and the position in which it lay.

Meanwhile Supt Roberts gave us a résumé of the crime, so far as the facts were known. The old lady was a Miss Salmon, who lived alone at "The Nook". From time to time, however, there came to stay with her an eighteen-year-old seaman, an orphan, whom she had befriended out of the kindness of her heart, and practically adopted. His name was Cusack.

On the night of the murder Cusack came home with a Canadian private. Both were drunk when they arrived at "The Nook", and both helped themselves from the old lady's cellar to more drinks. Miss Salmon, probably thinking it best to keep quietly out of their way, went up to bed.

The postman, calling at the house next morning, could get no reply, so he put a ladder against the back bedroom window, climbed up, and looked in. There was the old lady lying dead on the floor and the room ransacked.

The horrified postman called the police. When they arrived they found Cusack wandering drunk in the front garden and a Canadian soldier lying dead-drunk on the kitchen floor. Both had their pockets stuffed with valuables belonging to Miss Salmon.

Miss Salmon's bedroom door was locked on the inside, and barricaded too from inside by a chair. But whether Miss Salmon was responsible for these defences or not was a problem.

The post-mortem the two pathologists performed on her, in a pretty little mortuary surrounded by great scarlet dahlias and drowsy September bees, showed that this poor old soul of eighty-two had been punched and battered unmercifully and finally been left lying on the floor to die. Death was due to shock from her injuries.

Dr Simpson said she would have been too weak to lock and barricade her door herself, after the assault, so the detectives returned to "The Nook" and did some experiments with the bedroom door. They discovered that this door could be locked from outside and the key then be pushed back into the bedroom quite easily, and the door could be barricaded within the room, from without, too.

Cusack made two statements to the police. In the first he said, "I walked into the room and pushed at her with my hand, hitting her in the face with my right hand. She fell down on the floor and stayed there. She fell between the wardrobe and the dressing-table. She did not move after this."

But shortly after making this statement he evidently decided that discretion was the better part of valour, and so up came another statement, in which he accused his Canadian friend, McDonald, of the main violence, and even claimed that himself had shown concern for Miss Salmon. This second statement reads:

"She opened the door and McDonald caught hold of her, I believe round the throat. She did not have time to say anything. She struggled with him and tried to scream but she could not make much noise because he kept hold of her. He then laid her on the floor between the wardrobe and the dressing-table, and pulled a silk eiderdown off the bed and laid it over her. She was still struggling and knocking her heels on the floor. He said, 'Hold that over her.'

"I held it over her. The old lady then got her head out from under the quilt and said, 'What is all this?' I then struggled with her and put the quilt over her head again. I then went down the dressing-table drawers and I got out some jewellery. The old lady then started to struggle again and McDonald said, 'I will attend to her. I think I will have to tap her.'

"I said, 'If you are going to, do not hit her too hard, because she is old.'

"He then took the quilt off her face and said to her, 'Are you going to be quiet?' She started screeching and McDonald lifted her head just off the floor a little and hit her with his right hand in the face. She still carried on screeching and he then hit her hard in the face. She moaned a little and was then quiet. He then left her alone and we both went to the chest-of-drawers and took out some stuff. He said to me, 'I think she is kicked out, or dead.'"

Cusack and McDonald were charged with murder. Cusack didn't appear for trial, however, for at the time of the crime he had been in an advanced stage of pulmonary tuberculosis and he was dying in Brixton prison when, in January 1942, McDonald appeared at the Old Bailey.

McDonald was a big, husky dumb-bell, who could have felled his frail alleged old victim with one blow.

His defence was that it was Cusack who had assaulted poor old Miss Salmon and the jury agreed with him and found McDonald not guilty.

McDonald was able to return to his native Canada, a free man. But shortly after his return he was killed in a road smash. And Cusack had already died in prison.

CHAPTER
FIVE

Tale of Two Lovers

The September sun which had shone so warmly and brightly the day we had assisted with the "sticky job at Weybridge" waned to the paler light of October, and October, in its turn, faded into the first days of winter. The mortuaries became rather chilly places to work in, and I was always rather pleased when the lunch-hour came and I found myself at Guy's, in a warm dining-room, eating lunch with friends from the hospital administrative staff. For by this time I had many friends at Guy's.

Of course, we weren't able to get back to Guy's every day. Lunch was eaten everywhere and covered every variety of meal, from sausage rolls gobbled as we bowled along the Mile End Road in the car to repasts at The Ivy or La Coquille. Sometimes we even ate sandwich lunches in the mortuaries, and there was the famous day when Dr Simpson, who was always telling West that the floor of Southwark mortuary was clean enough to eat off, dropped a Spam sandwich on to the said floor, which, although certainly very clean, was nevertheless a mortuary floor. There was a heavy silence, during which West eyed Dr Simpson expectantly. Then Dr Simpson, with a half-grin, half-grimace, said, "Well, West, here goes, I said it." He stooped, picked up the sandwich and ate it. "Well done, sir!" exclaimed West.

But usually, two or three times a week, we lunched at Guy's and, just to ensure that devotion to the job remained at top level, once or twice a week there would be a p.m. to do, immediately lunch was over, in the hospital p.m. room. To these post-mortems, of course, the students came.

Their attendance varied. For some less spectacular autopsies our audience was meagre. But if the case was of any especial clinical interest the crowd was usually large, and if we had a criminal case it became necessary for C. K. S. and myself literally to fight our way into the p.m. room.

One Thursday at the end of October, C. K. S. informed me I would have to take a very quick lunch indeed, as there was a murder job in the Guy's p.m. room. So I swallowed a hasty plate of sausage toad-in-the-hole, skipped the chocolate mould which followed, got together my typewriter and brief-case — and a large supply of those little buff envelopes to pop hairs and fibres and fingernail scrapings into — and scurried away to the p.m. room.

As I approached, a strange sort of roaring noise was heard, and when I opened the door I found myself on the very edge of an enormous crowd of young men, all craning their necks and talking excitedly at the tops of their voices. I tried saying, "Excuse me, please," but nobody took the slightest notice, so then I punched one or two of them in the back, but they still ignored me, so finally I tried hitting them behind the knees with my typewriter and, in this unladylike fashion, fought my way through to the p.m. table which was the centre of all the excitement.

On the table lay a girl, gory with stab wounds. Beside the table stood Gibb (the now late-lamented and always much-loved Gibb), the p.m. room assistant, who usually ruled the students with a rod of iron but who was on this occasion permitting the uproar to pass uncommented, wisely realising, no doubt, that youth must occasionally have its fling. However, he exerted his influence sufficiently to clear a small space for me, my typing-table, my chair and my typewriter. Immediately, two students climbed on my table, to gain a better view of the p.m., and another swarmed up the back of my chair, perching like an acrobat. "Gentlemen," said Gibb, "you will have to get down from there." They got down.

At this point Dr Simpson arrived with Divisional Detective Inspector Hatton, Detective Inspector Keeling, and the Coroner's officer. Their entry was greeted by a deafening stamping of the feet, a form of emotional display common to students and convicts. On this occasion it implied a big bravo, as it were. Dr Simpson pointed out that the post-mortem was a very important and serious one, that it was only by the courtesy of the C.I.D. that the students were able to see it (another thunderous stamp for D.D.I. Hatton), and requested strict silence. Immediately all present became very grim, folded their arms on their chests and

assumed expressions suitable to incipient Spilsburys —
or, shall we say, Simpsons.

Certainly there was little to laugh at in the case
which now unfolded itself to the company. The girl
on the post-mortem table was a pretty blonde of
twenty-four, who came from the Old Kent Road, and
who had been stabbed to death the previous night by
her fiancé.

Her breasts, left side and back were crimson with
thirty-four stab wounds. Her hands had been slashed in
her desperate attempts to protect herself from the
young man's knife.

Brown, the fiancé, a twenty-year-old boy, so D.D.I.
Hatton told us, had known the girl, Rosina, for about
four years and they had become engaged the previous
April. Rosina's father was against an early marriage for
the young couple. Presently he began to suspect
intimacy between them and on the Sunday before the
murder he accused them of this. Both denied any such
thing. Rosina's mother said they were "not playing the
game". Her father told them "to keep the courtship
clean".

Brown replied he loved Rosina and if he could not
have her nobody else should. He was convinced by this
time that Rosina's parents were trying to break up the
engagement. He lay awake all Sunday night, worrying.
Finally he decided to kill Rosina, rather than lose her.

The girl had arranged to go to a dance with Brown's
sister on Wednesday evening, returning afterwards to
his home. At noon on Wednesday Brown phoned
Rosina and told her he wished to speak specially to her

that evening. So, after Rosina and Brown's sister had returned from the dance and had had family supper, Brown took the girl to an upstairs room, where they would not be disturbed.

A little later his stepfather, mother and sister heard screams coming from upstairs. The stepfather and daughter ran upstairs. They opened the bedroom door. There was no light in the room, so the old man lit a candle and went in. Rosina was lying on the bed with blood flowing from her. Brown was weeping and exclaiming he wanted his Rosina. In the general confusion which followed he left the house and at 10.45p.m. went up to a constable in the street and said, "Call an ambulance. I've stabbed my young lady." The constable went with Brown to his home. When the constable tried to examine the body Brown pushed him aside, sat on the bed, embraced the dead girl and cried, "Rosy, speak to me."

The constable examined the room and found a bloodstained dagger behind the door and a black-handled kitchen knife on the carpet. Brown said, "I have stabbed the girl and I hope she is dead and that I die too."

At the police station he began to talk. He said, "You don't know how I loved that girl. Her father has tried to part us. I intended to do this tonight. If I can't have Rosina, then nobody else will."

He made a statement in which he said, "I first met Rosy four years ago. We first had connection about five months ago and her father had suspicions about it. He found a letter from Rosina to me which confirmed his suspicions. He therefore accused us and told a cock-and-bull story that somebody had told him about us. Rosy's parents had always tried to guide our lives. I was determined they were not going to part us. I made up my mind before leaving Rosy's home that I would kill her."

Describing how he murdered her he said, "We sat on the bed and I told her how much I loved her. Then I told her I had made up my mind to kill her. I think she thought I was kidding. Then I picked up the knife. She screamed and I let fly."

This was the tale which D.D.I. Hatton now told the hushed throng in the p.m. room. Dr Simpson examined the girl's wounds; she had been stabbed thirty-four times, with great violence. A frenzied onslaught.

We saw Brown, the accused fiancé, next day at the inquest. He was in the custody of two prison warders. He shambled into the court; a wreckage of a youth, ashen grey in the face, his lower lip hanging, his nose red with weeping, his bespectacled eyes pink-rimmed and dull. During the inquest he huddled on the edge of a bench, his hands clasped between his knees, leaning dazedly forwards. His elder brother, a soldier on leave, was present in the public seats. Brown, as he left the court between the warders, made a brave attempt to smile and salute him.

Later the brother, with a pal, was allowed five minutes' conversation with the prisoner in the little ante-room next to the mortuary. Dr Simpson and I were waiting in the yard outside and we could hear the young men's voices and then, after a mere few seconds,

Brown's brother came out, weeping. He stood outside in the yard, blowing his nose into his handkerchief. A cigarette-end was flung through the door of the ante-room where Brown and the other young man were making disjointed conversation. Then Brown was led away by the warders. He was grey and helpless, like a piece of flapping old paper.

Soon after we saw him again, in the police court. He looked just the same; ashen and dazed and shambling. His stepfather appeared, as a witness. He was a small man, in a too-big overcoat, and he nervously handled an old cloth cap. He wore the same dazed expression as the accused.

The case came up for trial at the Old Bailey in November, before Mr Justice Hilbery. Brown had been considerably tidied up for this important appearance. Dressed in new clothes and with a haircut, he no longer looked so much like a derelict fragment of newspaper. He was still very pale, but quite composed, and bore himself with a quiet courage. He looked, in fact, as if he had come to grips with the situation, and so indeed he had. Apparently he had with difficulty been persuaded to plead Not Guilty. For he wanted to die. He knew quite clearly that he wanted to die. He had said so from the start, but now he really meant it. But other people concerned wished him to try to live and so, in a very quiet voice, he pleaded "Not Guilty".

Rosina's father told the court how he had found, and read, the fatal letter. He gave his evidence with understandable bitterness against Brown. But even Court Number One at the Old Bailey can react in an irrational fashion and this display of outraged fatherly virtue, sincere and perfectly appropriate as it was, annoyed the court, whose sympathies clearly lay with the lovers.

Describing how he had found the letter, Rosina's father said he had come home from work late and going into the kitchen had accidentally knocked Brown's jacket from the back of a chair. Three letters had fallen from the pocket. Two were in pencil, one in ink. He had read the letter in ink. Having read the letter he accused Brown of wrongful conduct with his daughter and told him to keep the courtship clean. Brown replied he loved Rosina and would not let anybody else have her . . .

When the angry father had left the witness-box, defending counsel set to work on the only possible line of defence: that Brown was insane. It was a pity he could not simply have appealed to the humanity of the court — nobody there wanted the boy to hang, excepting the boy himself. Everyone was intensely sorry for him. But our law says all murderers must hang, unless they be proved to have been insane at the time of the crime, or are unfit to plead, and it was impossible to prove Brown insane, even though his poor, tearful old stepfather climbed pitifully into the witness-box to tell us how Brown's granny had always considered the boy a little mental, and one or two other witnesses also appeared to give similar evidence. It was no use. There was not sufficient hard evidence. The judge began summing-up the case.

The court became very crowded as the trial drew to an end and I was obliged to squeeze into a seat on one of the public benches. I found myself next to Brown's stepfather. The poor old man had a heavy cold, he reeked of wintergreen and cough lozenges. Distress bowed him down. I could scarcely bear to glance at his face as the jury filed from the court to consider their verdict. We waited; they soon returned. The verdict was the only one possible, Guilty. Brown was sentenced to death. He was perfectly tranquil, standing very still and upright with his hands lightly resting on the ledge of the dock. But his poor old stepfather at my side burst out sobbing. He huddled weeping there, in his enormous old overcoat, helplessly wiping his face round and round with a stained handkerchief, and for the first time I understood what a murder really means in horror and anguish. I wished with all my heart I could say something to the old man to comfort him, but there was nothing to say. With tears in my own eyes I hurried out of Court Number One of the Old Bailey, where the sword of justice pierces so exceeding sharp.

As for Brown, he went cheerfully to the condemned cell at Wandsworth prison and there awaited his death, repeating constantly to his warders that he was happy at last because now he would soon be with his Rosina.

So ended the tale of two lovers, played not in sun-splashed Verona, but in the Old Kent Road. But whether in Verona yesterday, or the Old Kent Road today, the heart-break is always the same.

CHAPTER
SIX

Murder on Waterloo Bridge

One morning not very long after the sensational post-mortem at Guy's we walked into Southwark mortuary to do two not very exciting cases and found that West had a third body waiting for us; an ugly, weatherbeaten prostitute of about thirty-five to forty, dirty and slovenly, daubed with lipstick, rouge and river mud. She had been found, early that morning, lying on the Thames foreshore beneath the new Waterloo Bridge, which, at the time, was not yet open to the public.

She looked, at first sight, to be a suicide, but West hinted he thought there was something "fishy" about her. West claims to have a nose for "fishy cases". He added that late the previous night a man and woman had been heard quarrelling on the bridge and presently a soldier was seen leaving the bridge, but no woman. Later a woman's scarf was found on the bridge, beside the parapet, and when daylight came this woman was seen lying dead in the mud below.

Dr Simpson began the p.m. and before many minutes discovered the woman to be severely injured. He looked at West with a twinkle in his eye. "Quite right, West. There's something very fishy about this one. You had better ask the Coroner's officer to inform the C.I.D."

Further examination showed that a fierce attempt had been made to strangle the woman; there was a fracture of the voice-box, indicating a violent grip on the throat. Bruising on her back suggested she had been roughly forced against the bridge parapet. There were also severe internal crushing injuries with fractures of the ribs, and fractures of both thigh-bones, which were caused by her fall over the parapet on to the concrete piles and mud-flats below. The woman, said C. K. S., had died immediately following the fall.

It was at this point that Area Superintendent Reece, a shrewd man with a big laugh and amazing eyebrows, arrived at the mortuary. After he had discussed the case with Dr Simpson he hurried off to start investigations and we went back to Guy's and prepared a report for the C.I.D. Then for four days we heard no more about the matter. But on the fourth day came a very early morning phone call for me from C. K. S. saying that the C.I.D. wanted him to visit Waterloo Bridge with them, and could I be ready if he called for me in twenty minutes?

Twenty minutes later we were on our way to Waterloo Bridge.

It was a cold morning and the bridge, still in the process of completion, was broad, white and windy, like the deck of a huge liner. A party of detectives, all very burly in thick overcoats, escorted us along the bridge to the spot where the murder had taken place. We all craned over the parapet to stare down at the place, some thirty feet below, where the body was found. Knowing that C. K. S. didn't like heights, and fearing to see him plunging in the wake of the unhappy murder victim, I caught hold of the hem of his coat and hung on tightly.

While we stared, somewhat dizzily, down at the mud Mr Reece confided that the woman had been identified as one Peggy Richards, a prostitute from Deptford, and that the police believed she had been murdered by a Canadian soldier. "We haven't arrested him yet, but we've got him taped," explained Mr Reece.

There was some more discussion of technical aspects of the lady's fall from the parapet and then we all walked back across the bridge, admiring the view in general and commenting on the beauty of the Thames and the fairness of the morning. Then Mr Reece and his party drove off along the Embankment to the Yard, and we hurried off to start the day's post-mortems.

The Canadian soldier, a private named McKinstry, appeared at the Old Bailey some two months later. He was a stocky, bespectacled, balding man who stood stolidly in the dock listening to the case put forward by the Prosecution. This was that McKinstry had come up to London on fourteen days' leave and on arriving at Waterloo station had gone with a friend to a public-house close by, The Wellington. Peggy Richards was also at The Wellington and remained there until closing-time, in the company of several soldiers. At closing-time she was seen outside the public-house and a little later was noticed walking in the direction of Waterloo Bridge with a Canadian soldier.

At midnight a watchman on the bridge heard a man and woman quarrelling. He told a man who kept a store near the bridge and together they went out on to the bridge and there they found a Canadian soldier standing by the parapet. It was very dark, because of the black-out, so they helped the soldier off the bridge. Then they went back to see if they could find the woman. There was no woman to be seen, but by the parapet, where the soldier had been standing, they found a woman's scarf.

Between 12.30 and 1 a.m. McKinstry was in Waterloo station asking for a chit to sleep at the Y.M.C.A. He was noticed by a policeman to be in possession of a woman's handbag containing the identity card of Peggy Richards. McKinstry explained he had been drinking with a woman all evening and when they came out of the public-house at closing-time she hit him on the head with her handbag, and he caught hold of it, and then she ran off, leaving him with it.

Next day McKinstry went to stay with friends outside London . . .

Meanwhile the storekeeper by the bridge had been indulging in some of that amateur detection so dear to the Englishman's heart. The discovery of the scarf on the bridge had given him a hunch, so at the first peep of daylight he was out on the bridge again, back to the spot where he had found the scarf, peering over the parapet. And below him he saw, lying on the mud, what he had half-hoped, half-feared to see: the body of a woman. He went straight off to dial 999.

McKinstry was soon traced by the police and made a long statement to them, which was read to the Old Bailey jury. McKinstry in this statement said that he and his pal arrived at Waterloo and went to The Wellington, the pal saying, "What about some drinks and some women?" McKinstry said that was O.K. by him, so they had some drinks and bought some contraceptives a man was selling. McKinstry stood some drinks to Peggy Richards and suggested they should go out. They went into the street and he had her in a doorway. He paid her five pounds. (When questioned about this in the witness-box he said, "I gave that good and hearty," meaning that there had been no dispute about this financial transaction.)

Then they went for a walk. The woman was running along beside him chewing the fat about something and he said, "Oh shut up, you goddam bitch." They went to Waterloo Bridge and sat on what he later agreed might have been a parapet — apparently at the time he thought it was a window-sill, or so he said. There he had her again . . . After they had finished, insisted McKinstry, she struck him on the head with her handbag, and ran off leaving him with it.

Prosecution submitted that the end of this statement was false and that Peggy Richards had not hit McKinstry with her handbag and then run away, but that the two had had a violent quarrel by the bridge parapet, probably because she wanted a further sum of money from him, and that he had finally, in his temper, tried to strangle her and then pushed her over the parapet.

The case for the defence was that Peggy Richards *had* run away from McKinstry, but had then picked up some other, unidentified, man and it was this unknown warrior who had killed her and not McKinstry, who, said Defence, at the time of her death was in Waterloo station asking for a chit to sleep at the Y.M.C.A.

The jury accepted this defence and McKinstry was acquitted.

Like his compatriot, McDonald, McKinstry returned to Canada. And like McDonald he met his death there violently soon after his return. McKinstry perished in a fire.

CHAPTER
SEVEN

Portrait of a Merry Widow

At three o'clock one December afternoon we found ourselves driving round Bethnal Green with a young C.I.D. officer, looking for a block of tenements which we will call Berkshire Buildings. (These low-smelling places always have high-sounding names.)

Round and round the intricate maze of narrow elephant-grey streets we drove; the C.I.D. man as lost as we were, for he was new to the area. A melancholy landscape it was, of interminable dirty little brick houses whose little sooty windows stared, achingly bored, at the fog already uncoiling in preparation for the night. The more we searched for Tudor Rose Buildings the more we became lost, until finally we asked the way of two scruffy little boys who would have made admirable Dead End Kids, and they replied, "They's Berkshire Buildings, down there." But they were wrong, and we had to ask the way again, this time of a wizened old lady in rusty clothes, who was hobbling along on bad feet, carrying an unwrapped loaf of bread under her arm. She directed us correctly.

Berkshire Buildings were built according to the usual style: grey blocks of flats in grey asphalt yards. They were by no means modern; built, I should say, at the end of the last century when they were no doubt considered the ultimate word in working-class accommodation. Probably a lot of people declared them far too luxurious for workers.

The grey yards were deserted, for the children were not yet home from school, but women's voices echoed from the doorways, and everywhere babies were wailing thinly. A leaking water-pipe discharged a brown unsavoury deluge down a wall, splashing into large hideous puddles in the yard below, where paddled and piddled a very hairy, preoccupied-looking poodle. We entered dark doorways, encountered many odours, found flats 1 — 64, 99 — 145, but couldn't find number 82, which was the one we wanted. At last C. K. S. asked a vacuous, slatternly young woman who appeared with a little girl in a dirty pink coat, and she said, pointing, "Through that door there, mate."

The tenements were arranged on a system of tiers of corridors connected by staircases open on every landing to small balconies, which no doubt was designed to keep the buildings ventilated but which mainly succeeded in sweeping the place with perishing, dust-whirling draughts. The staircases were dark and their stone steps were worn by many, many weary feet. There was a great smell of rotting plaster, human dirt, latrines, cooking, and damp. The staircase and corridor walls were adorned with chalk sketches and scrawls of all kinds, from the harmlessly jocular and sentimental to the indecent. The buildings echoed with footsteps, babies crying, dishes clattering and radios playing. Silence was obviously unknown there.

The blocks were each four storeys high with a kind of penthouse communal laundry under the roof. Here were long stained sinks and fixed clothes-lines. On each floor, I discovered, was a lavatory, which one lavatory served all the flats on that floor, and a washroom with a very dirty sink — there were no bathrooms. For a bath the flat-dwellers had to go round to the local public baths. None of the flats had running water; all water had to be fetched from the wash-rooms.

The lavatories and wash-rooms were filthy, stinking places, their doors swinging wide open on to the corridors, up and down which the stinks wafted freely.

We found flat number 82 and, when we rang, the coroner's officer unexpectedly opened the door to us. He had already arrived on the job. He ushered us in and we stood looking around us. The flat contained two small rooms and a large cupboard, and was the home of a young widow who worked in a nearby factory and who extended her intimate favours to a commercial traveller who lodged with her whenever he was in London. She was, from all accounts, a lively, happy, easy soul, and now here she was, when we arrived, lying dead on her bed, wearing a particularly shattering magenta velvet frock with lipstick and chipped nail-varnish to match. She was plump, dark-haired, with blunt features. She had told a neighbour, the previous week, that she was four months pregnant and intended doing something about it. There was reason to suppose that the something had now been done, with drastic results.

She had also told the neighbour, during the conversation, that she had already tried slippery-elm bark (a popular but not very effective working-class abortifacient) and nothing had happened, so she would have to have "a go at something else". The morning of the day of our visit to her flat, the neighbour said, the young woman had complained of a pain, and about noon she had died.

Dr Simpson and the C.I.D. officer began looking for a syringe of the sort which is widely used for bringing about abortions, both by small-time abortionists and the pregnant women themselves.

We all poked about the flat, looking here, there and everywhere. It was a great opportunity for me to discover how a young woman factory-worker in Bethnal Green lives and I fetched out a notebook and began jotting down notes.

The living-room was small, untidy, confused, and by the standards of any select suburban housewife it was pretty squalid and dirty, but judged by the standards of many of the houses and homes we visited it wasn't too bad. Indeed, when one considered the plumbing facilities — or rather, the complete lack of them — the flat did its occupant credit. Certainly, it was all somewhat of a litter, but then there was really no room for a decent-sized wardrobe, or a chest-of-drawers. And the air in the flat was stale as old biscuits and when we tried to open the window we couldn't because the window had stuck fast years back and would never open again, unless somebody brought a sledgehammer to it, but that of course was not surprising because in many East London homes fresh air is looked upon as highly dangerous. A nice, warm, smelly, woolly fug is considered essential to good health and high spirits.

There was a large kitchen-type table in the living-room, a rather broken-down sofa and an aged easy-chair with boggly springs. There was a gas-stove, on which stood a frying-pan in which three sausages lay congealed in cold fat. Above the stove was a shelf with saucepans and cooking things. There was a kitchen range too, but that clearly had not been used for years. Over the range was a mantelpiece and I amused myself by cataloguing the things on it: an alarm-clock, two aspirins in a tiny unopened cellophane package, a box of rouge, a very dirty little powder-puff, three bottles of cough mixture, hairpins, a small woolly mat, cotton, needle ready threaded with white cotton, a letter in a stamped envelope, all ready for posting, and a coloured photograph of a small child in a turquoise-blue frock.

On hangers on the wall, strewn over the easy-chair, and on pegs on the back of the door were the young woman's coats and dresses. She had certainly indulged in plenty of clothes. Quite nice clothes, too. Cheap, but smart.

In her bedroom was a chair arrayed with more clothes. More dresses hung on the bedroom door. There was a shelved holdall with gingham curtains; here we found a pair of downtrodden shoes, a large roll of cotton-wool, a box of face powder, a hairbrush, combs, hankies, undies neatly folded, a pattern for a dress and a length of uncut dress material, scissors, nail-varnish, stockings, letters, face-cream and so forth, all neatly stowed away.

The bed on which the dead woman lay was tousled, tossed, unsavoury. Under the bed was a red-and-green wooden toy truck, brand new and obviously intended as a present for somebody. There was also an enamel chamber-pot. At the foot of the bed was a small zinc bath.

C. K. S. and the detective had so far found nothing they were looking for, so they turned their attention to the large cupboard which led out of the living-room. Such a very large cupboard, it was almost a sort of windowless closet, intended to be used as larder, brush-and-broom cupboard, boot cupboard, wardrobe, box-room, everything. (One can imagine what this cupboard would be like in a large, untidy family.) There was a food safe in it, and more clothes hanging on pegs, a bucket, a mop, broom, shelves on which were folded linen and blankets, pots and pans, kettles, cleaning powders and soap, matches, a few books, two or three bottles of beer and a bottle of gin, and, tucked away at the back of the top shelf behind some other things, the syringe C. K. S. was looking for.

So our search had not been in vain. And it had certainly taught me far more about life in Bethnal Green than if I had read dozens of books on the subject. I stood in this stuffy, yet damply cold, cheerless, waterless flat — let me repeat, not a drop of running water in any of these flats, all water, whether for washing, cooking or drinking, to be fetched from

47

the smelly wash-rooms — and I wondered what I would have turned out to be like had I been born and bred in Tudor Rose Buildings. I walked to the window, pulled aside a very grimy net curtain and stared down into the yards, now noisy with children. A glorious vista of grey asphalt, tall, dreary posts and sagging fixed clothes-lines, and a centrepiece of surface air-raid shelters, the brick sort, with flat concrete roofs. And I noticed that the roofs of these shelters were chock-a-block with every possible kind of junk and litter. Old bicycle tyres, old cloth cap, old gasmask case, old saucepans, empty tins and bottles, old cabbage stumps and vegetable peelings, cigarette cartons, mouldy loaves of bread, newspapers, jam-pot lids, apple cores, old bones, leg of an old chair, old lamp-shade. At first I couldn't understand how these things had got there. Then I realised they had all been tossed out of the windows of the flats by the irresponsible occupants and had landed on the shelter roofs instead of falling into the yards, where in due course, I suppose, such litter would either have been picked up by children or cleared away.

In short, if there was any light refuse knocking around your flat in Tudor Rose Buildings you just slung it out of the window — so long as you could open the window. Obviously quite a lot of people did manage to open their windows — to throw their rubbish out.

So I stood staring at the littered shelter roofs and the children and the clothes-lines and at all the dirty curtained windows of the other flats, where radios played and babies cried and harassed women scolded and shouted and dropped plates and clattered and cursed and coughed, and I was still staring gloomily when the undertakers arrived to remove the dead woman to the local mortuary, and we drove there too, leaving Tudor Rose Buildings behind us . . .

The post-mortem showed that the young woman died from a septic abortion. The syringe had been used to give her an injection of hot soapy water, which had started an abortion, but as the syringe had in little likelihood been sterilised before use, and as the circumstances and surroundings of the syringeing had no doubt been squalid — either a dirty bedroom or dirty kitchen — septicaemia had set in. There were no injuries to the uterus or surrounding parts and this strongly suggested that the woman had not performed the syringeing upon herself, but had sought aid from some other person — maybe the helpful neighbour, maybe a local abortionist — and maybe the helpful neighbour and the local abortionist were one and the same person. Who can say? In cases of this kind the police never get very far. The women who know what has been going on never talk.

The lack of injuries suggested the dead woman had had help with the syringeing, because women who try to perform these illegal operations on themselves usually fumble and cause bruises or tears. But there was nobody to come forward with any evidence of any kind, there was nobody to say what had really happened, and so, as in very many of these cases, the police drew a blank.

49

★　★　★

(The 1939 Abortion Committee reported that one out of every five to six pregnancies terminates prematurely, and that in some forty per cent of these there is evidence of criminal interference. This figure is probably an underestimate of the proportion of criminal abortions. But it is a social problem which, not being very glamorous, does not attract much attention. Moreover, to solve, or help solve, the problem would require straight and honest thinking on the subject of birth-control education. And as few people like, or are even capable of, straight and honest thought, the ignorance and criminal abortions will go on. Since the appearance of powerful bacterium-killing agents like M and B 693, penicillin and the like, the gravity of the problem of deaths from septicaemia arising from illegal abortion has faded to a remarkable degree. Abortionists have not been slow to avail themselves of the benefits of "chemotherapy".)

CHAPTER
EIGHT

Thoughts and Episodes of Spring

For some time it had been increasingly obvious that mortuaries are not the cosiest of places to work in during winter, but it was not until after Christmas that I really discovered what awfully uncomfortable places they can be.

Christmas itself was a warming time, with so many friendly faces and messages of good cheer I never noticed the weather. We worked on Christmas Eve, had Christmas Day clear, and were at work by 8.30 on Boxing Day morning. We spent the morning in the East End doing post-mortems, then lunched at Simpson's in the Strand, then did one case at Hammersmith. Then C. K. S. returned to his family, I had a lively Boxing Day tea with mine, and in the evening went to the ballet.

But the weather which followed Christmas was very cold and raw. The mortuaries with their stone floors, tiled walls, refrigerators, and constantly opening and shutting doors can best be left to the imagination. I became numb as I sat shivering at my typewriter and Dr Simpson had to have very hot basins of water to dip his hands in as he worked, for the bodies, brought from out the refrigerators, were petrifying to handle.

I remember one especially awful occasion when we found ourselves doing an early morning double job in North London on an elderly man who had murdered his wife with a hatchet and then gassed himself. The meagre morning light was just unfolding as we walked into the particularly uncomfortable mortuary. A chair and typing table had been thoughtfully placed for me — next to the refrigerator. The p.m. room door wouldn't shut, so an icy draught blew in from the mortuary yard all the time and wrapped itself round our feet. To add a hideous finishing touch, the p.m. table was of such inefficient design that a stream of blood spilled continuously over its edge, forming a pool by my chair. Two or three detectives, wrapped up to the ears, stood watching the blood dripping from the table with horribly mesmerised faces.

The mortuary attendant, a wild-eyed old man, dropped instruments in all directions and teetered about the place in a kind of trance. Dr Simpson's taut expression and ice-cube voice indicated to me that he was inwardly seething. When we finally drove from that place I prayed never, never, never to go there again. And, thanks be, we never never did.

To add to the delights of that winter, an influenza epidemic arrived. The post-mortem figures mounted and mounted, until we found ourselves frantically busy. One Monday, for instance, I recall we did thirteen p.ms., attended one — very long — inquest at Stratford-by-Bow, and went to the Old Bailey. We ate a sausage-roll lunch dashing along in the car from Stratford to the Old Bailey. It was a non-stop day, from

8.30 to 6. Tuesday was just as frantic, and by Wednesday evening we had done forty-two p.ms. in three days . . .

But spring always comes. The frosts vanished, the air grew warmer, the birds began twittering, the work slackened its furious pace. Gradually I peeled off the layers of heavy woollen clothing I had accumulated and began to look a little less like an Eskimo and a little more like my slender self. Pretty soon I was able to buy a spring hat and get out my spring coat.

Now those were the days of clothing coupons, and at all costs one tried to avoid buying a new coat, for a new coat left one practically bankrupt of clothing coupons for the rest of the year. My spring coat was by no means new, but I thought it would do for one more season if I shortened it, so the night before I intended wearing it I turned up the hem. The next morning was an early start; I met C. K. S. at King's Cross at 7.45. Just as I was getting into his car I discovered the hem of my coat still had white tacking-thread stitched all round it. White, on a blue coat. Yes, it certainly showed.

I tried pulling out the thread as we drove to our first mortuary of the day, but it was all so securely stitched and back-stitched — my own idea of what a good strong tack should be — I couldn't move it. And, of course, we hadn't been at work long before a call came to go to the Old Bailey. So there I was at the Old Bailey, complete with tacking, walking down Court Number One, trying to look very confident and poised and feeling worse than a low-grade tramp. But that wasn't the end of the story, ah, no. A message was

53

brought to C. K. S.: Mr Justice Humphreys wished to have a word with him. I accompanied my employer into the presence of the great and I was so aware of that white tacking I felt it was all lit up with neon lights. What a dreadful experience — to meet Mr Justice Humphreys the very day one's coat was fastened with white tacking cotton. A nightmare notion come true.

Besides overhauling my spring wardrobe I did what every right-minded woman does in April — indulged in a new *coiffure*. This meant that much spare time had to be spent at the hairdresser's, because I am a sucker at doing my own hair. So one Saturday afternoon I was under the dryer in a tasteful off-white and mushroom-pink cubicle, reading *Vogue*. The mortuaries were behind me for the weekend and I was all set for a chic, gay time in town. Or so I thought. But suddenly an assistant peeped under the dryer at me, "Miss Lefebure, you're wanted on the phone." Arrayed in white dust-cover and hairpins I hurried to the phone, to hear C. K. S. asking, "Miss L., how far is your beautifying process under way?"

"I'm under the dryer."

"How soon will you be dry?"

"In about twenty minutes."

"Can you come out slightly damp and pick me up at Guy's? There is a murder in Shoreditch mortuary."

"I'll be right along."

The hairpins were removed and a limply becurled Lefebure scurried into the Underground. By the time I reached Guy's I looked alarmingly like a French poodle. C. K. S. kindly made no comment. We whizzed away to Shoreditch and a few minutes after our arrival there I was sitting on a stone slab — originally intended for corpses — dashing off shorthand notes while C. K. S., Mr Heddy, the Coroner, Chief Superintendent Greeno (at that time an Area Superintendent) and D.D.I. Kean bent over the body on the p.m. table.

The only person who was ever tactless enough to mention my astounding appearance that afternoon was the Coroner's officer, and he couldn't resist whispering to me, "Now, Miss Molly, I know what you'd look like if you were a Fuzzy-Wuzz."

I would have liked, that afternoon especially, to have looked *soignée* and efficient, because it was my first encounter with that famous detective, Mr Greeno, and as Dr Keith Simpson's secretary I did not want to create a poor impression with high-ups at Scotland Yard. Moreover, the high-ups at the Yard all made terrific impressions upon me; indeed on first meeting them I was generally scared quite literally stiff. Mr Greeno was no exception. More than anything he resembled a huge, steel-plated battle-cruiser, with his jaw thrust forward instead of a prow. He spoke little, noticed everything, and was tough, not in the Hollywood style, but genuinely, naturally, quietly, appallingly so.

I found myself misquoting Hilaire Belloc, on the subject of the Lion — but it did just as well for Mr Greeno:

"His eyes they are bright
And his jaw it is grim,

And a wise little child
  Will not play with him."

Thus was the Area Superintendent, Mr Edward
Greeno, when he came stalking into Shoreditch
mortuary with two lesser detectives crunching on his
heels. The grim light of battle glimmered in his eyes,
and he started asking questions in a rather rasping
voice that sent shivers down my spine. He was on the
war-path, and I thought: God help the poor fool he's
after.

By the time the post-mortem had been in progress
for some ten minutes any sympathy I felt for the killer
concerned in the case had dwindled away, for it was
one of those brutal, senseless, ugly coshings which reek
of stupidity and cowardly violence.

The dead man was an aged pawnbroker who had
kept a shop in the Hackney Road, a poor, little, skinny
old man. Nine days previously he had been beaten up
in his shop by two men, who had got away, leaving him
unconscious on the floor. They had dealt him five
savage wounds on the head; the only thing which had,
amazingly enough, prevented him from being killed
outright was the felt hat he had been wearing. Dr
Simpson examined this hat, which had been brought to
the mortuary, with great interest, remarking how
astonishing it was that a mere felt hat could, to some
extent, protect the head.

But in spite of the felt hat the blows on his head had
ultimately proved fatal to the old pawnbroker and nine
days later he died, and a murder hunt began.

Besides beating up the old man the thieves had also coshed, and killed, his dog, presumably to stop it barking.

During the p.m. Mr Greeno showed us a big, heavy spanner, with which it was suggested the old man might have been struck. Certainly the spanner did seem a likely weapon, but, as it turned out, it was not the one the killers had used.

We soon learned the true story of the case, for within a few days of the p.m. at Shoreditch Mr Greeno arrested and charged two youths with the murder.

Their names were Dashwood and Silverosa. Both were ex-Borstal boys, both had criminal records stretching back to their early teens. Civilised, enlightened attempts had constantly been made to convert them into good citizens, but without success. They had been given lectures and lessons and handwork and physical training and fresh air, and interviews with psychologists and dozens and dozens of reports had been made about them; everything had been tried, except a good hiding. Nobody had thought of that. Or, if anybody had thought of it, the notion had always been dismissed as impossibly barbaric. So these two young men had drifted on their merry way, using their Stone Age tactics without compunction, till finally they had bit an old man — and his dog — a little too hard, which removed Dashwood and Silverosa abruptly from the hands of the reformers into the incipient clutches of the hangman.

As there is no honour amongst thieves, and especially not amongst the younger generation of pseudo-gangsters, Dashwood and Silverosa both made statements in which each did his best to pin the actual violence upon the other. Silverosa said:

"Two weeks ago last Thursday I went with Dashwood to a café where we had dinner. He told me he had a gun and he showed me a revolver. He told me he was going to do a job. I asked him, 'Where?' and he said, 'Anywhere, I don't care as long as it is something.' We went along the Hackney Road and he said the gun was only for putting the frightening powder in. We were going past a pawnbroker's. He said, 'We might as well go and do this if you are coming.' I said, 'All right, only no violence.' He said, 'All right.' We waited until closing-time as it was early-closing day and only one o'clock. We saw the pawnbroker come out and put the shutters up and go back into his shop and we walked in after him. I closed the shop door and when I turned round I saw the old man falling down. I didn't see Sam strike him but I surmised what he had done. I said, 'You silly sod, what did you do that for?' He said, 'I had to, he was going to blow a whistle.' I wiped some blood off the old man's head with my overcoat. I said to Sammy, 'Well, we've done the damage, we had better do what we came here to do.' We took some rings from the safe and off the table. We walked into Mare Street and took the bus to Walthamstow High Street . . ."

Dashwood, in his statement, admitted striking the old man, but tried to suggest that it was Silverosa who had started the struggle with the pawnbroker. His statement reads:

". . . On Thursday, 30th April, we went to a pawnbroker's . . . The dog started barking. I hit the dog between the eyes. George and the old man were scuffling, and we both jumped on him to hold him down and he started shouting. I said, 'For Christ's sake quiet down, or you will get hurt.' The old boy went on shouting. George said, 'Look out!' I bent over the old boy to shut him up and he put his arms round my neck, I bent over him and hit him on the top of the head with the revolver . . ."

Actually, of course, it did not matter which of the two had struck the fatal blows. Both had been present at the time of the murder and therefore both were guilty of murder. But this was something beyond their stunted powers of comprehension. Less than uneducated, reared solely on a culture of picture papers, blaring radio, films, cigarettes, back streets, pin-table saloons and easy money, eternally bored, fed up to the back teeth with everything and everybody, including themselves, bad-tempered, impatient, and carrying great, Great Big Chips on Their Shoulders, they were brought, like two sulky, bickering children, into court. They were at loggerheads with one another and they were soon at loggerheads with their counsel, the famous Serjeant Sullivan, with whose services they presently abruptly dispensed, saying they preferred to conduct their own defence. Their method of defending themselves was for each to accuse the other of striking the old man. Alas, they had no revolvers with them at the Old Bailey, they couldn't shoot the judge, or frighten the jury, or silence the prosecuting counsel by coshing him on the head. They could do nothing except bluster and lie, and snarl and scowl at one another, and so they were sentenced

59

CHAPTER
NINE

"In the Spring a Young
Man's Fancy"

Spring 1942 was made for romance. There were a great
many young men home on leave, the most beautiful
sunshine, all the birds singing, and all the trees bursting
into bud all at once, like delicious green explosions of
summer.

My days were spent happily round the mortuaries,
on my job, my evenings gaily gallivanting round town
with my escorts; a perfect combination of work and
pleasure. Unfortunately the escorts were, almost
invariably, appalled by the idea of my work and read
me long, severe, prosy lectures on the subject. (Males
have a weakness for long, severe, prosy lectures.) When
they had finished their leaves and returned to the
wars they bombarded me with long, prosy, lecturing
letters.

My girl friends, on the other hand, all envied me my
job, and were constantly pressing me for gruesome
details. "Do give me the latest news of any *good*
murders, darling," they would write. "And how are the
mortuaries getting on? Still as great fun as ever?"

Whereas a boy friend's epistle would say, "Next time you write, please don't mention stiffs. They give me the willies . . ."

But oddly enough, when the sexes get together at my flat over a supper party or some such, I discover that they reverse the process. If the subject of crime arises, it is the males then who clamour, in true he-man style, to hear gruesome details, see photographs, while the women, much to my interest, stage an equally determined *volte-face*.

The little lady who, when alone with me, adores discussing a case in full detail and laps up any pictures I have, now, for example, curls up in a chair and says weakly, "Oh Molly *please*, not more about that awful job, I can't bear it."

"Poor Mary," murmurs her husband, or boy friend, as the case may be, bending protectively towards her, "she just can't stand that sort of thing. She's not like you, Molly. You're tough, but Mary's very feminine and foolish."

Mary flutters her eyelashes, exchanges a meaning look with me, and then heaves a long long feminine foolish sigh.

"I was going to show Mary my pictures of the Wigwam case," I say briskly and brightly. "Wouldn't you like to see them, Mary darling?"

Mary, who last time she came to visit me, alone, could not be torn away from the Wigwam pictures, now gives a cry and waggles her head in violent protest, covering her eyes.

"For Heaven's sake," says husband, "if you show her things like that she'll never get over the nightmares. She just can't stand that sort of thing. I don't mind seeing 'em" (bracing himself, like Gary Cooper going to shoot-up a posse), "but Mary'd better hide her face, she can't stand that sort of thing. She's very feminine and foolish . . ."

Women are much harder-boiled than men, but they'll fight to the last ditch before they let the men know it . . .

To return to Spring, 1942. One evening I was getting ready for a stroll on Hampstead Heath with a *Forces Françaises Libres*, a young man who liked to lean over the rather muddy waters of Ken Wood lake and recite Verlaine with great meaning. I was in the middle of doing my hair when Keith Simpson came through on the phone, exclaiming happily that as it was such a fine evening, and as there was a very interesting shooting case at Wandsworth mortuary, he proposed to pick me up in the car and then drive over to Wandsworth to spend an hour or so sorting out the case with the C.I.D.

It was a strict rule with me my job always came first — and, of course, to be honest, I felt much more inclination to spend the evening at Wandsworth mortuary sorting out an interesting shooting case with the C.I.D. than meandering beside Ken Wood lake with a youth gloomily chanting:

"Un grand sommeil noir
Tombe sur ma vie;

63

Dormez, tout espoir,
Dormez, toute envie!"

So I rang the *Forces Françaises Libres* and explained to him that Ken Wood must be some other time, as a C.I.D. case had suddenly, etc., etc. A voice from the other end of the line demanded with Gallic point, "But why, why do you not prefer me to a corpse?" Then came the customary lecture, and I made my stock speech about finding my work absolutely fascinating, whereupon the F.F.L. burst into furious yowls, said some very nasty things about necrophilia, and ended abruptly and rather hysterically, exclaiming, "There must be something WRONG with you . . . to prefer a corpse . . . it's so unnatural . . . you wait, when next I come home on leave I will SHOW you!"

Shortly afterwards I was well on the way to Wandsworth — and I suppose the F.F.L. was comforting himself with appropriate stanzas of Verlaine. Or, much more probably, a drink at The Spaniards.

The case at Wandsworth was very interesting. The body was that of a young soldier, found lying dead in a pond on Wimbledon Common, with a bullet through his head. The C.I.D. thought at first that it was a murder, but after a long and painstaking examination of the body Dr Simpson found that it was a suicide.

Next morning we drove with the C.I.D. across the Common to look at the pond where the body was found. The C.I.D. had now learned more about the dead soldier than they had known the previous night. He had recently had V.D., but also, which was worse, a series of army lectures on the subject, and these latter had so alarmed and depressed him that he had decided to shoot himself.

So he had gone to the pond and there, standing on the bank, had shot himself, falling forwards into the water. A rather unusual suicide, which at first not unnaturally led to suspicions of murder.

Dr Simpson spent some time at the pond, examining the ground around and reconstructing the soldier's death. I stood on the bank, under the green springy trees, and looked into the water, where clots of blood and fragments of brain still floated, like exotic crimson water-flowers. And I thought that if the soldier had only been a young middle-class intellectual, instead of a respectable working-class boy, he would have written a short story about his experience, and joked about the V.D. lectures, and built up his ego with it all, until he was bursting with superiority, like Maupassant and Hemingway rolled into one.

But, alas, he was a nice boy, that soldier, so he ended by blowing his brains into a pool. If only he had written short stories! For, as Somerset Maugham says, anything is grist to the writer's mill. A pen, some paper, and anything, but anything, can quickly be worked out of the system.

CHAPTER
TEN

Case of a Lifetime

Now every detective dreams of that great, big case which is going to come rolling along one day to bring him fame and promotion. And every crime reporter dreams of a similar great, big case, his own exclusive scoop, which will make him the idol and envy of Fleet Street. While pathologists (though, of course, in a somewhat more dignified manner) dream of that great, big case which will turn up one day, to make Spilsbury with his Crippen, and Glaister and Brash with their Ruxton, look slightly insignificant. And every pathologist's secretary dreams of being around with her chief when that great, big case comes rolling along.

Well, a great, big case did come rolling along, and it was great and big, but, in the way of this world, the detective didn't welcome it because he was already up to his eyes in work, the pathologist was very careful not to become too enthusiastic about it because he didn't want to be disappointed, and the gentlemen of Fleet Street, God bless them, never even got a sniff or whisper of it until all was well under way. Aha, there was I, sitting, literally sitting, on one of the most interesting corpses of the century, one of the best murders in this country's crime history, and the Fleet Street gentlemen didn't know. I would see them all at the Old Bailey, polite exchange of smiles, "good-mornings". Gentlemen, back in my little back room at Guy's there is a corpse that is literally making murder history, and you just haven't got a clue. Aha, *what* a scoop! (And the late journalist in me wriggled for pure joy.)

It all began very lethargically, on Friday, July 17th, 1942. A squad of demolition workers were toiling in the hot sunshine, clearing the bombed premises at 302 Kennington Lane, Lambeth. Presently one of them prised up a stone slab with his pickaxe and there, underneath, lay the remains of a body. The demolition worker was not in the least excited by this. The remains, he thought, of just one more old air-raid casualty, or one more old corpse out of this here old graveyard — for they were working in a cellar which adjoined an ancient graveyard. He stooped to pick up the body; parts of the arms and legs were missing, the skull rolled loose as he moved it. Casually he dumped the body on one side while he and his mates finished clearing the ground around; then they went to the local for a drink, and it was not until the end of the day that their foreman reported the discovery of the body to the coroner.

The Coroner's officer next morning telephoned Dr Simpson. "We've got a p.m. here for you to do, sir, and there's some old bones been brought in too, bits of some old air-raid casualty. The Coroner would like it if you'd just take a look at them after you've done the p.m., though there's not much in them." It was a hot, lazy July Saturday morning and, as we hadn't much to do, we were able to go right away to Southwark mortuary.

When we arrived the p.m. case was lying ready for C. K. S. on the p.m. table. (It was just some ordinary non-inquest case.) West was standing by the side table, trying to improve the appearance of a large, very untidy brown paper parcel.

"What's that, West, our old bones?"

"The old bones, sir. But I've just taken a dekko at 'em, sir, and they look a bit fishy to me. The D.D.I.'s been told they're here, sir."

"Well, I'll take a look at them in a minute, when he arrives, but let's polish this p.m. off first."

We were just finishing the p.m. when in came Divisional Detective Inspector Hatton, followed by Detective Inspector Keeling.

Mr Hatton is a very big, round-faced man, devoted to what he called "hard facts". He was, at that time, up to his eyes in work — Black-Market offences, I believe he once said — and so he very understandably hoped that the "old bones" were those of an air-raid casualty, or an old body from the graveyard, and nothing more. He frankly said so. D.I. Keeling said nothing. Keen, quiet, very interested, he watched C. K. S. untie the string of the brown paper parcel . . .

The body . . . but one could scarcely call it a body. It was really no more than an incomplete skeleton, with a few withered tissues adhering. The skull was loose from the trunk. Dr Simpson, at that first examination, could say no more than that these remains were of a person some twelve to eighteen months dead, and that without doubt they were female, as the uterus (womb) was discernible. The body was small, so he added it might be that of a girl, maybe a young woman bomb-casualty. He asked to be allowed to take the remains round to Guy's, where he could work on them at his leisure, for any attempt to reconstruct them would obviously require hours of painstaking work.

So West presently carried the parcel round to Guy's for us.

When C. K. S. and I went into the Gordon Museum on the following Monday, there lay the brown paper parcel, and this time it was Ireland who was contemplating it with interest. C. K. S. untied the string again and then we stood staring at this withered dried thing. Corpses, subjected to modern methods of examination, do talk, talk plenty, but it did look as though it would require a miracle to extract much more than a peep from this one.

The first thing Ireland did was to exchange the lady's brown paper wrappings for a more respectable white dust-sheet. Meanwhile, C. K. S. remarked, "Well, the probability is that she's no more than an air-raid victim, but even so she will provide me with a very interesting essay in reconstruction; some entertaining spare-time work." And he gave me a grin. "Spare-time work" was a joke between us by that time.

On that Monday evening, when I went home, I left him happily in the Gordon Museum, cleaning the body with little bits of rag. Next day it was greatly improved in appearance. Cleaned of the dust and grit and the withered tissue it looked, even to me, to be considerably more informative. Dr Simpson pointed out to me that the body did not seem to be an altogether normal air-raid casualty. The skull, for example, had been severed from the trunk very cleanly. The lower jaw was missing, there was no scalp tissue adhering to the skull, excepting one very small particle at the back of the head — and bomb-blast does not scalp its victims like that. Neither did any of the facial tissue remain, not even a small tag. The lower parts of the arms and legs were missing; these amputations scarcely tallied with mutilation by falling debris — the limb extremities might have been chopped off, but scarcely shattered. Lastly, there were marks of burning upon the head, down the left side of the body, and at the level of each knee.

Could it be that the remains were those of a murder victim, and that an attempt had been made to dispose of the body, and destroy all clues to identity, by chopping off the head, stripping it of all face and scalp tissue, removing the lower jaw, chopping off the hands and feet and then burning? If so, the job had been crudely done; a body is a difficult thing for an inexperienced person to dismember; somebody seemed to have had a grisly time carving and hacking at this one.

A light of anticipation now began to shine in Keith Simpson's eye. He set to work to see to what extent he could establish the identity of the remains. He began by estimating the height of the dead woman in life by means of the famous Pearson's formulae mathematical formula; applied to one of the long bones of the body. The only bone available here was the left humerus — upper-arm bone. I was asked to work out the problem.

Now at mathematics I am a complete dolt. Even simple arithmetic of the adding-up and taking-away sort stumps me. So I huddled desperately over Pearson's formulae, finally announcing to my distinguished employer that I estimated the dead woman to have been eight foot nine in life. There was a strained silence . . . Then he took the pencil and paper from me and worked it out himself. Correct result, five feet and a half-inch-five feet one inch.

The next step was to discover the age of the woman. This was done by X-raying the various bone fusions, or sutures. The palate suture confirmed that the woman had been between forty and fifty.

Examination of the small piece of scalp still adhering to the back of the skull showed her to have had dark brown hair, going grey.

Examination of the remains of the womb showed that she had suffered from a fibroid growth.

So now we knew that the body was that of a woman aged between forty and fifty, height five feet and a half-inch-five feet one inch, with dark brown hair going grey, and suffering from a fibroid tumour of the womb. She had been dead between twelve and eighteen months.

It was at this point that D.I. Keeling came to call on us with a significant gleam in his eye, and a most interesting story.

Mr Keeling had discovered that the wife of a former fire-watcher, one Harry Dobkin, at 302 Kennington Lane — the premises where the body had been found — had been missing for the past fifteen months. And Mr Keeling had a hunch that this shrivelled corpse now lying in the Gordon Museum was Mrs Harry Dobkin.

Dr Simpson told him the details of height, age and so on, that he had established, and confessed his own suspicions that the remains *might* be those of a murder victim. Thereupon Mr Keeling, not daring to hope too much, but nevertheless in somewhat of a delicious twitter, hurried away to see if he could check these facts with actual identity data of the missing Mrs Dobkin. He went, in short, to visit Mrs Dobkin's sister. (Who had fifteen months ago reported Mrs Dobkin's disappearance to the police.)

And Dr Simpson, in an heroic endeavour to control his own excitement, remarked to me, "If she is Mrs Dobkin, and we can reconstruct her, it'll be a classical case, the kind of case that comes once in a lifetime. But it's almost too much to hope for. In all likelihood, Miss L., she's nothing more than an air-raid victim . . ."

Next day — July 21st, it was a date to remember — Dr Simpson came into the Gordon Museum after lunch, tucked the body, still wrapped in the dust-sheet, under his arm, and requested Ireland and myself to follow him; Ireland with the microscope, myself with typewriter. Away marched our small procession, to the Pathology Block; Keith Simpson, myself, Ireland. We climbed four flights of stairs — owing to air-raids the electric lift was out of order, which was hard luck on

Ireland, for the microscope was very heavy — and found ourselves in the Department of Clinical Chemistry, through which C. K. S. guided us, to conduct us finally into a very small room leading from the main laboratory. Triumphant and corpse-encumbered he flourished a welcoming hand. "Miss Lefebure, Ireland, allow me to usher you across the threshold of the Guy's Hospital Department of Forensic Medicine."

We stepped, with respect, into the Department of Forensic Medicine. All three in there together, we could scarcely turn round for want of space. C. K. S. said solemnly, "From small births grow great institutions."

"Hear, hear, Dr Simpson," said Ireland, putting down the microscope, with relief, on the laboratory bench. I put down the typewriter, C. K. S. put down the queried Mrs Dobkin, and that was the christening ceremony of the Department of Forensic Medicine, Guy's Hospital.

It was, so far as accommodation went, indeed a small birth. Our new "Department" was about ten feet long and five feet wide; a rather brash visitor observed that there literally was no room to swing a cat. He received the frigid reply, "I see no reason why anybody should wish to swing a cat."

A long bench ran the length of the room, and there was a very large window over the bench, affording a view of a brick wall, above which was a strip of smoky Southwark sky. The room contained two laboratory stools, Keith Simpson's microscope, his reference books, a huge blotter, my typewriter, and the scales and weights of Dr Ryffel, the Home Office analyst, head of the Department of Clinical Chemistry, whose weighing-room this really was; he had, as it were, kindly sub-let to us.

In addition, of course, there was the body; that fragmentary body, wrapped in a dust-sheet, which might perhaps be Mrs Harry Dobkin. Might be a "case in a lifetime".

The hopes which we pinned upon this body, very tentatively at first, gradually gained strength, for Mr Keeling was working hard at his end of the case and his discoveries tallied remarkably with those of Dr Simpson. For example, Mr Keeling learned that Mrs Dobkin, missing from home for fifteen months, had been five feet one inch tall, aged forty-seven, with dark brown hair going grey. She had attended the London Hospital for fibroid tumour of the womb, and had refused an operation to remove this tumour.

All this corresponded exactly with the data C. K. S. had extracted from the remains: woman with fibroid tumour of the uterus, some fifteen months dead, estimated height five feet and a half-inch-five feet one inch, aged between forty and fifty, with dark brown hair going grey. Within the privacy of Guy's we began confidently calling the body "Mrs Dobkin". "Miss L., would you take Mrs Dobkin down to Surgical X-ray, please? I want Miss Newman to take some photographs of her." So down to Surgical X-ray I would go, with Mrs Dobkin (in her dust-sheet) under my arm — she weighed very little — and for a while I would sit with her perched on my knee before a galaxy of lights while

74

Miss Newman took photographs. (I had better add that I did not appear in the photographs.)

On the Saturday following the opening of the Department of Forensic Medicine, C. K. S. and I went with Mr Keeling to the premises in Kennington Lane where the body was found.

Number 302 Kennington Lane was a disused house partially rented out as a paper store, and it was here that Harry Dobkin had worked as a fire-watcher. Number 304, next door to 302, was a bomb-wrecked Baptist Chapel, and it was in the cellar at the back of this chapel that the body was found.

It was rather a gruesome spot, this chapel, damaged by blast and fire. The cellar had previously lain buried under the fallen vestry, but this debris had been cleared by the demolition men, exposing the cellar to open air. A crazy little spiral iron staircase which once led from the chapel down to the vestry now clung airily to the charred chapel wall, its bottom step leading foolishly into space. The cellar contained nothing but the flagstone under which the body was found, and a rotten old wooden box in which the body may have been temporarily concealed.

We spent about half an hour in the chapel that first visit. We returned the following Monday, along with Area Superintendent (now Deputy Commander) Rawlings, Chief Inspector Davis and Detective Sergeant (now Chief Inspector) Dawes, as well as D.D.I. Hatton and D.I. Keeling. Chief Inspector Davis had been in charge of the investigations which had taken place some fifteen months earlier when Mrs

Dobkin was first reported missing by her sister, Miss Dubinski.

Miss Dubinski had told the police that her sister was living apart from her husband, Harry Dobkin, and had constantly to press him for arrears in the maintenance money he paid her. On April 11th, 1941, Mrs Dobkin told her sister she was meeting Dobkin, presumably once again to ask him for arrears. After lunching with her mother and sister at their flat Mrs Dobkin went out — and was never again seen by them. But at 6.30p.m. she was seen by a waitress in a café at Dalston, having tea with Dobkin. They left the café together; after that nobody ever saw her alive again.

Next day, April 12th, her handbag was found at Guildford post office. As it contained her identity card, ration book, and rent book the loss would certainly have been a serious one for her, yet she never made any attempt to claim this handbag. The police view at the time was, and still is, that Dobkin planted the bag in the post office himself, as a false clue.

At 5p.m. that same day Miss Dubinski reported the disappearance of her sister to Commercial Road police station. She insisted her sister had come to some harm at the hands of Dobkin — who in the past had frequently treated her violently. Dobkin was interviewed by the C.I.D. on April 16th. He made a statement describing the meeting with his wife on April 11th. He said that after they left the café in Dalston his wife got on an eastbound bus and he hadn't seen her since. He thought she had lost her memory and wandered off. He added that though his wife knew the Kennington

Lane address where he fire-watched she had never visited him there.

Four nights after Mrs Dobkin disappeared, the night of April 15th — 16th, a somewhat mysterious fire broke out in the cellar of the Baptist Chapel. There was no enemy action that night, so incendiary bombs were out of the question, and no inflammable material was known to have been kept in the cellar. Dobkin, the fire-watcher, said the fire started at 1.30a.m., but he didn't call the fire-brigade. Neither did he put the fire out. At 3.23a.m. a passing constable saw the fire and called the brigade. Dobkin was there, very flustered. The fire was fierce by that time and, although there can be no doubt Dobkin started it, it seemed to have become a much larger conflagration than he had intended. The brigade made no search of the premises when they had extinguished the fire. But at 5a.m. the minister of the chapel, Mr Burgess, arrived. He went down into the cellar, where the fire had obviously started. Dobkin had gone off duty, but the minister found in the cellar remains of a straw mattress — where certainly no straw mattress had ever been before. Moreover the mattress had been ripped open and straw taken from it and scattered in small heaps over the cellar floor. Mr Burgess reported this to the fire-brigade. At 2p.m. he again visited the cellar. During the intervening period somebody else had been down there, the straw had been tidied up, and a garden fork left in the cellar. Now thoroughly suspicious, Mr Burgess visited the cellar yet again at 7p.m. to have a little talk with Dobkin, who by that time was on duty. Dobkin was not very clear in his account of the fire. He seemed very jumpy, too. He advised Mr Burgess not to go down into the cellar as it was dangerous; he said he himself had been down there and it was very rough. Mr Burgess was not at all satisfied with this interview and more than suspected that Dobkin had started the fire himself. He confided these suspicions to his private diary.

A description of the missing woman was circulated, with a photograph, in the *Police Gazette*. Miss Dubinski herself inserted a photograph and description of her sister in the *News of the World*, three times. But all with no result. Meanwhile, Inspector Davis and Sergeant Dawes searched the chapel on April 28th and again on May 1st and 2nd. They made a very interesting discovery. The cellar extended for some distance under the floor of the chapel itself, and away under here they found a freshly dug hole, shallow, like a grave, some six feet long by two feet wide. But it was empty. Had it been dug as an intended burial-place for Mrs Dobkin?

Sergeant Dawes searched the place on all fours till he wore his trousers away at the knees, to use his own expression, but he found no body anywhere. Dobkin gave up his work as fire-watcher on May 20th, the police, having drawn a blank, reluctantly abandoned their investigations, and the matter was forgotten, until the sunny Friday, fifteen months later, when the demolition workers prised up the flagstone . . .

And now here we were all at the chapel, with Sergeant Dawes once again crawling on all fours under the chapel floor, to show Dr Simpson and Mr Keeling, also on all fours, where the intended grave had been.

I wanted to crawl under the floor too, but was firmly assured by a stern male chorus that it was too dirty for me. So I had to remain in the chapel above, with Messrs Rawlings, Davis and Hatton, peeking down at the three explorers from time to time through the cracks in the rotting floorboards.

The chapel was by now a very dilapidated, jim-jammy old place indeed, especially in the rain — it was raining that morning. It made me think of a Tom Sawyer — Huck Finn ghost haunt. The roof was full of holes, through which the rain dripped on to the rows of dirty mute pews below, where hassocks and old hymn-books mouldered together. On the dais at the end of the building a battered harmonium lolled like a lunatic and pages of holy music lay scattered round it like grimy snow. The place seemed to be awaiting a congregation of Baptist ghosts.

Presently C. K. S., D.I. Keeling and Sergeant Dawes emerged from the cellar, all three rather red in the face from being bent double so long, and very dusty. It certainly did seem, observed C. K. S., that a hole had been dug under there as an intended grave. "Yes, and he never put her in it, miserable old swine," said Sergeant Dawes, angrily rubbing his knees. "There was I sniffing round that empty grave, and the body not twenty yards from me, under the slab. So near, and yet so far!"

And both he and Mr Davis looked extremely glum, while Mr Keeling grinned delightedly, for the case had now passed from the hands of Chief Inspector Davis to D.D.I. Hatton, under the supervision of his Area Superintendent, Mr Rawlings.

This was because Miss Dubinski had originally reported her sister's disappearance to Commercial Road police station, where Mr Davis had at the time been D.D.I. He and Sergeant Dawes had consequently made the first investigations, which had resulted in such a disappointing blank. But now Mr Davis was a Chief Inspector at the Yard, and, moreover, the body had been unearthed in Kennington and reported by the coroner, Mr Wyatt, to the Southwark C.I.D., and the chief of that C.I.D. division was Mr Hatton. So the Dobkin case had become his pigeon. And Detective Inspector Keeling, his aide-de-camp, positively glowed with excitement to think that such a plum of a case had come his way, but Mr Hatton looked very phlegmatic, standing with his hands in his pockets, staring moodily at the cellar where the body had been found. He was up to his eyes in work, he grumbled, and really hadn't wanted a murder just then.

The next day we were all at the chapel again. It was a blazing hot day, but C. K. S. had had an idea, and Mr Rawlings had agreed it was an excellent idea, so here we all were: Mr Rawlings, Chief Inspector Davis, D.I. Keeling, Sergeant Dawes, the coroner's officer, two or three police constables who had volunteered to assist, and two demolition workers who had been more or less press-ganged by Mr Keeling. Mr Hatton was absent; he was tracking down some black-marketeers, explained Mr Keeling.

Dr Simpson's idea was this: the demolition men, on the day they discovered the body, had removed all the rubble from the cellar and deposited it in a big pile in the old graveyard. For all they knew — or we knew — this rubble contained other fragments of the body; important identity clues, perhaps, such as the lower jaw, which was missing from the skull, the hands, or the feet. So now this pile of rubble, all three tons of it, must be sifted.

"Well, Mr Davis," said C. K. S., taking off his jacket. "Well, Dr Simpson," said Chief Inspector Davis, taking off his. And beneath the baking sky, hot and blue as an enamel plate straight from the oven, the company picked up shovels and began digging into the pile of rubble. Two police constables held a sieve. The two demolition men propped themselves on *their* shovels, and stood gaping and grinning like zanies. Probably they had never seen people work so vigorously as that before. Certainly something struck them as very funny. But after a while they were persuaded to hold another sieve between them, and they grew quite interested.

I had to stand by, noting the findings. These were not inspiring. A large number of mutton bones, rabbit bones, metal shoe-heel pieces, old metal buttons, hairpins, and shards of flower-pots appeared, but nothing else.

It took two afternoons of hot work to sift all the rubble, but at last it was done. Work, alas, that yielded nothing, but which proved, if further proof were needed, that it is true the C.I.D. leaves no stones unturned in the course of investigation.

There was by this time little doubt, if any, that Dobkin had murdered his wife and concealed her remains in the Baptist Chapel under the flagstone, after doing his best to mutilate the body and then destroy it in a fire. But the police were still a long way from being able to charge him with murder. The identity of the remains had still to be clinched and the cause of death established. Dobkin had murdered his wife, but how? It seemed that discovery of this might well prove impossible.

Mr Keeling now telephoned us to say he had a photograph of Mrs Dobkin. Judged by this portrait the lady had been a rather wan, damp, dispirited personality, but she had somehow contrived for this holiday snap to twist her features into a watery holiday smile. Dr Simpson was delighted to have this portrait. He was going to use it as the portraits of the two victims in the famous Ruxton case had been used . . .

A photograph was taken of a full-face view of the dead woman's skull and upon this the holiday portrait was superimposed. The two corresponded exactly.

This additional evidence of identification was, however, not enough to establish identity beyond all possible dispute. For the final evidence we turned to the upper jaw.

D.I. Keeling set about tracking down Mrs Dobkin's dental surgeon. Presently he was found, Mr Barnet Kopkin, of Crouch End. Fortunately he had kept the most detailed record cards of the treatment he had given Mrs Dobkin. He was able to draw a diagram of her upper jaw as he had last seen it, and then Mr

Keeling brought him along to Guy's to compare this diagram with the upper jaw of the body.

It was a very exciting moment: Mr Kopkin, standing in our Department, with Mr Keeling, looking rather grim, standing behind him; Dr Simpson politely handing Mr Kopkin Mrs Dobkin's skull, Mr Kopkin taking it in both hands and then saying, without hesitation, in a tone of mingled triumph and amazement, "This is Mrs Dobkin's upper jaw. That is the jaw I attended and those are my fillings."

The diagram he had drawn corresponded perfectly with the actual jaw.

A further detail established the jaw as Mrs Dobkin's to an even more indisputable degree. Mr Kopkin's record card mentioned that in extracting two teeth from the left side of the upper jaw in April 1941 fragments of the roots of the teeth had been left in the jaw — not an uncommon occurrence. Sir William Kelsey Fry, the famous Guy's dental surgeon, X-rayed the jaw on this side and discovered these roots.

The police now considered the identity of the remains was established without a doubt. They could charge Harry Dobkin with murdering his wife, Rachel Dobkin, if they could find out how he had murdered her.

Dr Simpson bent all his energies to this task. And found that Harry Dobkin himself had done his best to help him.

For Dobkin, in a last attempt to destroy the body, had sprinkled slaked lime over it, particularly round the neck. But slaked lime doesn't destroy; rather, it preserves. In this case the slaked lime had preserved injuries to the throat, especially to the voice-box, and these injuries told Dr Keith Simpson everything.

I remember leaving him, one evening, seated at the laboratory bench, with a large sheet of white blotting-paper spread before him, and on the blotting-paper the bones of the voice-box, delicate and intricate as pieces of a Chinese puzzle. At these he probed, lightly but firmly, with a slender steel probe. He was in for a long, quietly satisfying session of "spare-time work".

Next morning, when he picked me up at Euston, I saw at once from his smile that it had been a very satisfying session indeed. As I settled myself in the car, he said, "It's murder, Miss L."

"It is?"

"Yes, without any possible doubt. When we get to Guy's I'll show you."

When we arrived at Guy's we went up to our small, but so soon to be famous, department, and there C. K. S. showed me what he had found. The bones of the voice-box still lay carefully set out on the blotting-paper. C. K. S. took up the probe again, pointing with it.

There was some dried blood-clot around the upper horn of the right wing of the voice-box; this clot indicated bruising and meant that there had been great pressure upon the throat while Mrs Dobkin was still alive. Under the bruising was a fracture of this upper horn of the wing. Now, this was of enormous importance, for such a fracture never occurs excepting in cases of manual strangulation. Without a doubt Mrs Dobkin had been strangled manually.

There was one other injury, to the back of the head, where there was more blood-clot, indicating heavy bruising. This injury suggested that Mrs Dobkin had either fallen backwards to the ground under the weight of her assailant, or had had her head bashed against the ground by the man who gripped her throat with frenzied hands, battering and strangling her.

So the moment for which we had all been working had at last come. For three months we had guarded the secret of the discovery of Mrs Dobkin's body. No word had leaked out, even to the Press. For three months we had all worked, quietly but doggedly. In July the remains had been found, now it was October, and the time was ripe for D.D.I. Hatton to arrest Harry Dobkin.

Like so many murderers, Dobkin, undoubtedly, was convinced he had outwitted the police. He had killed his wife — though whether in a fit of fury, or after cold-blooded premeditation, we shall never know. He admitted she had said to him, at that last meeting on the fateful April 11th, 1941, "If you don't make peace with me I will make trouble for you." As she had already on two occasions had him imprisoned for not paying her maintenance he obviously had good reason for wishing her out of his way. She was becoming an awful nuisance. Therefore, coolly or heatedly, he put her out of his way by murdering her, and then set about disposing of the body with ghastly determination and considerable cunning; chopping, scalping, stripping away the face, gouging out the eyes, cutting away the lower jaw, and finally, after four nights of bloody toil, attempting to burn what was left. And when the lady would not burn he sprinkled slaked lime over her and left her under a heavy slab.

There is little doubt that from time to time he revisited the cellar and probably took peeps at the decomposing body under the stone slab. Its condition reassured him that if it were ever uncovered it could never be traced as Mrs Dobkin. The authorities would accept it as an old air-raid victim. He believed — what reason was there for him to believe otherwise? — that he had got away with murder.

It is definitely known that Dobkin paid one of these visits to Kennington Lane on August 8th, 1942, two and a half weeks after the discovery of the body. (Perhaps he had heard a rumour that the demolition workers had found some old bones there.) At any rate, a passing constable saw Dobkin go into 302 Kennington Lane, where he had no reason to go, for he had given up fire-watching there long ago, and presently open a window and peer out.

Dobkin, surveying the chapel from his vantage point, could not fail to notice that the demolition workers had cleared and tidied the cellar of all the old debris, exposing it to the light of day, and that they had moved the stone slab from its old position. Obviously the body had been discovered at last.

Did his heart sink suddenly then? Or was his confidence so great he felt no qualms? I think it was the latter case. Like most people, Dobkin had absolutely no notion of the extent to which the police use modern science to help them in their investigations. He never dreamt, for a second, that the body had been taken to an up-to-date laboratory and examined by a pathologist, an analyst and a dental surgeon who were all leading experts in their respective spheres, and that it had been X-rayed, photographed, taken to pieces and put together again like a jigsaw puzzle. Lastly, Dobkin greatly underestimated the intelligence of the C.I.D. Detectives are no longer, if they ever were, flat-footed boys of the bull-dog breed plodding about, laboriously counting up two and two on their fingers and, just about, making the answer four. Writing of the Dobkin case later in the *Police Journal,* Dr Simpson said, "The case . . . is a good example of the versatility of the C.I.D. officer. The most scientific investigation the C.I.D. have ever had to perform was completed without a slip, extensive technical reports being compiled by an unselected group of officers with a competence which amply justifies its reputation."

Dobkin, like so many people, didn't know the C.I.D.

But now October had come — a strangely fateful month, October, an eternal month of reckonings — and Harry Dobkin *was* to get to know the C.I.D.

D.D.I. Hatton had Dobkin brought in to Southwark police station; into his office with its little high windows, its files, its paper-stacked desks. And Mr Hatton said to Dobkin, "In fairness to you I am now telling you that human remains were found in a cellar at a chapel next to where you were fire-watching in April, 1941, and we are satisfied they are those of your wife." To which Dobkin, a born blusterer, replied, "I don't know what you are talking about. I don't know of any cellar at the chapel and have never been down there. In fact, I don't believe it is my wife, but if you tell me so, I suppose I must accept it."

He was told that a police constable had seen him looking out of the window at 302 Kennington Lane, surveying the chapel and debris-cleared cellar in early August, whereupon Dobkin flew into a violent rage and jumped up, shouting, "Show him to me, the liar, show him to me."

The constable was brought in and asked if Dobkin were the man he had seen at Kennington Lane. He said, "That's the man. I've spoken to him several times at Kennington Lane about lights he has shown. I know him well." Dobkin, purple with anger, bellowed, "That's a lie. I've never seen him before, and I wasn't there. He's lying! He's lying!"

Now Dobkin, from the start, was much given to writing memoranda and statements for the police. He had, for instance, sent Chief Inspector Davis a long voluntary statement (incidentally quite untrue) at the outset of the investigation, and he sat down now, quite of his own accord, in Mr Hatton's office, pulled an old grocer's bill from his pocket and on the back of it wrote, in a big, rambling scrawl, a statement for Mr Hatton. It began:

"Divisional Inspector, Dear Sir,
    "In respect to what you say that my wife has been found dead or murdered, and that you say I

88

know something I am holding back from the Police . . ."

and off it roamed, but Mr Hatton, on Dobkin handing it to him, didn't bother with the roaming rest of it, for the first three lines were enough. "In respect to what you say that my wife has been found dead or murdered . . ." Ah, but nobody had uttered one word to Dobkin about his wife being *murdered*. How much better for him if he had not been so fond of writing voluntary statements!

Without more ado D.D.I. Hatton charged Harry Dobkin with the murder of his wife, Rachel Dobkin.

During the following days Dobkin continued to pester Mr Hatton with scrawled literary effusions: never, possibly, was a murderer so anxious to write notes to the police. Mr Hatton, when we visited him in his office one afternoon, brought out handfuls of these "*billets-doux*" as he called them, all scrawled on odd scraps of paper, any old scraps of paper, in Dobkin's big, round, rambling hand. "Always writing to me, always! Thinks I haven't anything better to do than read letters!" exclaimed the exasperated Mr Hatton, with an impatient gesture that sent Dobkin's communications scattering over the floor. Mr Keeling, grinning, picked them up.

We first saw Dobkin when he arrived at Southwark Coroner's Court for the opening of the inquest. A stocky, very powerful, somewhat stupid, albeit cunning man, with small, quick, cunning eyes and a big, shovel-shaped, inquisitive nose. He was taken into the mortuary yard to await the inquest and there he asked to see his wife. This, of course, was an impossibility. Very confident, he smoked a cigarette and offered West one too.

When he came into court he seemed very easy, almost contemptuous. He looked around at us all, and his expression plainly said, "Now let's hear what you've managed to cook up against me."

Nothing was said on that occasion to shake his confidence. Mr Harvey Wyatt merely adjourned the inquest until the trial should be over and Dobkin lurched, with a smug expression, out of the court.

Next time we saw him was at Lambeth Police Court. He sat in the dock there, his hands comfortably resting on his knees, wearing that same smug expression on his face. He remained so until Dr Simpson began giving his evidence. Then, gradually, a ghastly change came over Dobkin.

Keith Simpson spoke clearly, slowly, sentence by sentence piling the facts. And Dobkin, realising that the veil had been miraculously torn from his secrets, began to sweat. He pulled out his handkerchief and mopped his forehead, the back of his neck, the palms of his hands. His face became white. He shifted in his seat, gripped his knees with his big hands until the knuckles gleamed. If ever a man was shattered, Dobkin was.

On Tuesday, November 17th, 1942, Dobkin appeared for trial at the Old Bailey, before Mr Justice Wrottesley. Mr (now Mr Justice) Byrne and Mr Gerald Howard appeared for the prosecution and Mr F. H. Lawton for the defence.

Dobkin at the trial was fearfully nervous, impatient, very angry, darting furious glances round the court, and especially at Dr Simpson, Mr Keeling and myself, who sat at a table directly below the dock. Mr Keeling whispered to me, "If looks could kill, we'd certainly be dead."

From time to time Dobkin scribbled little notes which he passed to Mr Lawton. Mr Hatton, noticing this, grinned. "Still at it," he commented.

Mr Lawton put up a magnificent and grimly tenacious struggle on Dobkin's behalf, but in the face of Prosecution's overwhelming evidence he could achieve very little. And what he did achieve was successfully sabotaged by Dobkin himself when he went into the witness-box.

During the first stages of the trial Dobkin, as I have said, was nervous, but also very angry. By the time he reached the witness-box himself he appeared less angry, more apprehensive. He faced Mr Byrne as if he did not quite know what to expect. Mr Byrne's eye flickered, as he measured Dobkin with a cold, cold gaze, and then in even colder tones he began, "Were you fond of your wife?"

Dobkin, startled, hesitated and then, of course, had to reply, "No."

Mr Byrne questioned Dobkin about his arrears of maintenance money and terms of imprisonment imposed for these arrears, and then asked, "Did your wife tell you that if you did not make peace with her she would make trouble for you?"

"She said if I did not make peace she would make trouble for me."

"You would have felt much happier if you had never seen your wife again after that?"

Dobkin countered warily, "I would have been more content if she had kept away."

Mr Byrne pressed his point. "You had no desire to see your wife again at any further date?"

"No, sir," replied Dobkin, "I did not want to see her again."

"And after the eleventh of April," said Mr Byrne, again with that sinister flickering of the eye, "nobody saw your wife again?"

Dobkin was obliged to stammer that it was so.

This was the opening gambit of a long and brilliant cross-examination during which Mr Byrne played Dobkin as a skilful matador plays a bull. Indeed, the simile was singularly apt. The lumbering, massive Dobkin, sniffing suspiciously with his broad raised muzzle, faced the dark and graceful Mr Byrne, under the bright light, before an audience almost stiff with excitement, in an atmosphere charged with drama over which brooded the ultimate shadow of death. Mr Byrne, utterly self-possessed, beguiled Dobkin here, goaded him there, incited him to charge full-tilt and then brought him to a sickening, thudding halt, by degrees reducing this man, thereby, to a great, bewildered, panting hulk. All the good Mr Lawton had done for his client was speedily destroyed. Dobkin accused all the witnesses — excepting the medical witnesses — of lying. Of everybody else, from chapel

minister to C.I.D. inspector, he shouted, "He's lying!"
He insisted he had never been down in the cellar, had
never even known the existence of the cellar; although
two reputable witnesses had already described how they
had seen him go down into it, and Mr Burgess, the
minister, had been warned by Dobkin not to go down
into the cellar as it was dangerous!

In his panic Dobkin scarcely knew what he was
saying. Lying, blustering, floundering, sweating and
shaking, he gave us a hideous and unforgettable
portrait of terror. The jury stared at him in a kind of
hypnotised horror. The strong circumstantial evidence,
the astonishing medical evidence, must have weighed
heavily with them, the judge's summing-up was a
pattern of what a lucid summing-up should be, but
without a doubt it was Dobkin's performance in the
witness-box that set the final seal upon his fate.

The jury took only twenty minutes to find a verdict.
The court was packed to its limit with people waiting
with truly bated breath for the *coup de grâce,*
the *descabello.* And then word went round that the
jurymen were coming back. Dobkin was brought up
into the dock again; stood there, very pale, poking his
big, anxious nose into the air, as if trying to smell the
verdict in advance, as the jurymen, never looking at
Dobkin (a bad sign, this), filed into the court.

"Members of the jury," cried the clerk of the court,
"are you agreed upon your verdict?"

The foreman of the jury replied, in a low voice, "We
are."

"Do you find the prisoner, Harry Dobkin, guilty or not guilty of murder?"

"Guilty, my lord."

"You find him guilty of murder, and that is the verdict of you all?"

"That is the verdict of us all."

All eyes were fixed on Dobkin's face. When he heard the word "Guilty", falling heavily as a black stone into the solemnity of the court-room, he turned green, a vomiting green of the sea.

The clerk of the court resumed, after a short pause, "Prisoner at the bar, you stand convicted of murder. Have you anything to say why the Court should not give you judgment of death according to the law?"

Dobkin was always ready to say something, and even at this dire moment he produced a sheet of paper and began reading one of his long rigmaroles from it, accusing the police of having fabricated the case against him and asserting that not all the witnesses had been called. He had witnesses who could prove, he said, who could prove who could prove ... but his speech became more and more disjointed, we could not understand what his witnesses could prove, for his words stuck like a cracked record and then gradually whittled away, leaving him lamely and huskily concluding, "I hope I have not said too much."

Mr Justice Wrottesley put on his black cap and Dobkin stared at it helplessly as the judge began to speak, very slowly, very clearly.

"Harry Dobkin, after a patient hearing the jury have come to what I think is the right conclusion on this matter. The sentence is the sentence laid down by law for the offence which you have committed, and it is that you be taken from this place to a lawful prison and thence to a place of execution, and that you be there hanged by the neck until you be dead, and that your body be afterwards buried within the precincts of the prison in which you shall have been confined before your execution. And may the Lord have mercy on your soul."

"Amen," said the chaplain.

There was a moment of utter silence. Then Dobkin turned and walked down from the dock to the cells below; very pale, with a sudden strange vagueness about him, as though his strength and bulk had been driven from him at one blow.

That was the last time I saw Harry Dobkin, alive, though his face as he stood there in the dock listening to the death sentence still haunts me, as no other condemned man's face has. I wonder if those other people who were there watching also find it so impossible to forget.

The next and last time I saw Harry Dobkin was shortly after he had been hanged.

It was a foggy, cold morning when Mr Wyatt the coroner, Dr Simpson, Mr Rawlings, Mr Hatton, Mr Keeling and myself met in the outer yard of Wandsworth prison. After tolling the dismal doorbell we were admitted within the chilling, escapeless walls, and made our way to the prison mortuary, a small building amongst coal dumps and outhouses. It was clammy in there and we stamped our feet and shivered as we waited. Then there was the sound of cartwheels rumbling and clattering (the noise, I imagine, the tumbrils of Paris must have made; creak, clank and rattle) up to the mortuary door. The mortuary assistant opened the door and there, on a rough hand-cart, lay the body of Harry Dobkin, clad in vest, trousers and socks, with the deep mark of the noose round his thick, muscular neck.

They lifted him into the mortuary and placed him on the p.m. table. He looked very peaceful. His debts were settled at last.

The assistant stripped him. Mr Keeling murmured, contemplating those brawny shoulders and muscled arms, "It couldn't have taken much of his strength to kill that poor little woman."

We were told Dobkin had died quietly and bravely, praying ardently.

And that was the end of Harry Dobkin, and the epilogue to the famous Baptist Chapel Cellar Murder, which made medicolegal and C.I.D. history, brought promotion to several detectives, set the Guy's Hospital Department of Forensic Medicine off to a flying start, and added one more great murder story to the list of great murder stories marching gruesomely, but with horrible fascination, down the weirdly echoing corridors of time.

CHAPTER
ELEVEN

The Wigwam Murder

We must now go back to the beginning of October and those days when D.D.I. Hatton was in the throes of arresting Dobkin, and was receiving all those wordy notes, "Divisional Inspector, Dear Sir . . ."

That was in Southwark, among sooty warehouses and grey old streets. In Surrey, against a background of autumn-tinted trees and windy heathland slopes, another outstanding murder drama came to light.

On October 7th C. K. S. got a call from the Surrey police, saying that a body had been found buried on Hankley Common, near Godalming, and they were anxious for Dr Simpson to come at once. We cancelled all other appointments and by midday we were driving fast in the direction of Godalming.

Hankley Common was a former beauty spot, all heathery slopes, broken with graceful spinneys of birch and oak, and surrounded by wide vistas of wooded countryside and windswept sky. The Army, noting its loveliness, had of course taken it over as a battle-training ground. Camps had been built in the neighbouring woods and every day young men were taken out and toughened up amidst a welter of anti-tank obstacles, mortar ranges, field telephones and trip-wires.

We arrived at Hankley Common to find a large party of policemen, headed by the Chief Constable of Surrey and Supt Roberts, and fortified by Dr Eric Gardner, the pathologist, awaiting us in a muddy hollow. Greetings were exchanged and then off we set to climb a windy ridge which reared itself, rain-swept and dismal, ahead of us.

(It is odd how it invariably begins to rain when one reaches the scene of a crime. Up till that time, for instance, it had been quite a bright sunny day.)

As we struggled up the ridge, Supt Roberts told us how the body was found. The previous day two marines, busy training, had discovered an arm sticking out of a mound of earth on the top of the ridge and had immediately reported this to the police. The body had been left buried until the pathologists should arrive.

The top of the ridge was gained and there was the mound of earth with a withered arm sticking out from the side of it. Rats had gnawed away parts of the fingers. We stood contemplating it, shivering a little in the wet wind, and trying to warm ourselves with cigarettes, while the Chief Constable, Dr Gardner, Dr Simpson and Supt Roberts held a quick consultation. Below us a party of soldiers were busy at mortar practice, their shells whirling and whining over our heads every few minutes.

The two pathologists now took shovels and began very carefully uncovering the rest of the body. They had not been long at the job before a great stench of rotting flesh set everybody else busily judging the direction of the wind and then moving accordingly. The pathologists continued to dig, oblivious of everything but their task, and I was obliged to stay beside them, taking from them specimens of beetles, maggots, earth and heather, which I placed in the famous buff envelopes. And so the work went slowly on, until there lay exposed the sprawling, badly decomposed body of a girl.

The body was clothed in a green and white summer dress, light summer underwear, woollen ankle-socks, and a headscarf which lay loosely round the neck. The head had been battered in by some heavy, blunt implement.

It was decided to move the body to Guy's, and there was some discussion as to whether C. K. S. and I should travel back to London in a van with the body or by police car. Much to my relief the police car was finally chosen.

The body soon arrived at Guy's and C. K. S. had it placed in a large carbolic tank so that he might study it at his leisure, or, if you prefer it, in his "spare time".

"Spare time" mostly came at tea-time, so, for the next few weeks, C. K. S. arranged for us to take our tea beside the carbolic tank and its gruesome contents. This, I thought, was a very unattractive idea, for the smell of the body combined with the carbolic was enough to put the most insensitive off anchovy-toast and tea-cakes. However, it was not my place to complain, so there I sat with my tea-tray and memo-pad, jotting the notes which C. K. S. dictated to me as he stooped, all concentration, over the body.

Dr Gardner frequently came up to Guy's to assist with the examination of the body. The two pathologists discovered that the girl had received stabbing wounds to the left side of the top of the head, accompanied by similar wounds to the right arm and hand; these last resulting from the victim putting up her arm in an attempt to ward off the attack.

The pathologists came to a very interesting conclusion about these stab wounds. Because of certain characteristics it was clear they must have been inflicted with a hook-pointed knife. Neither Dr Simpson nor Dr Gardner had ever seen such a knife, but the nature of the wounds convinced them that such a knife must have been used.

Secondly, there were injuries to the mouth in keeping with the girl having fallen heavily on to her face, knocking out her front teeth.

Thirdly, there had been a single very heavy, blunt blow to the back of the head. Dr Simpson and I spent a whole afternoon wiring together all the fragments of shattered skull; it was like doing an exceptionally thrilling and elaborate jigsaw puzzle. When we had finished we found there was a vast depressed fracture of the skull, five inches in length and one-and-three-quarters in breadth, across the back of the head, as from a blow with a stake, or bough, or rounded bar. Such a blow would have killed the girl immediately.

A crush fracture of the right cheek-bone showed that she had been lying face downwards on the ground at the time she received this blow.

Lastly there were dragging wounds to the right leg, which had occurred after death, and which indicated that her body had been dragged over rough, open ground before burial.

So, from these tea-time sessions beside the carbolic tank, C. K. S. was able to tell the police that the girl had been stabbed at with a strange hook-pointed knife, had fallen on her face, knocking out three teeth, and while lying thus had been dealt a tremendously heavy murderous blow to the back of her head with a round, blunt instrument such as a bar, or stake, and finally, being dead, had been dragged over rough ground to the top of the ridge.

Meantime things had not been standing still in Surrey, either.

The Surrey police had decided to call in Scotland Yard, and Mr Greeno, now a Chief Inspector, had gone down to Godalming, on what was to prove one of his most exciting investigations.

It did not take the police long to identify the dead girl, through the clothes she was wearing and a portion of scalp with bleached blonde hair. A blonde girl in her late teens, wearing a green and white frock and a headscarf, was already known to the local police; she had for some time past caused them concern by her mode of life, for she lived rough like a tramp and consorted with soldiers. She was not, the police thought, a really bad girl, but she had run away from her home, and was in need of proper care and protection, or she would, they surmised, rapidly come to grief.

Her name was Joan Pearl Wolfe, she was a Roman Catholic with a strong religious conviction and, alas, poor girl, she surely came to grief.

She had last been seen alive on September 13th, which tallied with Dr Simpson's estimate of the time which must have elapsed since death.

Mr Greeno on his arrival set his men to searching the ground round Hankley Common ridge. Day in, day out, they searched.

Bit by bit they collected clues. First they found the girl's shoes, lying some distance apart from one another, and some way from the body's burial place. Then a bag with a rosary in it was found near one of the shoes, close by a small stream where there was a military trip-wire. Sixteen yards away was found a heavy birch stake. Clinging to this stake were a number of long blonde hairs.

Later, in a small dell up the hillside above the stream, Joan Pearl Wolfe's identity card was found, with a religious tract, and a document which was issued by the Canadian Army to men applying for permission to marry. There was also a green purse, an elephant charm, and a letter from Joan to a Canadian private called August Sangret, telling him she was pregnant by him and hoping he would marry her.

Mr Greeno learned that Joan, since July, had been living in the neighbourhood in rough huts, or "wigwams", which August Sangret had built for her, and where he had spent his leaves with her.

A deserted cricket pavilion which had also been a favourite rendezvous for Joan and Sangret was visited by the detective. Inside, Joan had drawn and scribbled all over the walls. She had drawn a wild rose, writing under it, "Wild Rose of England for ever — September 1942." And there was another sketch of a cabin, "My little grey home in the West." And a prayer written in pencil:

> "O holy Virgin in the midst of all thy glory we implore thee not to forget the sorrows of this world . . ."

There was also pencilled the address of Private A. Sangret, of Canada, and the address of Joan's mother in Kent.

The girl, at one stage, it was discovered, had been admitted to a local hospital, where she kept a photograph of Sangret, her "fiancé", on her bedside locker. From hospital she had written to tell him she was pregnant; pathetic letters explaining that the nuns at the convent where she had been brought up had taught her that an illegitimate baby was a terrible sin, but, she naïvely added, when she and Sangret were married and happy together with the baby everything would be all right.

She bought layette patterns, and people who saw this girl-tramp in the woods in the weeks before she was murdered noticed she was knitting baby-clothes . . .

Chief Inspector Greeno now went to the nearby Canadian Army camp where Sangret was stationed. Sangret was a young man half French-Canadian, half Cree Indian. He had recently asked his C.O. for a marriage application form, but had not returned it filled in. He admitted to Mr Greeno that he had associated with Joan, but added he had not seen her since September 14th, when she had failed to keep a date with him. He had reported her "disappearance" to his provost sergeant, saying, "If she should be found, and anything has happened to her, I don't want to be mixed up in it." He had told a friend that he had sent Joan home, as she had no clothes, and he told another friend that she was in hospital. These friends of Sangret admitted to Mr Greeno that they thought Sangret's behaviour over Joan's disappearance "very strange". First he had said one thing, then he said another, and seemed very much on edge over the whole business.

While Sangret was waiting in the guard-room for this first interview with Mr Greeno he excused himself and went to the wash-house. Nobody thought anything of it, at the time . . .

Mr Greeno, after this interview, came hurrying up to Guy's. He arrived in a van, in the back of which he had what appeared to be a section of Hankley Common. There were furze and bracken, hummocks of grass, and a small tree. These were to be examined for bloodstains. There was, in addition, a Canadian Army blanket, and a battle-dress, and the birch stake that had been found by the stream.

Dr Simpson and Mr Greeno spread the blanket and battle-dress out on a table in the lab and examined them. Both belonged to Sangret and both had recently, but not very effectively, been washed. (Sangret apparently could not, or would not, explain why he had washed them.) On the blanket, despite the washing, were faded bloodstains, distributed exactly in keeping with a person bleeding from the head and right hand that had been wrapped in the blanket. Dr Simpson decided that the body, prior to burial, had been wrapped in this blanket — and probably concealed among bushes. This would explain the very heavy maggot infestation of the body, which had clearly not been buried immediately after death.

The bloodstains on the battle-dress no doubt occurred during Sangret's attack on the girl.

The hairs on the birch stake were examined, compared with the hank of the dead girl's hair already in our possession, and proved beyond doubt to be hairs from the head of Joan Pearl Wolfe. The birch stake, too, exactly fitted the huge fracture at the back of the reconstructed skull. This was certainly the weapon with which the girl had been murdered.

"Now all we want is to find the knife," said Mr Greeno. And returned, accordingly, to searching the ground that had already been searched and searched. For it is infinite patience which so often wins the detective's day. But the knife was not lying amongst the grass and bracken of Hankley Common. Very dramatically it turned up in quite a different place . . .

In mid-November, long after all the leaves had blown down from the trees of Surrey, and Mr Greeno's investigations were plugging doggedly, but not very rapidly, along, up at the Canadian Army camp the waste-pipe of one of the wash-house basins was cleared of an obstruction which had been blocking it for the past five weeks. This obstruction turned out to be a clasp-knife; not a Canadian Army issue, but an unusual-looking knife with a hooked point; a point like a parrot's beak. And it was immediately recalled that Sangret had excused himself and gone into the wash-house while waiting for that first interview with Mr Greeno, five weeks previously. Was this Sangret's knife, and had he dropped it down the pipe in an attempt to hide it from Mr Greeno, knowing what a vital clue it would be to the detective?

It was Sangret's knife all right. One of his fellow soldiers recognised it as such. This soldier had found the knife, he said, during the summer stuck in the trunk of a tree by one of the shacks Sangret had built for Joan. The soldier had pulled it out of the tree and shown it to Sangret, who had immediately claimed it as his own.

The knife was now brought to Guy's and shown to Dr Simpson. Its peculiar hook-tipped blade was, of course, precisely the sort of thing the pathologists had described after examining the stabbing wounds.

The last lap of the investigations had now been reached. C. K. S. travelled down to Surrey again and there, with Chief Inspector Greeno, made a final reconstruction of the murder at the actual scene.

It was clear now what had happened on that September afternoon when Sangret and Joan had their last date. They had quarrelled in the dell up the hillside; probably over the marriage application form which Joan was so anxious for Sangret to fill in and sign, and which he was so loath to complete. Sangret attacked the girl with his knife. She managed to escape him and, terrified, wounded and bleeding, ran down the hill away from him, but at the bottom, by the stream, she fell over the military trip-wire, landing heavily on her face, smashing her teeth. As she lay there, stunned by the fall, Sangret overtook her and murdered her by a crashing blow on the head with the birch stake, which he afterwards flung away. He then wrapped her body in an army blanket and hid it under the bushes for twenty-four hours or so, after which he dragged his victim to the top of the ridge, a distance of some four hundred yards, and buried her.

This reconstruction of the murder must have fitted the actual circumstances very closely, for at the trial Sangret's Counsel never questioned it.

It seemed odd, perhaps, that Sangret should have troubled to drag the body up a fairly steep hill for burial, but perhaps, almost unconsciously, he was following the ritual of his Indian ancestors, who always buried their vanquished enemies upon a height.

Sangret was charged with the murder on December 16th in the presence of Mr Greeno. He said, "No, sir, I did not do it. No, sir. Somebody did it and I'll have to take the rap." He added, uselessly, "She might have killed herself."

The trial was held at Kingston Assizes at the end of the following February. Dr Simpson took the skull along with him to court. We arrived just before the court adjourned for tea. Dr Grierson, then the Chief Medical Officer at Brixton prison, asked C. K. S. if he would care to take some tea down in the gaoler's room, beneath the dock. C. K. S. accepted the invitation, and I was invited too. So into the dock we climbed and thence down the short flight of steps leading to the gaoler's cellar-like quarters below.

It was a rather grim apartment, with stone floor and bare walls and several cells opening on to it. In the middle of the room was a big wooden table, laid for tea, and the gaoler, one or two policemen, two prison warders and Sangret were standing talking together. We all sat down round the table, with the exception of Sangret and the warders, who took their tea standing, buffet style; pretty obviously because Sangret didn't wish to join the tea-party. The atmosphere of the gathering was somewhat out of this world. Dr Simpson, Dr Grierson and the gaoler chatted together on the subject of juries. The policemen were discussing football. I couldn't overhear the conversation between Sangret and the warders, but it sounded amiable enough. I sat silent, eating bread-and-butter and drinking good hot thick tea from an even thicker tea-cup. Every now and again I tried to stare at Sangret without staring at him.

Sangret was a strongly-built young man of medium height, with his Red Indian blood clearly predominant. Straight features, quite impassive, cold, glittering dark eyes, straight dark hair, and a red-bronze skin. With an appetite not at all impaired by the ghastly predicament in which he found himself he enjoyed a large tea, eating and drinking noisily, holding the thick slices of bread-and-butter in both hands. Not a gracious individual with whom to share a wigwam, I mused. And not likely to make anybody a doting, devoted, baby-dandling husband, either. Did he let out a blood-curdling whoop as he crashed Joan's skull in? One could very well imagine it.

However, although he was not a very sensitive-looking man, I did not like to stare at him too much. So I sat quietly sipping tea and listening to the conversation about juries on the one hand, the conversation about who was going to be top of the League on the other, and wondering what Sangret and the warders were talking about. It was certainly the strangest tea-party I ever went to.

At length it was over, the two medical gentlemen and I returned upstairs to the court, and the gaoler and the policemen began clearing away the tea things in nice domestic style. A few minutes later Sangret was back in the dock, facing Mr Justice Macnaghten across the crowded court, and Dr Simpson was in the witness-box, telling the jury how Joan Pearl Wolfe had been murdered.

And now came an historic moment. Dr Simpson took up a cardboard box, raised its lid and lifted out the dead girl's skull, in order to demonstrate to the jury the fracture and the peculiar stab-wounds. It was the first time a murdered person's skull had ever been produced at a trial. All present craned their necks to see, including the judge; all, that is, save one, and that one was Sangret. I watched him, but only the merest twinge of curiosity flickered over his face. Indeed the impassive Redskin.

The medical and circumstantial evidence combined made an overwhelming case against Sangret and the jury found him guilty, but rather unexpectedly added a recommendation for mercy. Why they felt he deserved mercy was a bit of a puzzler to me. The girl had not been killed accidentally, during a scuffle, for the blow to her head had been a truly savage one, delivered with full murderous intent. Nevertheless, the jury felt Sangret deserved mercy.

This plea was duly considered when Sangret appealed, but it was of no avail, and he was executed at Wandsworth a week or so later.

Dr Simpson did a p.m. on him. He lay there on the p.m. table, muscular, well-built, almost good enough for one of Fenimore Cooper's novels, his handsome bronze skin marked only by the imprint of the hangman's noose around his neck, and tattooed on his arm, ironically, the name "Pearl".

CHAPTER
TWELVE

The Gentle Art of Hanging

The first post-mortem on an executed person I attended with Dr Simpson was that of the spy who sold to the Germans the information which resulted in the sinking of the famous *Jervis Bay*. This wretched man, British by nationality, was a large, flabby, plethoric-looking person, suffering from various antisocial ailments and altogether nauseating. He had been hanged at Wandsworth prison, and it was there we did the p.m. on him in the cold, old-fashioned little mortuary with the derelict bird's-nest in the roof and a pile of ancient, unvarnished coffins standing by the door — I always used one of these as a typing-table.

During the course of years we did many p.m.s in this mortuary, some on prisoners who had died natural deaths, some on suicides (but suicide is very rare among prisoners), and the rest of the cases, the majority, on persons who had been judicially hanged.

Post-mortems must be done on all executed persons, because on each one the Coroner must hold an inquest, attended by a jury and Press representatives, to ensure that the execution has been "expeditiously performed".

All the hangings were most expeditiously performed.

The bodies used to be trundled up to the mortuary on little wooden hand-carts which, as they rumbled over the rough stones of the prison yard, always made me think of the tumbrils. A scrunchy, rumbling, rattling sound the little cart made, with the tramping of feet instead of the clopping of horses' hooves.

The dead man would then be lifted from off the cart by the warders who had wheeled it, and carried to the p.m. table. He was clad in trousers, singlet, socks; no shoes. Around his neck was the deep, livid mark of the noose. Otherwise he always appeared perfectly peaceful and in many instances, I thought, positively relieved to be dead.

A condemned man is given a good breakfast, if he wants it, on the morning of his execution and before he goes to the execution shed he receives a tot of brandy — I believe he can have whisky if he prefers it.

The execution is at nine. The law demands that the body must remain hanging for a certain stated period of time after the execution. The autopsy and inquest generally take place about eleven the same morning. Directly the man has been executed notices of execution are pinned up on the prison doors.

There is no doubt that judicial hanging, compared with many natural deaths, is merciful. There is no strangling; the scientific combination of noose and drop jerks the head from the trunk and everything is over in a second or two. Nobody need have any doubt of the swift efficiency with which hanging is practised in our prisons today. It is as quick, humane and efficient a method of execution as any in the world.

It seems to me that the days of waiting in the condemned cell must be the worst part of the ordeal. The actual hanging is quickly over.

Afterwards the body is buried within the prison precincts.

In fact everything is carried out just as the judge declares it shall be when he reads the death sentence to the prisoner, ". . . that you be taken from this place to a lawful prison and thence to a place of execution, and that you be there hanged by the neck until you be dead, and that your body be afterwards buried within the precincts of the prison in which you shall have been confined before your execution. And may the Lord have mercy on your soul."

To which the court chaplain solemnly cries, "Amen."

I have lost count of the number of times I have watched a judge don the black cap and sentence a prisoner to death, but with one or two exceptions all the persons sentenced in these awful terms have behaved with fortitude.

Most people who are hanged die bravely, too.

Prison officials are humane, they do not gloat over executions. The police do not gloat over them. Nobody gloats over them excepting the great general public. The appetite of the public for murders and hangings seems to be insatiable and the Press feeds and stimulates this appetite; for which I think the Press is not to blame, for people only buy the kind of newspapers they want to read. As Tom Clarke started his first lecture of the first term of my year of the London University Journalism Course, "Journalism is not a bloody priesthood." The public gets the kind of newspapers it deserves.

I have sometimes thought that if murderers were not hanged the public would not take such a bloodthirsty interest in the subject of murder and that if public excitement were not so intense there would not be so many murders.

Of course, the English have always had a passion for murders and murderers. Shakespeare, the most popular playwright of his, or any, period, knew this and introduced killings and killers and hangmen into his plays with abandon. He knew that, the more morbid scenes there were, the more audiences would flock to the theatre. "Ho Barnardine, come forth and be hanged, sirrah." And among these plays is *Macbeth*, the greatest murder play ever written, with its intensely moving and terrible scenes and astonishing grasp of criminal psychology.

During the Tudor era public executions took place on Tower Hill and beheading was the usual form of execution, with burnings at the stake second on the bill. We are told that during the reign of Mary Tudor even the public became sickened by the non-stop beheadings and burnings.

Later Tyburn became the scene of public executions. Tyburn Tree, as the gallows was called, stood roughly on the spot where Marble Arch now stands and these occasions of public execution drew immense crowds. The condemned were driven in carts from Newgate prison — on the site of which the Old Bailey now stands — to Tyburn, and the route was lined with crowds, sometimes jeering and cat-calling, but on other occasions cheering and offering encouragement and even refreshment if the condemned were a popular figure; some celebrated highwayman, for example. Jack Sheppard, for instance, the young highwayman who escaped from prison four times before he was finally hanged, rode in positive state to Tyburn and was a national hero.

Tyburn Fair was considered a great entertainment. Pedlars and tumblers and buskers of all kinds were there to amuse the crowds before the executions took place. Men, women and even children thronged to Tyburn with, Samuel Richardson tells us, "a kind of mirth, as if the spectacle they had beheld had afforded pleasure instead of pain".

Boswell, who once went to Tyburn to satisfy his curiosity, describes the crowd as "most prodigious". Scaffolds were erected all round the gallows, rather like grand-stands. Boswell "got upon a scaffold very near the fatal tree, so that we could clearly see the dismal scene . . . I was most terribly shocked, and thrown into a very deep melancholy."

But Boswell was considerably different from most of the other people, who flocked to Tyburn without suffering a qualm.

Hanging in those days was not the scientific matter it is today. There was no proper drop, the prisoner's neck was not dislocated, death was not instantaneous. For some time after the prisoner had hanged he — or she — kept the crowd entertained by convulsively writhing in mid-air; "dancing on the air" it was popularly called. In order to hasten the wretch's end relatives were allowed to pull at his legs. Actually, of course, he became unconscious very soon after he was hanged and the convulsive movements were purely reflex. Neither did pulling the legs hasten death.

Sometimes relatives would bribe the executioner to cut the hanged man down quickly so that the "body" could be hurried to a waiting apothecary, who in some instances was able to revive the "corpse".

In 1783 Tyburn Fair was abolished, much to public disgust. Public executions were now held instead outside Newgate prison. The crowds were still enormous and enthusiastic. With the great bell of the prison tolling and the crowd roaring, the prisoners were brought out to be hanged. There is a terrific description of such a morning of execution in Defoe's *Moll Flanders*.

In 1788 a new kind of gallows was brought into use. By employing a falling trap-door a long enough drop was created to break the prisoner's neck, so that death was almost instantaneous and the famous "dancing on the air" no longer occurred. But enormous crowds still turned up to watch.

Pirates were not executed at Newgate, instead they went to a gallows at Execution Dock, Wapping. Their bodies were afterwards hung in chains, as were the bodies of highwaymen.

England must have been a gruesome place in those days. Imagine walking home along a dark road late at night and having to pass a body strung up at the crossroads, rattling a little as it swayed with the wind. Or entering a town and looking up to see a row of bloody heads impaled above the great gate. And yet perhaps these things were no more gruesome than our own photographs of the "mushrooms" of experimental atom bombs.

The last public execution took place in 1868, not a hundred years ago.

If executions became public again today I suspect that crowds of people would attend them; those people who swarm outside a police court to catch a glimpse of a murderer, who queue up all night to hear a murder trial at the Old Bailey, who gather outside prisons at the hour of execution, in some cases creating hysterical scenes, on other occasions merely standing there as if fascinated and afterwards staring at the small, bald notice of execution which is put up on the door.

As a result of the Royal Commission one reads a good deal about hanging these days. The most interesting observations on the subject that I have ever heard came from the Public Executioner, Mr Albert Pierrepoint, junior, whom I once met at Wandsworth prison.

We were there doing a post-mortem on a murderer, a young Burmese who had kicked his wife to death. Suddenly the mortuary door opened and in came a young man in a blue suit, who stepped in briskly, gave us a cheerful smile and said, "Good morning, Dr Simpson. If you don't mind I'd like to take a look at my handiwork."

We stared at him with some astonishment, whereupon he introduced himself as Albert Pierrepoint, who had just taken over the job of Public Executioner from his uncle, Tom Pierrepoint.

We had already heard quite a lot about Mr Pierrepoint, junior, as a matter of fact. We had been told that the senior Pierrepoint had recently resigned because he felt he was growing too old for his work of hangman and that he had been busy training his nephew to take his place. Although the junior Pierrepoint had so far performed only a few executions he had already proved himself to be greatly and naturally skilled as a hangman.

The Pierrepoints, of course, have provided public executioners for generation upon generation past and are very proud of this family tradition.

Mr Albert Pierrepoint, the newly appointed hangman, our unexpected visitor, was short in stature but powerfully built, with a ruddy face, a round head, bright blue eyes and a quick, cheery manner. There was nothing mawkish about him. He explained he wanted to see a post-mortem because he wanted to know exactly what happened to people when he hanged them. Would Dr Simpson mind showing him? Dr Simpson was agreeable and demonstrated how the neck vertebras had been severed right apart by the jerk of the noose drawing tight at the finish of the drop. Our visitor, deeply interested, asked a large number of highly technical questions.

Mr Pierrepoint assured us that hanging is much more of an art than a science. Certainly it has a strong scientific basis, but a really first-class hangman is born, said our visitor, not bred. Hanging must run in the blood; it requires natural flair. The judgment and timing of a first-class hangman cannot be acquired, they are a gift.

He stressed that technically the most important detail of all is to get the highest point of the noose on the left side of the neck, not too high up.

Finally we asked him if the work upset him. He appeared surprised for a moment. Then he smiled a little and said, "No. I look upon it this way. It's a job that must be done by somebody, and it must be done as well as possible. It is my aim to do it as well as it can possibly be done."

Our visitor then thanked Dr Simpson for demonstrating the body to him, beamed all round the mortuary in a friendly farewell and hurried off, brisk and compact. Since then he has established for himself a great reputation as a hangman. He has even been flown to other countries to perform executions. For my part I shall never forget that morning when he walked into the mortuary to "take a look at his handiwork" and talked to us about the principles of his art, the ancient art of hanging.

CHAPTER
THIRTEEN

Interiors

Bouts of war-weariness now began to grip me from time to time, rather after the fashion of bouts of malaria. One would feel a bout coming on, endeavour to fight it off, fall victim to it, shiver and shake in its grasp, finally to emerge from it bored, depressed and listless. It was a real illness, this war-weariness, and, as the war went on, almost everybody fell victim to it. Many, many people in the world today are still suffering severely from its after-effects.

Of course war-weariness didn't take everybody the same way. Some it made drink a lot. Others took to bed — with others — a lot. Some became hideously gay, brave and hearty. Others became sardonic and bored. Some seriously depressed. The Cockneys sharpened their celebrated wit until it had an edge which cut as painfully and bitterly as grass. A few took to prayer, or started work on a second vegetable allotment, or began a new baby. My grandmother, who was over ninety, crocheted a full set of dinner mats and read right through all the big Russian novelists. She would look up at me from her Turgenev or Gogol — "He's a wicked man, this Fyador, and look what he's done to that poor Masha —" and, breathlessly, would plunge back into the book.

Of course I was really one of the last people with a right to complain, for I had a deeply interesting job and Dr Simpson allowed me three weeks' holiday a year, all in one lump, and often I got an extra fortnight later in the year, too. So when my holiday came I was able to rush up to Cumberland and there work all my war-time spleen out of my system in a marvellous orgy of rock, rope, and long long tramps over the fells. Part of the time I might manage to get my sister or some friend to come with me, but often I was alone up there, on the fells all day without seeing a soul, for the war had removed all the hikers and hostellers, along with their wretched orange peel, and had left the district as God intended it: for sheep, shepherds, ravens and climbers.

These interludes devoted to trying to break my neck on rocks, or capering twenty-mile stints over the tops, purged my system and Lefebure would return south in fine fettle, ready to have another bash at being a perfect secretary — and taking the war on the chin.

I realised how lucky I was to have these breaks, when so many people were going through the war without any breaks at all.

Dr Simpson had a very delightful cottage at Tring, where he had installed his family, and I paid frequent happy visits there. It was wonderful at the end of a day's work to whisk out of dirty old Euston into the quiet of a country summer evening.

It was always marvellous, during the war, for a Londoner to get away from London, even if only for an hour or so. Others flocked to London to spend giddy leaves, but we all wanted to get away from London. We had had London, with a vengeance. London was the fortress we held and where so many of us died, and it was a relief to escape sometimes from its grey, scarred battlements.

As the war went on, Dr Simpson got more and more "country jobs". These trips were always intensely interesting, even if not enjoyable in the ordinary sense of the word, and they introduced a spicy variety into a job which already was very far from being dull.

One spring day in 1943 we were called down to Kent on a queried murder. It was our first visit to Kent. C. K. S. observed that, quite apart from the murder, it should be rather a nice outing.

Very soon we were on our way. The train moved swiftly into the Garden of England and I stared hard out of the window. I didn't know Kent at all. Of course I had realised it would be flat, but not *so* flat. A flat landscape makes me sink, very sinky, and this landscape soon had Lefebure in the depths. Oh, those rows and rows of little fruit trees, planted in dead-straight lines, all gesturing stiffly and singing despondently "Spring will be a little late this year . . ." Ah, that flat earth, which never at any point rose towards the cold March sky. I remembered the comment a friend once made to me about the fen country: "Such desperately platonic scenery, strictly no interesting protuberances." It was the same, I found, with Kent.

When we arrived at Maidstone we were met by a very trim little policewoman driving a very trim little car. She took us to the H.Q. of Kent County Constabulary, where we met Chief Superintendent F. H. Smeed; a very big, burly, charming man with a slow, warm smile. He was about the only thing I approved of in Kent, that afternoon, anyway.

Now we all bundled into a very large car and drove off into the wilds of the Garden of England. The landscape was as pancake-flat as ever and, in this part of the Garden, entirely devoted to cabbages.

Our destination was a very small hamlet, little more than a single row of cottages, set at a crossroads. They were not the sort of cottages you automatically visualise at the mention of cottages. These dismal habitations huddled about the crossroads, gritty-faced and grey-roofed, each with a long, narrow front garden all mud and sog and withered wintry plants.

The cottage we had to visit was sandwiched in the centre of the main row. Waiting in the garden for us was a young detective who let us into the cottage. It was very dark inside and icy cold. Directly we stepped into the place a fearful stench greeted us; the acrid, clinging, clanging odour of positive habitual filth.

The rooms were unbelievably dirty and although you couldn't see the bugs you knew they were there. There were filthy old chairs and curtains and broken furniture, and bits of food lying around, and newspaper on the kitchen table instead of a tablecloth. Filthy clothes and muddy old boots were slung about. There were broken, unwashed crocks and hideous saucepans. The place was rotten and reeking with dirt.

On the kitchen floor, between a chair and the table, lay a dead, middle-aged woman, as filthy and unkempt as the cottage. She was fully dressed and had on a muddy overcoat and boots.

The Coroner's officer began telling us about the case. This woman, he said, had left her husband and come to live in this cottage with a labourer and their two illegitimate children. She and the labourer were given to drinking bouts and the previous evening had gone off on a pub-crawl together. They had arrived back home at about eleven; neighbours heard them quarrelling and banging about.

According to the labourer, he had gone up to bed, leaving his woman sitting in a chair in the kitchen. When he came downstairs in the morning he found her lying dead on the floor.

The neighbours, however, told the police about the quarrelling and banging around and the C.I.D. accordingly decided to look into the matter.

Dr Simpson and the detectives now moved gingerly about the filthy kitchen, taking measurements and searching for an explanation of what had really happened.

"Don't touch anything, miss, or you'll pick something up," advised the Coroner's officer. "It's the dirtiest place I've ever been in."

It was ghastly to think of children living in such a cottage — which was only fit as an abode for black beetles, and not highly particular beetles at that.

I wondered, as I frequently still wonder, why the State cannot prosecute people for being dirty. After all, filth is a menace to the entire community. It seems odd that people can be prosecuted for bad morals, but not for being physically dirty. If this woman had taken up the career of a prostitute she could have been fined, but as a filthy housewife she could not be fined. Personally I feel that a clean prostitute is better than a stinking, dirty housewife who lets her children live like cockroaches.

Of course parents can be fined for neglecting their children, but the neglect has to reach the most appalling proportions before anything can be done about it. I suppose this woman was a borderline case.

Dr Simpson and the detectives had now decided that the labourer's account of the incident was true; there were no signs of a struggle having taken place in the kitchen and the injuries to the woman's head were simply in keeping with her having fallen and struck her head on something as she fell. The body was removed to the local mortuary and the p.m. C. K. S. performed there confirmed this. She had fallen, struck her head, and died of a cerebral haemorrhage.

So that was our first trip to Kent.

One of the things which never ceased to give me a feeling of surprise in my job with Dr Simpson was this business of being able to go into other people's homes. Criminal investigation is an Open Sesame. Nevertheless, I always felt a trifle amazed when I found myself as a matter of course walking into some stranger's house — even though I was in the company of the C.I.D.

Shortly after this Kent case we went, for example, to a North London surburb to investigate a murder. We found ourselves, with the local D.D.I., inspecting a nice, clean comfortable house in a nice, tidy, respectable surburban street. We looked into slightly disordered bedrooms, into a nursery with a dolls' house, rows of dolls, a large rocking-horse. We glanced into the drawing-room with its piano and upholstered furniture, the dining-room with its highly polished table and chairs. But the kitchen was the room that mattered most to us, for there in dressing-gown and pyjamas lay the mistress of the house, murdered.

She had been stabbed, and there was blood everywhere. A tap of the gas-cooker had also been turned on and the room was full of gas. The police opened the window and doors. The murderer had perhaps turned on the gas-tap to make it look like a case of suicide — though this was a forlorn hope — or perhaps (this seemed a more likely theory) to ensure that if the woman did not die from her stab wounds she would die from coal-gas poisoning.

It was an awfully strange thing to stand in this clean, modern, well-kept kitchen, very much like one's own kitchen at home, to see a stabbed woman lying on the floor at one's feet and blood spattered all over the nice clean kitchen. It was such an amazing combination of the ordinary and the outrageous. Something day-to-day and homely slashed with complete horror.

What had really happened in that kitchen? What had been said, what so violently and dreadfully done? Dr Simpson was able to tell us what was done, but nobody but the murderer could tell what was said and why the violence which was done was done, and some of all this he would rapidly forget, or would not care to repeat. A murderer can give a bare description of that last scene between himself and his victim, but he can never tell everything.

Tolstoi, in *The Kreuzer Sonata*, makes the murderer tell the tale of how he killed his wife, but although he leads up to the killing in great detail, and can tell you in great detail how the dying woman looked after the attack, propped up in bed, swathed in bandages and full of speechless indignation and shock, the actual account of the killing is jerky and vague — as accounts of killings by the killer always are jerky and vague. Tolstoi knew exactly how a murderer describes the murder, how his mind afterwards is a medley of memory and blank.

The violent actions of the moments of assault, the overwhelming emotions accompanying the actions, are too much for the mind to assimilate, it is all movement and no reflection, like a torrent rushing headlong over a rocky steep. Afterwards, when the hand has dropped the weapon, or the fingers relaxed from the throat, and the actual *feel* of the killing gone — and these purely physical sensations cannot survive more than a second or so — there is nothing to remember because there is nothing truly to remember with. One can, for example, remember a conversation with a lover long, long afterwards, but the sensation of physically loving cannot truly be remembered. It can only be recaptured by loving again, and then no two episodes of love will be exactly the same twice over. Moments of physical love and moments of murder are ephemeral; they cannot be preserved in the memory. They can never be adequately described because they are simply experienced in the flesh, the mind never has a chance to reflect. Everything in murder and love is *felt*. Anybody who thinks about love doesn't love. He — or she — is merely a coldblooded Gallup-poll type. And if a person about to do murder stopped for one instant to think, the result, in ninety-nine cases out of a hundred, would be that he wouldn't become a murderer. Only a very few murders are premeditated and thoughtfully carried out. It is when the moments jump up and chase each other round and round in a frenzy that passion exists — and afterwards the person who was in the middle of the whirl just cannot remember. Lovers can't remember, neither can murderers. Never truly remember.

The murderer in this North London case, the murdered woman's husband, was arrested, tried, found guilty and executed, but the real, inside story of the crime never emerged. Only the bare facts came to light. The murderer was a quite brilliant Indian research chemist in his early forties. His wife was a nice, healthy, unspectacular Englishwoman of the same age. She was, so far as could be ascertained, a tranquil, devoted housewife and mother. There were two children — both at boarding-school at the time of the murder. This took place early one May morning. A neighbour described afterwards how he had heard screaming just before seven and, on looking from his window, observed at the bedroom window of a nearby house a woman in blue pyjamas shrieking for help. Then a man, also in pyjamas, appeared behind her and pulled her away from the window and the screaming stopped.

The neighbour left it at that. The English carry their belief in personal freedom to a fantastic degree; if wives wish to hang screaming from their windows and husbands want to pull their screaming wives indoors and slam the windows shut — why, then let them. It's a free country, and it'd be pretty bad form to interfere.

A little while later this same neighbour saw the husband of the erstwhile screaming woman leave his house burdened with two suitcases and walk away up the road.

Not long afterwards a charwoman discovered the wife dead in the kitchen.

The cause of her death was shock from blunt wounds of the head, accelerated by coal-gas poisoning. She had clearly been chased round the house by her attacking husband and killed, after a struggle, in the kitchen. But why?

Only the husband could say why, and he never offered any explanation.

Dr Simpson could reconstruct the actual killing. The C.I.D. could search the man's house and investigate his private affairs and build up the salient outline of the case. Nobody could look into the murderer's mind and probe the quick and heart of the matter. There was no Open Sesame for that.

It is this ultimate secrecy of each one of us which makes the story of everyday life so fascinating. Each one of us has a secret room which is inviolate.

CHAPTER
FOURTEEN

Portrait of a Fairy

The Dobkin case had involved us in an aftermath of quite considerable literary activity, for C. K. S. wrote — and read — a paper on the case for the Medico-Legal Society, and after this he wrote an article on the same subject for the *Police Journal*.

Dr Simpson, as a Home Office pathologist, subscribed regularly to the magazine, and it was felt that his secretary might also read it. Some articles, however, were not unnaturally far above my simple secretarial head, such as "A Numerical and Dual-Purpose System of Finger-Print Classification" or "Spurious Gems and Their Scientific Detection". But there were other articles, for instance "Drunk In Charge; Some Hints on Evidence and Procedure" by Inspector Frederick Pickard of the Birmingham City Police, that I studied avidly, for it was crammed with hints which I felt might one day come in very useful. For example, this quote of advice of Sir Henry Curtis-Bennett to a motorist:

"If you are ever stopped by the police, don't for goodness sake touch the car in any way, as you will be said to be leaning on it for support. Don't sway at all when you are walking, or you will be said to be staggering under the influence of drink. Spring smartly to attention, stand upright outside the car, and say, 'I am not guilty of whatever you are about to charge me with doing'."

The Dobkin case article was such a success Dr Simpson wrote another on the Wigwam Murder, and after this he contributed regularly to the *Journal,* with accounts of his more important and interesting murder cases.

Besides these articles he had begun writing his students' textbook on forensic medicine, so I found myself with a lot of "spare time" typing to do. The "spare time" came mostly in the afternoons, when it did come. C. K. S. would leave me upstairs in our Department, while he went to work downstairs with Ireland in the Gordon Museum. I would sit typing, seated on my high stool at the departmental bench, under which still lay the remains of Mrs Dobkin, wrapped in her dust-sheet.

At first there were other people up there with me, at work in Dr Ryffel's big laboratory, but as the light dimmed, the short, dreary light of English winter afternoons, they would finish their work and go home, for there were no black-out arrangements on the top floors of the Pathology Block (ours was the top floor but one), so no electric lights could be used after black-out time and consequently when dusk fell it was necessary to end laboratory work for the day. The Pathology Block, built just before the war, was the work of an optimistic architect who had designed the laboratory walls almost entirely of wide glass windows and these proved very difficult during the war; during air-raids they were rather a menace to the people working doggedly in the laboratories and so far as black-out went they were impossible to cope with. Consequently in mid-winter work in the upper floor labs ended about four o'clock.

I had instructions from C. K. S. to join him in the Museum for tea round about 4.15. By that time all the upper floors were deserted save for myself, and just after four a porter, somewhere in the bowels of the building, switched off all the lights on the upper floors with a master switch, thereby plunging me abruptly into near darkness. Then, foolish as it sounds, I became hideously aware of my lonesome state and of the murdered Mrs Dobkin lying under my bench, an inch or so from my feet. It was not so much that I feared her — poor, stupid, inoffensive little woman, nobody could have feared her, either in life or death; but I had a terrible phobia that if I looked up I should see Harry Dobkin glaring at me through the window-pane, pallid and sweating, as he had glared at me at the Old Bailey. Directly the lights went out, therefore, Lefebure leapt up, gathered together her typewriter and papers and beat a precipitate retreat down the four flights of stairs (the electric lift stopped working, of course, when the porter switched off the juice), and after a final nervous canter along a dark corridor arrived at the Museum, trying to appear as casual as possible, although by that time severely out of breath.

132

Presently I began timing myself so that I had packed up and left the Department just before the lights went out. This worked nicely, but then the wretched porter began switching off the electricity earlier and earlier, and therefore I arrived in the Museum earlier and earlier too, thereby creating an impression of one unduly eager for her tea, and finally calling from C. K. S. the comment, "Miss L., you're turning up at ten-to-four these days, although you know there's no tea until quarter past. You won't get enough typing done if you stop so early. It isn't all that dark upstairs, surely you can manage the last quarter of an hour up there without a light?"

I didn't like to tell him I was afraid of being alone in the twilight with the Dobkins; it sounded so silly, especially from the cool and collected Miss Lefebure. So I steeled myself to those horrid little afternoon sessions and even tried to force myself to walk calmly down the stairs when 4.15 arrived, but I rarely succeeded in this final *tour de force* and generally descended them in a wild dash for light and company.

However, as nobody saw me behaving in this illogical and foolishly feminine fashion it didn't matter. And, anyway, I had gained a reputation for being forever on the hop, skip and jump. C. K. S. was fond of pointing out that when I first joined him I "strolled" around, but that now my pace had "appreciably quickened". He himself never walked but always ran everywhere, and I had got into the same habit. We streaked in and out of mortuaries and leapt and bounded about the hospital buildings in a positive excess of energy. Because of my constant hopping and skipping I came, in certain circles, to be known as "The Fairy". My light build, fair hair and ceaseless dancing about no doubt earned me this name. Personally I felt more like a performing flea than a fairy.

Of course I was called other things besides a fairy. I recall a very gallant old doctor who came to Poplar mortuary to see a p.m. he was interested in; as I walked into the p.m. room with the notes of the case he caught me up and exclaimed, "My dear young lady, I don't like to see you in this sort of place, no, I don't like it at all. I'm of the old school, and I find it most unsuitable."

"I find it all very interesting," I said, "I should miss it if I had to give it up for other work. And why shouldn't I work here?"

"Ah," he said mournfully, "a suffragette, yes, yes, a suffragette."

I had delightful visions of myself chained to the mortuary railings, waving my typewriter and vociferously demanding the right to work among corpses.

However, most people took my presence in the mortuary more or less for granted.

A lot of people came to watch the p.m.s, many of them doctors and, of course, many officers of the C.I.D.

Among the C.I.D. personalities was a suavely dressed, good-looking, exceptionally genial Detective Inspector, who carried a most beautifully rolled umbrella which he brandished jauntily as he came into the mortuary. This was the famous Robert Fabian, whom we first met in Southwark. But later he turned up at Hammersmith, flourishing his umbrella even more gaily. He had become a D.D.I., and he accepted congratulations with infectious laughter. Although he was without a doubt a terror to the crooks he pursued, so far as we were concerned he was fun to work with. He had a terrific sense of humour and made jokes about everything. Sometimes he would hum to himself happily. He also had a genius for pithy comments.

I only once saw him disconcerted in any way, and that was when C. K. S. remarked upon the soubriquet which one of the Sunday newspapers had bestowed upon him: "D.D.I. Fabian, the Humphrey Bogart of Scotland Yard". The Humphrey Bogart of Scotland Yard turned the slightest degree redder in the face and then grinned. "Well, Humphrey Bogart can have a bash at my job if he'll let me have a bash at his salary."

One job we did with Mr Fabian was the case of an ex-Broadmoor man who battered his wife to death with a rolling-pin and then gave himself up to the police. We went round to the house where the murder had taken place. It was a neat, tidy little house, complete with lace curtains, ferns in pots, artificial flowers on the sideboard and a collection of family photographs on the mantelpiece. I began looking at these photographs and Mr Fabian came over to me, picked one of the photos up and said, "That's the devoted husband. Loved children and animals — particularly cats."

"Did he have any children?"

"No, but there was a tabby cat."

I looked at the bland, round, pop-eyed, broadly-smiling face. He was sitting on a low wall, with two

135

little children and a black dog. They all seemed very pleased with themselves.

"Was that since he came out of Broadmoor?"

"Oh yes, he'd been out several years."

"Why did he go there?"

"For trying to murder his wife."

"Why on earth did she have him back?"

"She wanted him back."

"I suppose she never thought he'd try it a second time."

"Lord, no; thought him the kindest, dearest soul on earth."

I went on looking at the photographs, so many of which featured this round-faced, jaunty householder and ratepayer, the man who, according to his photographs anyhow, was always beaming like a sun. Obviously very popular with his friends and relations and the life and soul of every party. In one photo he had his arm round his wife, in another snap he was cuddling the cat. And always smiling . . .

Back came Mr Fabian from a brief search of the premises, carrying a bloodstained rolling-pin. Adhering to the congealed blood were several long dark hairs.

"The weapon, Dr Simpson."

"Without a doubt, Mr Fabian."

"Considering he'd given her a pretty thorough battering the first occasion, she must have been a wonderfully trusting type. And now back he'll go to Broadmoor. Ah well."

Mr Fabian later presented Dr Simpson with the rolling-pin, which was given a prominent position among the murder weapons exhibited in the Gordon Museum.

We collected many interesting trophies during the course of our work. One we obtained about this time, and which I especially liked, was a huge metal weight, impossible for me to lift, attached to a piece of rope. With this went a succinct suicide note: "I expect you will find me over Battersea Bridge — if you are interested."

They did find him over Battersea Bridge.

Another collector's piece was a geyser vent-pipe, complete with starling's nest blocking it; this had caused the accidental death from carbon-monoxide poisoning of a housewife taking her Friday night's bath.

The felt hat of the murdered pawnbroker at Hackney was added to our collection of interesting garments.

When I first joined Dr Simpson one of the things that most intrigued me was the C.I.D. officers' knowledge, or ignorance, of ladies' underwear. Victims of crimes would be undressed, garment by garment, in the mortuary, one officer undressing the body and another tabulating the clothes as they were removed. The other officers present joined in, in a kind of male chorus. Shoes, stockings, dress, petticoat — or "slip" as they always called it — panties, vest, bra, these caused no trouble, everybody could identify such things; but some items of wear puzzled the gentlemen very much and they would turn to me with enquiring, bothered faces. "Miss Lefebure, what's this?" — holding it up suspiciously, at arm's length. "A camisole," I replied, after a moment's staring. "Never seen one of them before," was the rejoinder. "No, they're just coming into fashion again, along with the new waist petticoats," I explained. "Oh, thanks, Miss Lefebure." Then, briskly, "Item, one camisole."

"Miss Lefebure, *whatever's* this?"

"Oh, it's one of those boned, strapless brassières."

"She's wearing it in a very funny place."

"It's slipped down."

"Oh. Thanks, Miss Lefebure. Item, one strapless bra."

There was one garment they always recognised immediately, all greeting it with triumphant shouts, "CamiKNICKS!"

Some of the clothes removed were occasionally so extraordinary even I couldn't put a name to them. The results of home dressmaking courses, perhaps. "Why not make your own lovely lingerie, and save pounds?"

These disrobing episodes always amused me, but I always sat there very straight-faced, giving advice when asked.

I could never get them to appreciate the difference between a corset and a roll-on. But perhaps it didn't really matter.

Many of the senior officers from the Yard filled me with considerable awe and at first meeting one or two of them quite scared me. One of these was Chief Superintendent F. Cherrill, for so many years head of the world-famous Scotland Yard fingerprint department. Mr Cherrill recently retired, but when I knew him he was at the zenith of his celebrated career, and indeed a man to be reckoned with, as famous in his own line as Spilsbury was in his.

We first met at Hammersmith. I recall it vividly.

In Hammersmith mortuary yard there grew a large castor-oil plant. Why, nobody knew; not even MacKay, the mortuary keeper, who generally knew everything concerned with his mortuary, and a lot more besides. But why there was a castor-oil plant in the yard MacKay just didn't know. "Do you like castor-oil plants, MacKay?"

"Not particularly, Miss Molly, do you?"

"No. Does the Coroner like castor-oil plants, MacKay?"

"I've no idea."

Dr Simpson definitely disliked the castor-oil plant. It got in his way when he parked the car.

One afternoon he had parked the car so close to this plant that when I climbed out of the car I became entangled in its greenery. I was dickering about with the wretched thing when a very loud, highly amused voice boomed, "Hullo, Eve. Looking for a fig-leaf?"

Disentangling myself I looked up in some horror. There, standing in the mortuary doorway, grinningly surveying me, was a very large, solid, rather portly gentleman, even larger because of his vast grey overcoat. There was something about the goblin humour of his grin that sent me scurrying off to the Coroner's office for refuge. "Who's the man in the grey coat and the bowler hat?"

Said the Coroner's officer, with bated breath, "Why, that's Mr Cherrill, the fingerprint expert. You've heard of him, haven't you?"

Of course I had.

Gathering my courage I went back to the mortuary. Mr Cherrill gave me another grin; he could see he had scared me, and it tickled him.

Gradually, in the course of several encounters, I got to know him and ceased to be so scared of him, although his quality of gnomish humour always kept me on the *qui vive*, ready to jump. He knew it too, and, I suspect, enjoyed teasing me.

Dr Simpson frequently sent specimens from post-mortems to Mr Cherrill at the Yard and I would be sent to take them to him. Visiting a high-up at the Yard was quite a business, at any rate during the war. I had to fill in and sign a chit, which was then taken to the officer to be visited, who would scan it and say, "All right, let her come up." Then a large police sergeant escorted me to the office of whoever I might be visiting; perhaps Chief Constable (now Commander) Hugh Young or Deputy Commander Rawlings, or perhaps one of the Chief Inspectors, but most often Mr Cherrill.

One day as I walked into his office he waved my chit ferociously at me and growled, "Can't you write better than this?"

"It's the awful pens the Yard provides, Mr Cherrill."

"Don't blame our pens."

"They're dreadful."

"So is this scrawl." He contemplated it and shook his head.

"Can you read character from handwriting, Mr Cherrill?" I ventured.

"I certainly can. I'm an expert at it. Want me to tell you yours?"

"No thank you. It might be too disconcerting."

"I know all about you," he said, tapping the chit and grinning.

"I expect you do. At the Yard you all know everything about everybody, with or without the aid of handwriting."

However, despite my horrible writing he not long afterwards asked me if I would like to be *his* secretary. The offer didn't seem to be a leg-pull either, for he assured me I would come in most useful in his Department, and rising briskly from his chair took me for a brief tour of the amazing place, pointing out this or that job I would be useful for.

I found it all absorbingly interesting, although it was very hard to believe there were enough crooks in the country to necessitate those vast stacks of fingerprint files. It gave one an alarming glimpse of the size and extent of the underworld. Record after record after record of criminals' fingerprints. The efficiency of the system of filing was impressive to a degree. Mr Cherrill was rightly very proud of it all, but when he again said, "Now, wouldn't you like to be my secretary?" I repeated, in the style of a Mrs Micawber, that much as I appreciated the offer I would never, never, never desert Dr Keith Simpson.

At one stage we kept Mr Cherrill supplied with fingers, with which he did several important experiments.

Another time, when C. K. S. and I had been visiting him about some fingerprints on a revolver, he remarked as we were saying good-bye, "Oh, Dr Simpson, before you go I wish you'd do me a favour."

"Anything, Mr Cherrill, anything," responded C. K. S. affably.

"I've got one or two bits of a young woman here," explained Mr Cherrill confidentially, "——— ———" (giving her name), "you remember the case, Dr Simpson? Some time back now."

Dr Simpson said he remembered.

"I had one or two odds and ends of her brought up here for me to look at, pickled, you know, of course, and I put them away in a cupboard afterwards and forgot all about 'em, but I don't want them cluttering the place up, we're very short of space here, so I wondered if it'd be too much to ask you to pop them in your hospital incinerator; would that be too much trouble?"

"No trouble at all, Mr Cherrill."

"Let me find her, then." He began poking round his cupboards, pulling out parcels and packages, shaking his head, pushing them back and muttering, "I know she's here somewhere. I've got her somewhere. Bother the girl, where on earth is she?"

After a bit C. K. S. said, politely "What about leaving it till some other time, Mr Cherrill? You can find her at your leisure, and I'll take her next time I call."

"But damn it, I know I had her here in one of these cupboards."

A stickler for efficiency, he was most annoyed at his failure to find the lady, or what portions he had of the lady, and fumed around his office, grumbling, "I know I've got her here somewhere."

We had to leave without her. The matter was never mentioned again, and I could never summon the courage to ask Mr Cherrill if he *had* found her.

CHAPTER
FIFTEEN

Severe Testing of a Secretary

When August came C. K. S. retired to his cottage for a fortnight's "rest". He took me with him for part of the time, for he was in the middle of writing his textbook and it seemed to him that a rest was a splendid opportunity for doing some concentrated dictating and typing.

Most of the work we did out in the garden; the weather was lovely, and it certainly was a pity to stay indoors. I am not, however, perhaps so fond of fresh air as I should be, and I felt a slight exasperation with the playful little breeze that used to come along and create lively havoc with the pages of the manuscript. It was especially trying as we had reached the section of the book on poisons, and the section of the book which dealt with poisons struck me as somewhat nightmarish — from a typist's point of view:

"Dinitrocresols; dinitronaphthols; dinitrophenols: dinitrothymols.

"Para-aminobenzenesulphonamide; its salts; derivatives of para-aminobenzenesulphonamide having any of the hydrogen atoms of the para-amino and sulphonamide group substituted by another radical; their salts (substances of the sulphonamide group) —"

And so on.

Nevertheless, in spite of the intimidating aspect of the typescript, it was very nice in the garden, with the sunny countryside spread before me, terminating in a horizon of gentle blue sky and Dunstable Beacon, while in the cornfield at the back of the cottage the harvesting machine went round and round with a familiar clank and rattle which reminded me, vividly and pleasantly, of the Exmoor farm Augusts of my childhood. And the work on the textbook was enlivened with bouts of gardening, picnics, jaunts to Whipsnade, climbing trees, swimming, going to look at some neighbouring pigs — a delightfully snoozy pastime — and entertaining Americans from a nearby Army Air Force camp. The beautiful weather held, everything was honey-balmed, warm and tranquil, and then . . . along came the wasps.

They were everywhere; in the larder, the kitchen, the dining-room, on the buns and in the jam at tea-time, they even prowled round the toothpaste in the bathroom and investigated our ginslings before dinner. Obviously there was a nest of them somewhere in the immediate neighbourhood. We scouted around, but found nothing.

Then, during a game of badminton, a shuttlecock fell into a small thicket of elderberry bushes and when C. K. S. emerged from retrieving it he looked quite excited. "I've discovered the wasps' nest. A vast thing, hanging from a branch. When the children are in bed we'll deal with it."

"We" meant himself and me, for Mrs Simpson was visiting friends for the day.

So, when the children were safely in bed, C. K. S. said, "Come on, Molly, let's settle those wasps."

"Do you intend smoking them out?"

"No, I've a better idea than that."

He fetched a kitchen stool, garden shears and a very large glass specimen jar, with a lid to it; one of the jars you could pickle a whole baby in, if you wanted to. This he gave to me to carry. It was heavy and slippery and I put both arms round it and hugged it to my bosom, nervous of dropping it and breaking it.

"What are we going to do?"

"I'll cut the nest from the branch, drop it gently into the jar, and you'll clamp the lid on, presto!"

It sounded a highly daring scheme, a little too daring if the wasps got any inkling of our plan — and wasps are suspicious creatures, apt to draw hasty conclusions. No, I didn't think it sounded an awfully good idea, not really a good idea at all.

I tried to hint this tactfully.

"What about getting stung?"

"If we're quick and clever enough they won't have time to sting us."

That gave me even more of a sinking feeling. I knew he would be quick and clever enough, but what about me with the slippery jar and the lid?

We were now trotting across the badminton lawn, C. K. S. with stool and shears, myself with the jar. We climbed over the little wooden fence into the thicket and, after a couple of minutes' wary battle with brambles below and criss-cross branches and catchy twigs above, found ourselves face to face with a big, buff-coloured object which hung, like a giant and over-ripe pear, from a branch of a particularly large bush.

C. K. S. put down his stool and stood on it. He stationed me under the nest, holding the jar open and the lid at the ready. Everything was very still, no wasps around, no humming or buzzing. But who knew what little eyes were watching, what little black antennae quivering, what little zzzzzy conversations going on? "Chaps, he's after our nest!" And forth they'd seethe . . .

Lefebure, as you can see, was all of a twitter and very near flinging down the jar and bunking off. But somehow or other I managed to stay my ground, clenching my teeth and clutching the jar like a life-preserver and expecting to be stung all over in a twinkling. C. K. S. meanwhile balanced precariously on the stool, making tentative snips at the surrounding twigs.

"Clearing the decks a bit for action," he explained.

Still no sign of life from the wasps.

C. K. S. was very gingerly in his movements — this was the *clever* part. In a minute would come the *quick* bit.

"If wasps are like bees (and bees can communicate, according to the people who study them), then, if wasps are like bees, I reckon a big S.O.S. is going out right now," I thought. I peered up at the nest and C. K. S. braced himself with the shears.

"Steady with the jar, Molly?"

"Steady with the jar."

"Then here she goes."

147

He severed the branch one side of the nest, then the other, holding the branch dexterously at the second cut and steadying the nest as much as possible, then lowering it with infinite care into the jar. I had the lid clanged into place in a trice. We each drew a deep breath.

"Nice work."

With the air of victors we left the thicket and marched back across the garden to the little terrace, where a table with drinks was ready for the brave.

"They're a very quiet set of wasps," I observed. I put the jar on the table and we stared at its contents inquisitively. But the wasps remained strictly indoors.

"Do wasps retire for the night early?"

"I really have no idea. I've never studied wasps very closely."

"I would have thought they'd be out and about quite late these nice light evenings."

We studied the dormant nest thoughtfully as we sipped our drinks. Each of us nursed the same unbearable suspicion, but, womanlike, I was the first to voice such a thing.

"Could it be last year's nest?"

"Could be," said C. K. S. We stared at our prize some more. "Possibly," he said. "In fact it does appear to be deserted," he concluded.

"What a pity." But I didn't mean it. I was thinking how lucky we'd been. For wasps are belligerent insects and if the nest had been inhabited we should have been seriously attacked, without a doubt.

Presently a neighbour dropped in for a drink. He was something of a naturalist, so we showed him the nest. To our horror he didn't hesitate to lift it from the jar.

"Quite a nice one. Last season's, of course. Where was it?"

"Among the elderberry bushes."

He dropped it casually back in the jar. "Quite a nice one."

Next morning a farm labourer found a wasps' nest in a bank a few yards up the lane, and he smoked the occupants out, much to the delight of the local children and the dogs. The wasps, sure enough, came pouring forth in a frenzied crusade and one or two of the children and dogs were stung in the course of the battle. I only learnt of all this by hearsay, though, for at the time of the incident I was in the garden, typing.

CHAPTER
SIXTEEN

Underworld

Among the Americans who visited at Dr Simpson's cottage were several medical men and they used to enjoy coming up to London on their short leaves and spending a morning or afternoon going around with us. They were interested not only in the actual post-mortems, they were also fascinated by the glimpses these little tours gave them of London's private life, as it were; the peeps at her courts, her police, her criminals, slums and underworld dramas. Our formal, traditional court procedure never failed to thrill and impress our guests, while the fact that our police invariably went unarmed struck them as an astounding combination of the heroic and the foolhardy; they decided that our criminals must be less tough than the American variety and therefore our police were not in such danger as the cops back home, but then along came a tough case or two to disprove this theory, which left but one possible conclusion, voiced by a puzzled but frank visitor who exclaimed, "I guess you British must be crazy, after all." Our slums, I suspect, rather surprised and horrified them, although they were too polite to say so; they were all very courteous sightseers.

Generally, of course, they knew London only as a place of theatres, clubs and West End rendezvous — these trips with C. K. S. showed them the other face of this vast, schizophrenic city.

One really beautiful morning in September we had with us a doctor from Denver. A call came for us to go with the C.I.D. to a South London lodging-house where a man had killed himself. So we drove through the warm bright sunshine, which all the more exposed the dirt of the dingy streets, to a grey, sooty, dreary crescent, not so very slummy in aspect, but unpleasantly dim and drab.

Outside the house we were to visit a little crowd of local residents had gathered; people as grey, dim and drab as the houses they lived in. The D.D.I. led our party up to the peeling front door and knocked; a spiky woman with untidy, streaky blonde hair and a lined, thin face answered our knocks. She let us in and indicated the door of one of the front downstairs rooms. "In there."

We went in.

Immediately up jumped the smell and leapt at us; the overwhelming smell of real, thick dirt, a smell so intense it seems alive, a veritable animal. There was no genuine air in the room at all, there was only this atmosphere that you breathed and swallowed in slabs. The D.D.I. made a rush at the window, but of course it was not only shut tight but also stuck fast. Its panes were so dirty one could scarcely see out of them and the muslin curtains which draped them were

151

elephant-grey with grime and sheltered the corpses of long dead and shrivelled flies.

Despite the bright day outside, the room was extremely dark, so that we peered around. There was no electricity or gas to put on to help us to see, there was only a bit of old candle stuck in a little jar on the mantelpiece. However, we could, in the dim light, make out an iron bed with tousled clothes piled on it, and sprawling on his back on top of these, stripped naked to the waist, the dead man, with a streak of scarlet blood flowing across his lean and livid chest.

As our eyes became accustomed to the gloom we could make out more of this horrible room, which would have provided Maxim Gorky with some good material, from the once green-papered walls — now blotchy and peeling with damp, so that they appeared to be suffering from some ghastly skin disease, as did the lumped, clotted and pitted surface of the filthy ceiling — to the squat, slow, fat bug which was taking a trip along a crack by the fireplace. In one dark corner was a wooden table, spread with an old sheet of newspaper, and on this stood a filthy mug, some pieces of twisted cutlery and a tin plate heaped with fragments of cold potato and cabbage in congealed gravy. By the table was a rag-strewn chair and an old trunk. On a second table stood a pile of dusty gramophone records and an old portable gramophone. There was a small bedside stand with all sorts of filthy odds and ends on it, and beneath this was an unspeakable bucket which had been used for everything from chamber-pot to scrap-bin, and which had obviously not been emptied for several days. The last item to be dropped in it was an emptied Lysol bottle.

Over the mantelpiece were pinned pictures from newspapers of various leg lovelies.

This was the "home" of a Londoner in the year 1943.

The room, with its shapes, its shadows, its gloom, was all dull green, moody sepia and dismal black, and in the centre was the black iron bed with the tumbled filthy bedclothes and spread-eagled across it the dead man, his livid greenish-white face, arms and chest glimmering in the darkness around him, his dark-trousered legs dangling over the side of the bed, terminating in heavy — how heavy — black surgical boots; two club feet, booted, heavy as lead. One felt the eternal despair of those heavy feet. But one's eyes were torn from the tragic feet to the violently crimson, thickly brilliant blood flowing from the wound under the heart. His arms were flung out in a gesture of wild pain and final surrender. The right hand was deformed; close to these twisted fingers glittered a newly-bought knife, streaked with blood.

We all stood staring. It was indeed a picture dramatic and ruthless as a Hogarth, dark and haunting as an El Greco . . .

The body was presently removed to the mortuary and the suicide reconstructed by Dr Simpson and the C.I.D. The knife the man had stabbed himself with was very sharp and brand new; he had no doubt bought it to kill himself with. His stomach was full of Lysol; his courage to stab himself had failed at the last and he had tried to poison himself instead, thinking it would be an easier death. The poison was agony. He had therefore seized the knife and thrust it into his heart.

This was the grim drama of the cripple's last moments. But what had led up to those last frantic moments? At the inquest a few days later we learnt all about that.

The chief witnesses at the inquest were the streaky landlady, arrayed in all her dismal best, which included a coat with a large orange fox collar and a big shiny imitation leather handbag, and another crippled man, an emaciated, nervous, sick-looking individual, in dirty raincoat and an old felt hat, who propelled himself into court in an invalid chair with big wheels. His thin, colourless face, with its hollow cheeks and too-large, dark eyes, was not unintelligent, he bore the air of an aspiring intellectual. He bore, too, the impatient, overstrung, querulous manner of the chronic invalid.

This man had been a great friend of the deceased, for he had lived in the same lodging-house, just across the hallway, and the two cripples had spent their evenings together, talking. The man who had killed himself, Joe, had lived in the house for twelve years. At the time of his death he was thirty-five. He had two clubbed feet, a deformed right hand and a severe duodenal ulcer. He had supported himself for many years by playing the gramophone in the main streets of Fulham, Hammersmith, Putney. He had never been a very merry man, said his friend, but recently he had become depressed, and very very strange.

"How do you mean, very strange?" asked the Coroner, glancing up from his writing-pad.

"Delusions, sir, delusions. That, and his ulcer, you could see he was in a very bad way. He suffered awful agony."

"What kind of delusions were they?"

"He saw Jesus floating in a tree."

The Coroner began to write again. "Anything else?"

"Oh, yes, a lot of things. St Peter hanging from the peg at the back of his door, and the saints, and sometimes Jesus on the cross also hanging on the peg on the door. You could hear him, sir, shouting in there in the evenings, 'Get out of my room! Get out!' Because these visions, sir, they terrified him."

There was a pause — the Coroner's pen scratched a little.

"He kept a diary," went on the witness. "He was always writing in this diary about these visions he saw."

"Yes," said the Coroner, taking up a worn, rather large diary, "I have it here. He writes a great deal about religious matters in it, I see." The Coroner read slowly from a page, "I wish to be with God. I am going to join my God."

"He was a very religious man, especially at the end, in fact you might say he was almost a religious maniac," went on the witness. "He believed in all these visions he saw, thought they were all real. No use at all telling him he imagined 'em. He thought St Peter had come with a message for him. And he let himself get in a shocking state; hair grew long, wouldn't shave, wouldn't eat. All he did was to see these visions and talk about religion.

Quite a mania. In the end I wouldn't discuss religion with him. Anything else, but not religion, although naturally sir, I too believe in a Great Sublime."

"Quite so, quite so," murmured the Coroner. He wrote some more, then looked up again at the witness. "Did he see these visions only in his room?"

"At first, sir, yes, but in the end he was seeing 'em everywhere. He started seeing crosses and the like in my room, but I said to him, 'Get out of my room, I won't have you seeing things like that in here.'"

"'I am going to join my God,'" quoted the Coroner, glancing at the diary again. "That sounds as though he contemplated taking his life. Did you ever hear him threaten to take his life?"

"Toward the end he often did. Threatened to drown himself. I said to him, 'Don't do that, boy, the water is so cold.' But I had a feeling something of the sort would happen in the end."

The landlady now came into the witness-box and told much the same story as the previous witness. "You could hear him shrieking and shouting alone in his room in the evenings, shouting, 'Get out! Get out!' Once or twice I went to him and asked whatever was the matter. He said, 'It's St Peter, he's hanging on the peg on my door and he looks awful, I don't want him in here.' Of course, there was nothing there really, but he was certain there was. I didn't like it at all, my house has always been respectable."

"Didn't you tell a doctor?"

"He wouldn't see a doctor. He was in an awful way, though. Bloody crosses all round him, he said."

"Can you tell us about the evening he died?"

"About half-past nine I went to his room to take him some milk. It was all very quiet, no answer when I knocked. He'd been very quiet all evening, because usually, you know, you could hear him talking and calling out to himself, like, but that evening he'd been very quiet, which I'd thought unusual. So, well, I felt a bit nervous. In the end, after I'd knocked several times, I opened his door. The room was all dark. I shone a torch, he was lying on his bed, I saw blood, so I went into Mr Motspur's" (Mr Motspur was the previous witness), "and told Mr Motspur, 'He's been and done himself in.' Of course it did and it didn't come as a shock, because he'd been going a bit queer in the head lately, like I said."

"Was he regular with the rent?"

"Oh, yes, always regular with the rent." She gripped her handbag a little more firmly and explained, "It was all those crosses and things he saw worried him, and then he kept on saying he would go to God."

"Quite so, quite so," murmured the Coroner again.

"I didn't turn him out because he was always regular with the rent and, in a way, I was sorry for him, but I had to warn him about the shouting and seeing things because, naturally, others in the house didn't like it. But he didn't take no notice. Went on as bad as ever."

"Quite so."

"It was the visions worried him, especially that St Peter. And he kept saying he would join his God."

The Coroner found a verdict of suicide while of an unsound mind. After the inquest the landlady and Mr

157

Motspur left the court together, he propelling himself in the wheeled chair, she walking beside him, uncomfortable in her best shoes. I watched them going up the street, talking together, back to that dark and dirty house where the voice which had called to St Peter to get out was now silent, where Jesus no longer floated in a tree. But the landlady and her lodgers would talk about it all for many a long day: Joe, who had gone queer in the head, and seen visions, and in the end done himself in. Joe, the pal who had turned dotty, Joe, the lodger who had been so bad for a respectable house. Come, don't you remember poor old Joe? Used to play the gramophone in Putney High Street and the Broadway. Crippled hand and both feet. You remember Joe.

CHAPTER
SEVENTEEN

Murder in a Fog

There was one thing our London-exploring Americans did want to experience, more than any other, and that was a "pea-souper". They had read about London pea-soupers in Dickens, Wells, Conan Doyle, they had seen innumerable films about London with the characters groping in an impenetrable musty sea of fog. And now how they wanted to be able to write back home themselves about a pea-souper in which they had actually groped their way along Piccadilly! A genuine pea-souper when you couldn't see your hand in front of your face!

Well, on November 20th of that year, 1943, a genuine pea-souper of rich and ripe vintage came rolling down on London, but most unfortunately none of our Americans were up in town that day. They certainly missed a classic fog. The metropolis was engulfed in noonday night, thick, reeking and khaki-coloured. It blotted vision, choked noses and throats, and muffled all sound, so that all the traffic became creeping and ghostly, and all the pedestrians flannel-footed. Everything and everybody fumbled, mumbled and fumed in the woolly, immobile gloom. Only the telephone remained brisk and unhesitating. A call came through on ours from Scotland Yard, asking us to go with Chief Inspector Chapman to a murder job at Luton.

Our progress from mortuary to mortuary had already been brought to a standstill by the fog, so C. K. S. informed the Yard he would wait at his West End flat for Mr Chapman to collect him. We took a snack lunch in the City and groped our way back to the flat. The Yard phoned again to say that Mr Chapman had gone to his home to pack a bag, but he would be calling for us as soon as possible. So I lit the gas-fire in C. K. S.'s lounge, he opened a bottle of madeira, and we settled down in two easy chairs to fortify ourselves against the rigours of the coming journey, and to listen to a gramophone recital of Cesar Franck's "Symphonic Variations".

Far below us, bathed in fathoms of fog, the traffic moaned and bickered in muffled accents. In the lounge, where we waited, the madeira and music made a strange prelude to the murder investigation which lay ahead. Indeed, it was so novel an episode to be introduced into the middle of our day that we found ourselves exchanging sly glances of amusement. "Old Chapman will think we prime ourselves well for a murder," said C. K. S., pouring more madeira and starting off the "Variations" all over again. "I hope he turns up before it grows pitch dark. It's not going to be easy getting to Luton in this weather."

Just before three there was a ring at the front door and Chief Inspector William Chapman presented himself, together with Detective Sergeant Judge. (Now

160

Chief Superintendent and Chief Inspector, respectively.)
Mr Chapman is shortish, bulky, pink and smiling. Mr
Judge is tall, lean, dark and rather serious. They wore
heavy coats and thick scarves and advanced with wary
detective tread into our exotic atmosphere of madeira
and music. However, it took little persuasion to embark
them on a madeira each too, and for a brief while
everything was quite partyish, rather than murderish.
But soon we were all packing into the police car which
was waiting in the street below, Mr Chapman asked us
if we minded his pipe, we said we didn't, so he lit it,
and the journey began.

The driver of the car was a Flying Squad man who
had formerly been one of Sir Philip Game's personal
drivers and he obviously regarded the fog as an
interesting obstacle sent by a benevolent Providence to
enliven what would otherwise have been a rather dull
journey. With a grin of delight he plunged us into the
thickest pockets of gloom, losing his way and finding it
again repeatedly, laughing meantime hugely at the joke
which no other driver in London saw. We avoided
lampposts and the like by miracles, and every now and
again he asked us gaily if we thought the car was on the
pavement. There was not much way of telling whether
the car was on the pavement or not, so we pressed
merrily on, without accident, which suggested we were
in the roadway after all.

At last we were out of London, the dense yellow fog
melted into a dense white one, and our driver assured
us he thought we were on the right road for Luton. We
kept our eyes open for signposts, lost our way, found it,

161

lost it and found it again and finally arrived, via St Albans, at Luton.

I was already slightly acquainted with Luton, remembering it as a peculiarly dismal, drear, dank, dispiriting dump. Renewing the acquaintance I found Luton to be just as much of a dismal, drear, dank, dispiriting dump as ever. The fog pawed it with mangy pads, mud clotted its streets, its inhabitants meandered pallidly and moodily past the depressing war-time shops. Our car drew up outside the town's police headquarters — a heavily-sandbagged edifice — and we were greeted by Detective Inspector Thomas Finch, of Luton C.I.D., who took us into his office and regaled us with cups of tea and what slight information he had so far managed to collect about the murder.

"At quarter-past two yesterday afternoon, November 19th," said D.I. Finch, "two sewer men who were testing the water level of the River Lea, which flows through the outskirts of Luton, found the body of a naked woman bound with cord and wrapped with sacks lying in the water. A public footpath skirts by the river and along this path large numbers of people walk daily on their way to the Vauxhall factory, but yesterday morning was foggy, not many people noticed the sacked object lying in the river, and the few who did merely supposed it to be refuse of some sort or the other. So until the sewer men climbed down the bank to test the water level the sacks held their secret intact.

"The sewer men were testing water levels on the 18th, too, in that same part of the river, but they are certain the body wasn't there then.

162

"It seems to me," continued Mr Finch, "that the murder took place somewhere else, not in the actual vicinity of the river, and the body was brought there for disposal in the water on some sort of vehicle. I've searched the banks of the river and the waste ground around, but there's nothing to indicate the murder took place there. So far as traffic tracks by the river go, however, the only ones to be found are on a nearby bridge; we've checked on them and they belong to a milk lorry which stops on the bridge every morning, so it doesn't seem a very likely vehicle. All the same, I've had the tracks preserved. You never can be too careful.

"The sacks in which the body was wrapped have so far given us no clues, neither has the cord binding the body. But they may help at a later stage."

"And the body?" put in Mr Chapman, puffing at his eternal pipe. D.I. Finch shook his head. "Not a lot to go by yet, but we hope Dr Keith Simpson will be able to help us there. She's a youngish woman, completely naked, no rings or anything like that, no birthmarks. There's an old stomach scar, and one interesting thing is she hasn't any teeth, which seems a bit unusual at her age; might be useful. She's been pretty badly knocked about. But before you go to look at her I suggest you pay a visit to the river, just to see where she was found."

So we all drove to the river. But river, perhaps, is a misleading title for the shallow, muddy stream winding its way between dispirited acres of waste ground and allotments. The Lea, at this stage of its career, was a bare six inches deep, fringed with muddy banks tufted with unhealthy grass. To mark the exact spot where the

163

body had lain a small stake had been planted, surmounted by a piece of soiled white rag.

Dr Simpson and Mr Chapman stood on the footpath and stared at the stream. Then they slithered down the bank and stared at it some more. Then they climbed back up the bank, inspected the ground around, inspected the milk-lorry tracks, surveyed the dismal scene of stream, stake, banks and allotments again. There was nothing much to be learned from this riverside jaunt. The body had lain in the stream, some four feet from the bank; Dr Simpson thought it had most likely been rolled down the bank into the water and with this both Mr Chapman and Mr Finch agreed. Then we all returned to the cars and drove to the hospital to examine the body.

The Luton and Dunstable Hospital proved a very modern, attractive building, with a clean, white, light mortuary. The dead woman was lying on the p.m. table, still bound, but no longer wrapped in the sacks. At these sacks, ordinary coarse potato sacks they appeared to be, Dr Simpson and Mr Chapman peered attentively, but there were no clues — foreign hairs, fibres or so forth — visible to the naked eye; so the sacks were carefully put on one side, to be sent away for laboratory examination.

Police photographs of the woman, wrapped up as when she had been found, were shown to us.

C. K. S. then turned to the body on the p.m. table. The first thing he did was to take the body temperature — this had fallen to that of the surroundings. Full rigor mortis was also present. This indicated that the woman had died during the afternoon or evening of November 18th. She had clearly been dead when dumped in the river. Because the water was shallow she had lain only partly immersed, and skin changes suggested she had lain there for only a very short time, some twelve to eighteen hours at the most, which meant she had been put there probably during the darkness of November 18th — 19th.

The cords which bound her were carefully examined. Her legs had been tied before death, the trunk after death. So she died while she was being trussed up, no doubt, although she was unconscious when the murderer began the job of trussing her — but he, of course, was more than likely under the impression she was already dead.

There was nothing about the cord, at that stage of the investigation, which could provide the detectives with clues. It was put aside with the sacks to go to a laboratory.

Dr Simpson then began searching the body for anything which might offer identity clues. She was a well-built woman, with dark brown hair, worn short, brown eyes, aged between thirty and thirty-five, five feet three inches tall. She was completely nude. There were no rings on her fingers. She had no birth-marks, but there was an old appendix scar. Although she was only a young woman she had no teeth, which, as D.I. Finch had already observed, might prove a useful identity clue. The state of her gums showed she had worn false teeth, but these had been removed. She had had a child, or children, and she was five-and-a-half months pregnant again now, at the time of her death.

Police photographs, full-face and profile, were taken, but without very much confidence, because the injuries the woman had received to face and head had resulted in so much bruising and swelling that she obviously looked very different now, in death, from her everyday living self.

These injuries showed that she had been gripped across the throat by a right-handed person, from in front, and while gripped thus had been pressed against a wall, or on to the floor. There was no asphyxiation, however, and no serious attempt had been made to strangle her. She had, in fact, been killed by an extremely violent single blow, from the edge of some very heavy blunt weapon. This blow extended across the left side of the face, from chin to ear. The ear was split, so was the cheek over the cheek-bone. The upper and lower jaws were fractured.

Mr Chapman, watching Dr Simpson examining these injuries, remarked, "It's not going to be much use bringing people in to identify her when she's been knocked about like that. I doubt if her own mother, if she has one, could recognise her now."

This blow from the blunt weapon had clearly rendered the woman immediately unconscious and had felled her to the ground. In falling she had struck and injured her right temple and side of her head, splitting the scalp above the ear.

The actual cause of death was brain hæmorrhage and Dr Simpson thought it must have taken the woman some thirty to forty minutes to die, from the time she received the terrible blow from her assailant. But as she was unconscious her killer no doubt thought her dead and began undressing and trussing her soon after she fell, motionless and bleeding, to the ground. By the time he had completed the job she *was* dead.

He then somehow conveyed the body to the river, rolled it down the bank into the water, and left it.

So the police now knew, without a doubt, that the woman was murdered. They knew, in some detail, how she had been killed. They knew, pretty closely, when she was murdered (the afternoon or evening of November 18th). But they didn't know who the unhappy woman was — and until they knew who she was they couldn't discover her murderer.

Before we left the mortuary samples of her hair and her fingernail scrapings were taken. It was also decided to preserve her feet in the hope her shoes might be found. Her fingerprints were taken, and a specimen of her blood for grouping. (This proved to belong to group O.)

Night was quickly falling when we all left the hospital mortuary and returned to Luton C.I.D. headquarters. Mr Chapman and his faithful Sergeant Judge began discussing with D.I. Finch the problem of where they should lodge during their stay in Luton. C. K. S. and I interrupted this little conference to say good-night, for we were now returning to London, in the Squad car which had brought us down. Mr Chapman gave us a smile.

"You'll have a great journey in this fog, Dr Simpson."

"You'll be glad you are staying here, Mr Chapman."

"So long as we don't have to stay here too long. I'll be getting in touch with you to let you know how we progress, or to ask you for further help if we need it. And now, for the present, many thanks, and good-night. Have a good drive back to town."

And his smile spread in mischievous ripples over his face, as we all shook hands.

Cheerful man! He was going to need all his buoyancy, all his humorous optimism, before his sojourn in Luton was done . . .

Our driver was not quite so perky as he had been on the outward journey. An afternoon's waiting around at Luton had damped his spirits. He turned his car's bonnet towards London and the trek began.

The fog grew thicker and thicker, darker and darker as we neared town, till finally we were crawling gropingly about the northern suburbs, in a desperate miasmic gloom, with only the vaguest notion of where we were. We pulled down the windows and stuck out our heads, peering against an atmosphere slightly less transparent and congenial than a dirty horse-blanket. The fog engulfed us, choked us, seeped into us, while we stared unavailingly for some kind of street sign which would help us to decide our whereabouts.

Our driver was enjoying himself again now. "This is quite a fog. Can you see anything, Dr Simpson?" asked the man at the wheel.

"Not much," said C. K. S., peering hard at nothing.

"Am I on the pavement?"

"No, I can just make out the kerb. You're doing very well."

We forged slowly ahead and then, from out of the murk, came a furious hoarse yell. "Look out, look out, you fool! What kind of a driver d'you think you are?"

And the beetroot-red face of a madly indignant citizen appeared suddenly, mouthing and pop-eyed, right beside us. "Speed like that, night like this, pavement . . . might've . . . nasty acci . . ." and then he had dissolved back into the fog, was totally gone, as astonishingly as he had appeared.

Our driver, hugely tickled, repeated again and again, "What kind of a driver d'you think you are?" Then he added, "And what was that about speed? We're going about five miles an hour. I can't go any slower. Why didn't he look where he was going? We weren't on the pavement."

"I didn't think so," said C. K. S.

"He was ambling about in the road. Typical idiotic London pedestrian. Never mind, though. Worse troubles at sea."

In the end we found Russell Square Tube station and there they put me down. They shouted "Good-night," and crept away into the fog again, to look for Dr Simpson's flat.

By next morning the fog had almost cleared and we were able to continue our routine mortuary work without any trouble.

We looked forward to hearing from Mr Chapman. And so indeed from time to time we did. But all he had to tell us was that he and Sergeant Judge were groping together in a fog thicker and more enduring than the one we had travelled back from Luton in. A fog of complete mystery in which they peered and searched and questioned, week by week, without any ray of information to light them in their investigations.

Now every big detective has his special reputation, and Mr Chapman was — still is — famous for his tenacity. He will persevere with a case long after other men exclaim, "Give up!" Therefore, with the Luton sack murder, he stuck grimly to his searching. Every now and again he came up to the Yard for a conference and on these occasions he would also perhaps pop along to see Dr Simpson; the round-faced, pink-cheeked personality who has been nicknamed, rather well, "The Cherub"; only a cherub with a wearily determined glint in his eyes as the weeks with the Luton job wore on.

"How's it going, Mr Chapman?"

"Oh, we keep hoping," he replied always, with a sound that was half a regretful grunt and half a chuckle.

Photographs of the dead woman were being exhibited in Luton shop windows, flashed on the screens of local cinemas.

"MURDER. POLICE ARE STILL ANXIOUS TO ESTABLISH IDENTITY OF THIS UNFORTUNATE WOMAN. HERE IS HER PICTURE". The picture was accompanied by her description.

But her injuries, just as Mr Chapman had feared, had distorted her face to such a degree she was quite unrecognisable. Her seventeen-year-old daughter, for

170

example, saw the photograph at the cinema, but never recognised it as her mother.

The father had told his children that mother had left home after quarrelling with him, and since she had done this once before, and since, moreover, "letters from her" arrived regularly for grandma, the children suspected nothing.

The two boys saw the photograph in a shop window and they did tell their father that it looked like their mother, but he replied it couldn't possibly be, as she had called home to "fetch some clothes" only a day or so previously. After that the children nursed no further suspicions.

The police ran a house-to-house enquiry, "Do you recognise this woman?" One man, a neighbour of the murdered woman, did half-recognise the picture and told his wife, "You know, that picture, it's a funny thing, but I thought it looked a bit like that Mrs Manton down the road, that's been gone from home the past few weeks." His honest spouse told him not to be a damn fool. So he buried his suspicions. Nobody wants to look a fool.

The nail-scrapings taken at post-mortem had proved uninformative. Mr Chapman had had plaster casts made of the dead woman's jaws in the hope some dental surgeon might recognise them, but although the dead woman's dental surgeon was one of the people interviewed in the house-to-house search he did not identify either the casts, or the photograph of the murdered woman.

Everything that could be done was done. Four hundred and four missing women were accounted for in the process of the search. Six hundred and eighty-one addresses of women whose whereabouts were unknown to their relatives were traced. Thirty-nine identity visits were paid to the body and nine persons identified it in genuine error as the body of four other women.

Two hundred and fifty lorry drivers who had called at the Vauxhall works at about the time of the murder were traced and interviewed.

Cleaners' records were searched. Streets and refuse dumps were combed for discarded or fragmentary clothing. Enquiries were distributed through the Press, the BBC, in the *Police Gazette*, to all county and borough police throughout the country. Scores of persons were interviewed who had heard screams, or seen suspicious persons, or happenings, on or about November 18th — 19th.

During the house-to-house search a police officer actually called at the home of the dead woman, but nothing aroused his suspicions, for the two boys he spoke to there didn't think it necessary to mention that their mother had "gone away". They didn't recognise the photograph, either.

A neighbour saw the boys being questioned, but when her turn for questioning came she didn't say anything about her neighbour down the road who was missing from home — why should she? Bertie Manton, the missing woman's husband, had said his wife had gone to Grantham to visit her brother. The neighbour knew, too, that the absent Mrs Manton was pregnant, but why tell a policeman that? Goodness, there's nothing very special about that. As for the photo, once again it went unrecognised.

The midwife who had paid Mrs Manton ante-natal visits had been told, like the neighbours, that she had gone to Grantham. The Luton Food Office had been told the same story.

As for the dead woman's mother, she had no more suspicions than her grandchildren, for "letters" arrived regularly from her daughter, posted in London — apparently the absent woman had gone from Grantham to Hampstead. The old lady had to have her daughter's "letters" read aloud to her, for she was almost blind . . .

The English are a great race for detective fiction, and they enjoy murder on the radio, television, the films. Nearly all the people interviewed by the detectives must have had at least one murder thriller tucked away on a bookshelf, they must have switched on the wireless at night to listen to a murder play, or trotted round to the cinema to see a film with corpses, cops, killer and witnesses complete. But when a policeman arrived on their doorstep, showing a photo of a murdered woman, "Do you by any chance recognise this photograph? Here is her description," the crime-fiction addicts found it impossible to grasp the situation in all its reality. Murder is something you read about, listen to on the wireless, see at the pictures, discover in print every Sunday morning when you open your newspaper, but you never come across it in your own everyday life. It happens to other people, maybe, in other districts, but it doesn't happen in your family, or among your neighbours, or down your street. Now this description says a woman between thirty and thirty-five, height five feet three inches, hair dark-brown, bobbed, eyes brown, heavy dark eyebrows, no teeth of her own, five-and-a-half months advanced in pregnancy. Well, that's the very description of Mrs Manton who lives a few doors up and who's away from home, but you never even think of this because Mrs Manton's a neighbour, and things like murder don't happen to neighbours, only to strangers you read about in the newspapers. Even if you do think, "Well, that sounds rather like Mrs Manton," you know you're being silly, because Mrs Manton has gone to her brother's at Grantham, Mr Manton told you so. And besides, that photograph the policeman's showing you, you've never seen that face in all your life. So you tell him, "No-o-o. It isn't a face that's known to me at all." And he says he's sorry he's had to trouble you and you say no trouble at all and good-afternoon and go inside and shut the door, and you hear him knocking at the next house. Well, and what's the use of him going there? They won't know no more about it than you do. And you finish your housework and have a cup of tea, and the evening draws on, and your hubby comes home, and after supper there's that murder play on the wireless . . . Such is life.

Such was life in Luton. "No, I've never seen that face." "Sorry, I've no idea who it is." Hundreds of doorsteps, hundreds of questions and answers, hundreds of interviews. Hundreds of phone conversations, chits and reports and statements, hunches

174

followed up, dead-ends arrived at, hopes dashed. The days become weeks, the weeks months . . . one, two, three months.

It begins to look as if it can go on for ever, POLICE ARE STILL ANXIOUS TO ESTABLISH IDENTITY OF THIS UNFORTUNATE WOMAN . . .

At last, on February 21st, an extremely detailed re-examination was made of all clothing and property that had come into the hands of the police during the enquiries; a kind of "stock-taking", as it were. Among the items of clothing was a piece of a black coat, and as this was being meticulously re-inspected there was found, in the padding, a dyer's tag which had not been noticed before. So the dyer was immediately traced and interviewed. His record book showed that the coat came from a Mr Manton, of Regent Street, Luton, in March, 1943.

The detectives had already been up and down the length of Regent Street — so near, and yet so very far! And now back they were again, this time making some very discreet enquiries, which revealed that Mrs Manton had not been seen since November 18th, which was, of course, the date of the suspected murder.

Chief Inspector Chapman now called at Manton's house. The door was opened by a girl, and immediately Mr Chapman knew the search was ended, for, to use his own words, "The girl was the image of the dead woman." She was, in fact, the deceased's daughter.

Manton was interviewed that same day at a local N.F.S. station where he worked. He admitted to Mr Chapman that he hadn't got on very well with his wife;

they had quarrelled over her friendships with soldiers and his with a local barmaid. On November 25th they had had a big quarrel and she had "slung her hook". She had gone first to her brother's at Grantham and then to London.

Manton was shown the identity photograph of the dead woman and he said, "No, that's nothing like my wife." He added, "I wouldn't do a thing like that. Besides, she's alive, we have letters from her." To prove this point he identified four letters the deceased's mother had received from North London, between the end of December and the beginning of February, purporting to be written in Mrs Manton's hand, and signed "Rene", which was the name she used. The letters described how she was getting on in London.

Mr Chapman noticed that in these letters the name Hampstead was spelt without the "p". Manton was accordingly asked to write, "Hampstead". He did so, and left out the "p". There was no doubt he had written the letters himself, travelled to Hampstead and posted them to his near-blind old mother-in-law, who was unable to examine the handwriting herself. The postage dates of these letters coincided with the dates of his leaves from the N.F.S.

Manton said he remembered that his wife left him on November 25th because that was the last day of four days' leave he had had, and it was on that last day of leave that they had quarrelled.

Asked to describe his wife, Manton said she was dark-eyed, dark hair, five to six months pregnant, had an appendix scar, and no teeth. She had worn false teeth, he added, and he gave Mr Chapman the name of his wife's dental surgeon.

This dental surgeon — who had already once been interviewed by the police without result — recognised a photograph of Mrs Manton in life. He produced records of Mrs Manton's teeth which showed that roots remained in her jaws, but no teeth. X-ray photographs already taken of the dead woman's jaws corresponded exactly with these dental records. So did the plaster casts Mr Chapman had had made of the jaws.

There could therefore be no argument about the identity of the dead woman. She was Mrs Manton all right.

Mr Chapman made some more enquiries about Manton. He found that his leave in November had ended on the 18th, not the 25th. The neighbours and relatives insisted they had not seen Mrs Manton after the 18th.

Mr Cherrill was called to Luton, and he found a pickle-jar in the Mantons' house with a beautiful thumb-print on it which matched the thumb-print taken at the time of the post-mortem.

There was ample evidence now on which to arrest Manton and charge him with the murder of his wife. On being charged he broke down and made a fresh statement:

"I am sorry I have told you lies about my wife . . . I killed her, but it was only because I lost my temper. I didn't intend to."

They had quarrelled frequently, he said, and in 1942 she had left him, but had returned. However, the

177

quarrelling had continued as badly as ever. At last, on November 18th, when they were having tea alone together, they started quarrelling again and she flung a cup of hot tea in his face. He lost his temper, picked up a very heavy wooden stool which was near his feet under the table and hit her about the head and face with it, several times. She fell backwards on to the floor.

"When I came to and got my sense again I see what I'd done. I saw she was dead and decided I had to do something to keep her away from the children. I undressed her and got four sacks from the cellar, cut them open and tied her up in them. I then carried her down to the cellar and left her there. I had washed up the blood before the children came home to tea. I hid the bloodstained clothing in a corner near the copper."

After dark, continued Manton, he brought the body up from the cellar, got out his bike, laid the body across the handlebars and wheeled his gruesome load down to the river. Here he laid it on the edge of the bank and then watched it roll down into the water.

Next day he burned the clothes and the false teeth.

After this statement detectives made a detailed search of Manton's house and found old blood splashes on the living-room walls, the ceiling and the door-jamb. A bloodstained envelope was found on the cellar stairs. All these stains belonged to group O — the dead woman's blood group.

In the front room was a dismantled bike; Manton's.

The stool, Manton said, had been broken up for firewood and burned, not long after the murder.

Mrs Manton's sister recognised the portion of black coat, the vital clue, as part of a coat Mrs Manton had had dyed black for a funeral.

How the coat had been torn up and thrown on a rubbish dump — for it was on a rubbish dump a detective had first found it — was never fully explained. Manton had most likely destroyed all his wife's clothes and disposed of the fragments here, there and everywhere. He hadn't reckoned with detectives who even search rubbish dumps.

So this fragment of a torn dyed coat, in which was sewn a dyer's tag, provided, after three months' hard and fruitless investigation, the vital clue in the Luton Sack Murder. This clue turned up only just in the nick of time, too, because Mr Chapman was on the point of giving up the case as hopeless.

Manton was tried at Bedford Assizes and found guilty. It was considered, however, that there were extenuating circumstances and so he was not hanged. But he died, not long after, in prison.

And that is the story of the Luton Sack Murder. A story of tenacity and incredible patience. A story, I think, of how our police are really rather wonderful.

CHAPTER
EIGHTEEN

War Work

By this time, of course, the authorities had made a spirited attempt to call me up. I had, however, been able to persuade them that I was doing more useful work as Dr Keith Simpson's secretary than I would do if I were called into the Women's Services, or even put in a munitions factory. But at the start of 1944 another attempt was made to get me into uniform. Again I put forward the reasons why I considered I was more useful to the State in my present job than I would be as an A.T.S., Wren or Waaf, or factory hand wielding a spanner, and my eloquence this time persuaded the female official at the Labour Exchange that I had really best remain a civilian for the duration.

"After all," she observed kindly as she closed the interview, "we can't all expect to have a close-up view of the war. Some of us have to stay put in our ordinary jobs."

I thought of the stay-at-home view I had already obtained of the war and it seemed to me to have been quite comprehensive. The Big Blitz in East London, the bodies of scores and scores of air-raid casualties, including some of the victims of the Bethnal Green shelter disaster, several post-mortems on spies hanged at Wandsworth prison, and the gradual accumulation during the course of my daily round of innumerable war anecdotes: soldiers returning to shoot unfaithful wives, deserters holding-up and killing unfortunates in order to get money from them, timid youths taking cyanide to avoid their call-up, and a hundred and one other stories, combining to give me a broad and vivid picture of life in war-time England.

So when I heard I was to continue in my ordinary job I didn't feel I was being cheated of any war-time experience. It wasn't the more orthodox experience I would have obtained in the Services, but it was experience of the war for all that.

And indeed in the first month of the new year a case came along which was peculiarly a "War Crime", one of the first of the cases of that era of war-time crime which was to prove such a tricky period for the police, posing them innumerable new problems and straining their resources to the utmost; the era of a war-swollen, mobile population, troops on the move, deserters on the run, refugees drifting hither and thither, an era of Black Markets, new rackets, new racketeers, of smuggling and all manner of unlawful "larks", the whole of that war-time crime wave leading to the post-war wave of spivvery and violence, the gunnings and the coshings and the dismal dark-night exploits of the juvenile gangsters . . .

It was a cold, grey day in mid-January when we were called to a comfortable, middle-class Surrey suburb.

Our destination there was a half-timbered, pseudo-Tudor homestead standing in a tidy, privet-hedged garden. There, in the heavily oak-panelled lounge-hall, we found a large party of C.I.D. officers, headed by Area Supt William Rawlings and D.D.I. George Somerset. The burly figure of Mr Cherrill bustled in all directions searching for fingerprints, while Percy Law, the famous Yard photographer, was shooting off flashlights.

The focal point of this activity was the body of a middle-aged, grey-headed woman who lay, gagged and bound, on the hall floor.

D.D.I. Somerset told Dr Simpson the little that was already known of the case. The Tudor residence was the home of a Greek shipowner, who was at present away on business. The dead woman was his housekeeper, a forty-seven-year-old refugee named Klara Steindl. She had been living all alone in the house during her employer's absence.

The Greek was reputedly a man of some financial substance and in the house were several impressive-looking safes. Somehow the knowledge of these safes had leaked out. The house was visited by burglars who set to work to crack one of the safes. Miss Steindl, it seemed, had heard them and gone to investigate. She had been struck one or two — not very serious — blows and had been gagged and bound and left lying, helpless and dumb, in the hall while the burglars finished rifling the safes. They had then beaten a retreat, leaving Miss Steindl still lying, trussed and gagged, in the hall.

At first she had been unconscious, but Dr Simpson's examination of her showed that she had recovered consciousness and had struggled frantically to release herself. She was already in breathing difficulties from her head injuries and the gag, and her struggles precipitated asphyxiation. The dead woman was blue in the face and had clearly struggled wildly for some time to loosen her bonds, but had succeeded only in choking herself.

Thus a burglary became a murder case.

At first the detectives all seemed very hopeful. Mr Cherrill had obtained some good fingerprints and before long had definite suspects "all taped for the job", as Mr Somerset said. But then something went wrong. The suspected men vanished. Apparently they had left England in order to fight for King and Country, and that was that. Opposite the Steindl case had to be written the most unpopular word in any detective's vocabulary; UNSOLVED.

Quite a number of suspected murderers were to escape retribution during the following months by being drafted for overseas service just in the nick of time. The Steindl case was one of the first.

It was also our first murder case of the year, and one way and another 1944 was quite a year.

Dr Simpson and I often drove past St Paul's School on our way to Hammersmith. The boys, of course, had all been evacuated at the beginning of the war, but the school buildings seemed to be used as some kind of military headquarters. Especially in the first months of 1944 unusual activity could be noticed there;

183

military guards appeared at the gates, large and very impressive staff cars were drawn up outside, and various gentlemen sporting scarlet braid and decorations were glimpsed entering the driveway. "Some sort of Staff conference seems to be going on," observed C. K. S. "Now, if we were German spies . . ."

One afternoon we saw Monty leaving the place in a large limousine; our car drew up beside his at the traffic lights and we had an excellent view of the keen, penetrating, rather foxy face, which was so much more witty than one had expected.

We discussed these local excitements with MacKay of Hammersmith, who was gloomy about it all. "Let's hope Jerry hasn't noticed the goings-on," he said.

Jerry had, and St Paul's School and neighbourhood received several nights of intense bombing.

The school wasn't too badly damaged, but the streets around suffered.

The morning of February 24th, when we turned into the road which took us past St Paul's we saw sights which, though by now familiar, never failed to sicken. Gaps torn between the rows of houses, deep craters in front gardens, brimming with high piles of earth, rubble, plaster, laths, bricks, tiles, fragments of furniture. Houses with their sides or fronts torn away, exposing rooms where ceilings sagged, wallpaper flapped in tattered strips, pictures dangled crookedly, a tossed bed lurched, tables and chairs poised drunkenly. Everywhere was broken glass, not a window in the district seemed left intact. The car crunched over broken glass as we drove slowly along the road. The houses that still stood stared blindly and darkly at nothing; but how many holes had been torn in their ranks! Poor old houses, I thought, poor London houses.

When we had crunched slowly through the glass-sprinkled streets and had made a big detour because of a large yellow notice, "DANGER — UNEXPLODED BOMB", we finally arrived at the mortuary. That precise, white-tiled domain over which MacKay ruled so efficiently had become a place of chaos, and MacKay charged around it like a furious rhinoceros.

So many fatal casualties had been taken that previous night into the Civil Defence mortuary that there had been an overflow into MacKay's mortuary — which was, of course, intended for coroner's cases only. All over the floor of the Hammersmith mortuary now lay bodies, the bodies of bomb casualties, which are unlike the bodies of any other casualties, for they are so dusty, and raggled and crumpled; so tattered and degraded. Old people, young people, little children, lying there battered and begrimed, some shattered and crushed by falling debris, some with their insides blown out, some burned and blasted, blackened and charred, some literally blue in the face from violent asphyxia, and one or two, astonishingly, apparently unblemished, wax-pallid and tranquil, like novelette corpses.

MacKay and his assistants hustled round, tying identity discs to the bodies, putting any belongings found on them into little bags which were then tied to the bodies too.

In the yard outside the Coroner's office swarmed anxious people, searching for lost relatives. Their faces wore stunned, slightly astonished expressions. Not many of them wept. They were all too shocked for tears.

A youngish woman was talking to a big, broad police constable, who was bending towards her with a solicitous, almost tender expression. She was saying, in an odd, flat, matter-of-fact voice, "You see, I don't know quite what to decide about their funeral. My husband's at sea, in the Navy, and they were our only children, only the two of them, you see, and I don't quite know how he would like them buried."

She looked at him in that matter-of-fact way, and you could feel that she was stunned beyond all normal sensation, while the policeman looked down at her with eyes that were bright with tears and when he spoke his voice sounded thick.

"Well, if I was you, ma'am, I'd have them buried in the common grave. It's very nice, really, you know; there's a very nice ceremony, and they're all buried together, with a Union Jack put on their coffins, so it's a proper ceremony, very nice, and it'll save you all the anxiety and trouble and at the same time be much nicer for you to look back on, afterwards; the ceremony, you know, and the flag."

"Oh, yes, yes," she said quickly, "I didn't know they buried them so nicely as that, oh, yes, yes, that is a nice idea."

A nice idea to have one's only two children buried with the Union Jack, a nice idea, with a ceremony, I thought, as I scurried into the p.m. room, my throat suddenly rigid with a great hard lump, and the mother left in the yard discussing her children's funeral with the policeman. And in the p.m. room our inquest case lay perched high and singular, white and cleanly naked, on the porcelain p.m. table above the litter of dusty, tattered bomb casualties, among them, if I had searched, two children who were to be buried with the flag.

Everyone working in the mortuary had now assumed the stiff, impassive, chill expressions that the English assume when they are in a crisis and seething with emotion. MacKay didn't talk any more, he just barked instructions, and C. K. S. dictated to me in a frozen, beautifully detached style, as though he were reciting Shakespeare in ice. In short, everyone was brokenhearted and furious.

During the days that followed we all became progressively colder and stiffer and more and more impassive. The nights were torn with bombs and mornings brought more and more bodies to the mortuaries. Especially in the Hammersmith area. At Hammersmith, MacKay chugged around faster and faster and more and more bodies came in.

Among MacKay's assistants at that time were an affianced couple, and it used to intrigue me very much to watch them billing and cooing at each other as they busied themselves over the gruesome work, tying the identity discs on the bodies and exchanging happy smiles whenever they caught one another's eye. There certainly are some queer folk around.

Even MacKay had to relapse into a short, strangled chuckle when he caught them beaming lovingly amongst the dead. "Put that in a book, Miss Molly. Ah, but nobody'd ever believe you."

Of course none of these bodies should really have come into the Coroner's mortuary, but they overflowed into it in a torrent, till MacKay didn't know which way to turn. Finally, Mrs MacKay, a charming and indomitable Scot, came down to the mortuary to help her husband. She had never handled a dead body before, but MacKay was so tired he had to rest, so she took over from him. "There was a coroner's case to attend to, so I came down here to the mortuary in the evening and locked myself in with the body. I thought, 'If I faint, or cry, or scream or have hysterics or do anything foolish there'll be nobody to see me or know I'm being so stupid.' But luckily I was all right and didn't mind it like I had feared I might," Mrs MacKay told me afterwards, simply.

"I should think you've had enough of dead bodies now, Miss Molly, to last you a lifetime," remarked MacKay, threading his needle with string, preparatory to sewing up the anaesthetic death Dr Simpson had just been examining.

"I'm beginning to feel a trifle that way," I confessed. "What about you?"

"Yes, they're even getting me down a bit," sighed MacKay. "It wouldn't matter if you could get a good night's sleep in between the work, but you can't sleep in raids like these."

C. K. S. had arranged to meet three American doctors at Hammersmith on one of these mornings. When we arrived we found that bombs had fallen on houses just across the road from the mortuary. Deep, debris-filled craters marked the places where the houses had stood. Up the debris mounds struggled Civil Defence Rescue workers, wearily but determinedly struggling to save people still lying buried. In the mortuary were fresh rows of torn and dusty bodies and round the door of the Coroner's office stood the stunned-faced, agonisingly dry-eyed relatives.

Presently up drove a jeep, with three very smart American medical officers and a fresh-looking young driver. The officers were ushered into the mortuary, where they stood, bewildered, among the bodies. A short conversation with Keith Simpson ensued. The bombing had rather complicated our day and it was decided that instead of accompanying C. K. S. on his post-mortem rounds it might be better if the visitors went to the Old Bailey instead. I was to go with the party, to take care of them. C. K. S. added, with a twinkle, "Here you are, Miss L., here's your chance to ride in a jeep."

Like every right-minded girl I was curious to ride in a jeep, so I put on my hat and coat with alacrity and trotted out of the mortuary with the three officers; who, by the way, appeared scared stiff of me.

Now C. K. S. was lecturing that evening to the Medico-Legal Society, with a "Social" to follow, and I was due to attend both these functions. Therefore I was dressed in my very best — there being no time to slip home at the end of the working day to change. I was wearing, as part of my ensemble, a model black Paris hat that didn't like winds. Also I had on my only pair of silk stockings. Delightfully suitable for cocktails, but not for a ride in a jeep.

The jeep was in the mortuary yard, minus its driver. We found him over the road, watching the Civil Defence men with the interested but slightly remote expression of a tourist. He and the three medical gentlemen entrusted to my care had, in fact, only just arrived from the States and this was their first encounter with an air-raid, or rather, the aftermath of an air-raid.

"These bombs sure do a lot of damage," said the jeep driver. I gave him the look which veterans give novices, and then we all went back to the jeep.

The right way to ride in a jeep is to sprawl and yet brace oneself against the lurches and bounces, holding on to anything available with both hands. But in a tight skirt, silk stockings and high-heeled shoes sprawling and bracing both become virtually impossible. I had to cling on to my hat with one hand and direct the driver with energetic gestures of the other, for he, sweet youth, had never driven in London before, he had not yet even got into the way of keeping to the left-hand side of the road, and he had a distinct passion for driving head-on against streams of "One Way Only" traffic. This made the journey rather hair-raising, and by the time we reached Piccadilly I felt exhausted. All my muscles were aching, and I felt bruised all over, for I was bouncing about the jeep like a piece of pop-corn. We were beginning, too, to attract some notice from people on the pavements. A jeep careering erratically down Piccadilly, bearing four Americans and one young woman, the latter holding her hat to her head with one hand, gesturing like a Boadicea with the other, and endeavouring intermittently, with nervous and futile clutches, to restrain her brief war-time skirts from blowing above her knees, was quite a diverting sight. It requires a good deal to embarrass me, but I began to wish I had never taken that jeep ride. Meanwhile, I tried to maintain my poise and point out interesting landmarks to the gentlemen, who all jerked their heads to look where I pointed with gratifying promptitude — including the driver, which was not so gratifying.

When we reached Aldwych this jaunty New World personality plunged us, despite all my warnings and pleadings, full-steam-ahead into the oncoming tide of traffic, with the result we only escaped several collisions by mere hair-breadths, and finally caused a traffic block. I felt so terrible I just closed my eyes and thought, "Remember, when you are questioned by the police you don't understand a *word* of English." But somehow we sorted ourselves out of the congestion we had caused, and all the other drivers were very friendly and hands-across-the-Atlantic, and finally we were on our way again. Not for long, though, because I unwisely pointed out a famous church and the driver thought I was directing him and accordingly shot us into a cul-de-sac, from which we then emerged, almost as fast as we had entered, in reverse. A final ghastly spurt of speed, another frantic gesture from me, which the driver followed up with a misunderstanding swerve, and we found ourselves in St Paul's Churchyard, missing a picturesque old post by inches. And now two of the party decided they would rather see St Paul's than visit the Old Bailey, and the driver said he'd sure like to take a look at Saint Paul's too, so we all climbed out of the jeep, and I and the one remaining officer interested in the Old Bailey set off to complete the last short lap of our journey there on foot, while the other three climbed the pigeon-decorated steps of the cathedral.

The rest of the morning my officer and myself spent in Number Three Court, listening to the astonishing story of a young thing of fourteen who had made herself out to be seventeen and had had high jinks with an unfortunate soldier whom she had afterwards brazenly accused of rape. My American was very impressed with the court's traditional procedure, and extremely shocked by the young thing of fourteen. We were both pleased when the soldier was found Not Guilty. This case was then followed by a charge against an abortionist, and I suggested we should leave the Old Bailey in search of some lunch . . .

The Medico-Legal Society's meeting in the evening was as diverting as my morning had been, but in a vastly different way.

I once heard the Medico-Legal Society described by a reporter as "A crime club that hangs out in Portland Place." This is, in a sense, both true and wildly untrue.

The Medico-Legal Society is a very serious scientific society which meets once a month to discuss various subjects of serious medico-legal interest. These meetings take place at the Society's very dignified headquarters in Portland Place. The distinguished medical and legal members of this society range from famous women Harley Street specialists to celebrated judges. At the time of which I write Sir Bernard Spilsbury was Treasurer of the Society, and Sir Roland Burrows, K.C., the President. The reader will therefore understand why such an elevated Society, formed to discuss expertly medico-legal subjects, can scarcely be dubbed a "crime club".

On this particular evening, after a Council Meeting upstairs, everybody went downstairs to a small but very comfortable lecture-theatre, where C. K. S. gave a lecture on the Dobkin case, illustrated by lantern slides, the lantern manipulated very smoothly by the invaluable Ireland. The lecture nicely balanced the scientific with the stimulating, and the audience greeted it with enthusiastic applause.

Sir Bernard Spilsbury was the intended second speaker, but he failed to attend because the previous evening he had been at his club, the famous Carlton, when a bomb fell on that august place, covering Spilsbury, along with the other members present, with a deluge of plaster and soot. Sir Bernard therefore excused himself from Portland Place and remained quietly recovering at home instead.

Dr Simpson was kind enough to take me along to several of the Society's meetings, for he knew how I liked going to new places and collecting impressions. At one meeting he not only pointed out a famous woman doctor to me, but also brought to my notice a vast "potato" in the lady's stocking!

Perhaps she too had been bothered by bombs and hadn't been able to settle down to her darning.

Many of the members who attended these war-time meetings were, of course, in uniform. Everything was done in a manner which was typical of Britain at that time: the meetings held early, because of the raids and the black-out, the members arriving not in their cars but on foot, their dress sombre and simple, and everyone showing a firm, albeit quiet, determination to carry on with the monthly meetings and the erudite discussions of crime in spite of Hitler and all the bombs, blastings, hangings and blowings-up he could muster.

All the same, beneath this cool façade, nerves, by this time, were becoming a trifle frayed and people, from time to time, did rather odd things, as our daily work in the mortuaries revealed to us. One example of frayed war-time tempers, which I shall never forget, concerned a Lambeth costermonger family. They all lived together in a brave little Lambeth house: the old parents, their son, their daughter-in-law, and one or two other members of the family not specified. And after so many sleepless nights and narrow squeaks they were all beginning to get a bit snappy with one another.

The family tension came to a head during dinner one day, over the subject of the black-out. The local A.R.P. warden had been complaining recently about the household's black-out and had threatened they would be served with a summons if they didn't do something to improve matters. The head of the household, a peppery old costermonger of seventy-odd, said it was all the fault of his daughter-in-law; she just didn't bother to see that the black-out was properly done. Up jumped the old man's son, husband of the allegedly careless young woman, and said he wouldn't have his wife blamed for everything, his father could take his remarks back. Father, adopting a pugilistic attitude with raised fists and tucked-in chin, responded, "Even if I am turned seventy I can stand up *to you*." Amidst alarmed, shrill exclamations from the womenfolk the two men exchanged a flurry of trivial blows, one of which, from the old man, caught the son on the head, whereupon, much to everybody's horror, he fell to the ground and lay there motionless.

The poor old father, immediately overcome by remorse, dropped on his knees beside his son, kissed him wildly and called to him, "Wake up, John, wake up!" But John did not wake up. Various efforts were made to revive him, but without success. Finally the father decided on hot, stimulating applications in the region of the heart and being of the old, hardy school, chose the family flat-iron, heated on the stove, as the method.

The iron, very hot, was twice firmly placed on the unconscious man's chest, but there was no response even to this drastic treatment. (Indeed, if he had been capable of response this "stimulation" would surely have sent him leaping to the ceiling.) The fact was that the son was beyond all revival. The doctor, when called, confirmed he was dead and the body was taken to

Southwark mortuary, while the poor old father was arrested.

The body we found on the p.m. table at Southwark was that of a well-built man in his late thirties, with a clearly defined hot iron mark burned on his chest, just as if he had been a tablecloth or sheet on which a careless housewife had set down her iron while she turned her attention to something else for the moment. I stared at this burn in astonishment. "But what a thing to do!"

"Very old way of reviving people, a hot iron," said West. "And guaranteed to make a chap sit up, with a jerk and all — so long as he isn't dead."

"But, West, I think it's ghastly."

"I told you before, Miss Molly, that these coster-mongers are a real rough lot," replied West, with all the Cockney's supreme contempt for costermongers; costers, contrary to popular belief, not being Cockneys, but of Irish origin. Upon the other hand I have met costers who are intensely proud of being costers, who trace themselves back, with a superior expression, to their Irish forefathers, and who would not be labelled Cockneys on any account. Personally, being educated by West, I am all on the side of the Cockneys.

Dr Simpson, who was always very interested in West's erudite remarks upon South Londoners, and the people of Southwark and Lambeth in particular, now joined in the conversation. "Well, your old iron treatment didn't make this chap sit up, West. I'm afraid it would have taken a good deal more than a hot iron to revive this one." He looked thoughtfully at the burns.

"Beautiful specimens of post-mortem burning. I'd love a photograph of them. Miss L., can you slip your coat on, nip round to Guy's and see if Miss Treadgold can spare a moment to take a photograph for me?"

Accordingly, I slipped on my coat and sprinted across the big bomb-site, cleared and tidied of debris so that it rather resembled a desolate playground, beat my way up the home stretch of Great Maze Pond, skipped into Out Patients, bounded past Casualty, plunged into the Main Medical Block and hastened, first at a run, then at a panting stagger and finally at a weak-kneed lurch, up the five flights to the Photography Department, where presided the charming and talented Sylvia Treadgold, one of my very good friends at Guy's.

The Photography Department was in a sort of penthouse which had only recently recovered from a bomb. Sylvia was used to having me tumble in, gasping and clutching the air in the last stages of exhaustion after all those ghastly stairs.

"Treadgold!" (The hospital habit of always using surnames.)

"I'm in the dark-room."

I poked open the dark-room door and squeezed myself in through a cautious crack. It was like the cauldron scene from *Macbeth*. In a lurid red glow Treadgold and her assistant were bending over something, muttering.

"Excuse me," I interrupted them.

"Hold on a second."

I waited, gradually getting back my breath. The muttering went on.

"Coming," said Sylvia at last, and I explained my mission. Could she come round to Southwark mortuary right away to photograph some burns in a queried murder case?

"Love to."

We squeezed out of the dark-room.

"Why d'you always climb all those stairs? The lift is working again now," said Sylvia, as she collected her gear.

"I know, but for one thing stairs keep me in training, and for another thing I just don't trust that lift."

However, we made the descent by the lift; an emergency affair, all groans and squeaks and stops and jerks, but the pride and joy of the individual who had fixed it up and who met us on the ground floor with a happy smile and the observation, "Going smoother now, ain't she?"

"Mah-vellous," breathed Sylvia.

Back at the mortuary we found D.D.I. Smith (now Chief Inspector Smith, celebrated for being in charge of the Craig shooting case). Mr Smith, suave and deliberate, always carried the most perfectly rolled umbrella and I always wanted to ask him if he rolled it himself, for it was the veritable work of an artist. But I never did ask him, because I wasn't certain if it were the kind of thing a humble secretary can ask a dignified D.D.I.

The p.m., during my absence, had taken a dramatic turn. That the man was dead some time before the hot iron was planted on his chest was now amply evident, for examination of the brain revealed that it was not the blow from his father's fist that had killed him, but the sudden rupturing of a developmental cerebral aneurism. This meant, in other words, that the man might have dropped down dead at any time, and although the quarrel with his father might have precipitated his death because of his excitement it could not be considered to be the cause of his death in any way.

So the father had not killed his son, although I don't suppose remorse ever ceased to torture him at the memory of this foolish fight over the family black-out.

It was not long after this South London episode that we had a call to East London, to a murder in Leyton. Goodwin, the Coroner's officer for that district in those days (he retired after the war), explained that it wasn't much of a murder, "just a husband quarrelled with his wife".

He met us at the police station and escorted us to the house where the murder had taken place; talking non-stop all the way, telling us what was known of the case. (The time of our visit was about two in the afternoon.)

"The D.D.I.'s held up, Dr Simpson, says he'll be along as soon as he can, and same with the Coroner."

"In that case, Goodwin, we'll push on with the job."

"As I thought, sir. Well, sir, it goes like this. Screaming heard by neighbours at 12.15 pip emma today, sir. Husband seen to leave house in a hurry at 12.30 pip emma, sir. Encountered P.C. in street (one of our chaps, sir), and told him he'd just killed his wife. P.C. went to look and sure enough there she was, sir. Everything left as husband left it, for you to see, Dr

Simpson. Apparently he believed she'd been trying to poison him, at least, that's his story. The neighbours say they quarrelled together a lot. They'd spent all last night down an air-raid shelter. Here's the house, sir."

It was a little terrace house, divided into top and bottom flats, like so many little Leyton houses. How often had I, a nervous cub-reporter, stood on such a doorstep, come to collect the details of a wedding or golden marriage anniversary. And now here I was on the doorstep with Dr Keith Simpson and P.C. Jack Goodwin, waiting while the latter with real police aplomb took out a door-key and opened the front door and then led us up a narrow, steep, short flight of stairs into a little sitting-room.

The table was laid with the remains of a meal, and tea things, and there was a half-full cup of now cold tea and a plate of unfinished bacon and fried bread. But it was not an enticing table, being thickly spattered with blood, as were the carpet, the furniture, the walls, even the ceiling. On the floor lay a woman, stuck clean through with an enormous *Samurai* sword.

"Used to hang on the wall as an ornament," said Goodwin, indicating a hook over the mantelpiece.

C. K. S. got out his thermometer and tape-measure and I got out my notebook, pencil and little buff envelopes. Then we set to work, taking temperatures and measurements and collecting hair, fingernail-scrapings and so on. We were very absorbed in this work, so that we didn't precisely notice what Goodwin was up to, although I did think, in passing, that he seemed to be rattling and clinking and splashing a lot in the adjacent kitchen, very *hausfrau*.

Presently C. K. S. said, "O.K., Goodwin, I've done all I have to do here. Perhaps the undertaker could come round now and shift the body to the mortuary for us."

"Righty-o, Dr Simpson," says Goodwin. Then the astonishing creature adds, proudly, "Tidied things up a bit, haven't I?"

Tidied up he certainly had. He'd cleared the table. He'd washed up all the breakfast things; the china and the cutlery and the blood-spattered plates, everything. He'd swabbed up all the bloodstains from the furniture, the walls. In fact he'd got the room quite apple-pie and if it hadn't been for the lady lying skewered on the hearth-rug you wouldn't have known there had been a murder at all.

C. K. S. looked slowly around. "Goodwin, I just don't know what your D.D.I. will say. You've successfully abolished every clue."

Goodwin's jaw dropped. He had expected, I think, a word of praise. Poor old Goodwin.

I don't know if the D.D.I. did say anything. Fortunately it was a case in which fingerprints and bloodstains were not vital. The husband had given himself up to the police and had made a full confession, and at the trial he was found to be insane. As for the actual murder, one can scarcely ask for more evidence than a *Samurai* sword thrust into the front of the victim and protruding several inches from the back. A warning, as C. K. S. told the Guy's students afterwards, never to keep dangerous ornaments about the house . . .

Goodwin, I might add, was a constant source of joy to me, besides being quite a friend. I remember him once hurrying into Wanstead mortuary where there were two bodies awaiting post-mortem examination, one case of his, from Leyton, the other a case belonging to the Woodford Coroner's officer. Goodwin hurried in, exclaiming, "Dr Simpson, just take a look at my brain first, would you, to see if I've got a haemorrhage."

"All right, Goodwin, hop on the slab and I'll take a look," said C. K. S.

Goodwin snorted. He knew Dr Simpson knew he always referred to bodies from Leyton in the First Person Singular. For example, "Well, if you ask me, Dr Simpson, I've got a fractured femur." Or, "Dr Simpson, I've got a ruptured gastric ulcer, when can you do it?" "Dr Simpson, I've got a fractured skull and queried abdominal injuries, taken into Whipps Cross Hospital, dying."

A last word for Leyton mortuary; a small, concrete building presided over by Miles, the dour but really very kind-hearted and likeable mortuary keeper, a man very proud of, and devoted to, his job. We were there a few days after the *Samurai* sword case, quietly doing a p.m. on a natural death (a local A.R.P. man, I remember), when the door of the p.m. room opened and my dear, one-and-only P.C. Albert Bultitude looked in.

P.C. Bultitude was all bultitude, and adorable.

"Good-morning, Dr Simpson. Good-morning, miss. Excuse me looking in like this, but I wanted to see old Bill, if he's here."

"There's nobody here but ourselves, Mr Bultitude, and Miles, who is in the viewing-room. I don't think I've seen anyone else here this morning."

"Isn't that Bill you've got there, Dr Simpson?"

"Here, Mr Bultitude?" exclaimed the startled C. K. S., indicating the body.

Mr Bultitude drew closer, and peered.

"Yes, that's old Bill. He was a great pal of mine, poor old chap. Thought I'd like to drop in and take a last look at him."

"Certainly, Mr Bultitude. You are very welcome," said C. K. S., quickly recovering his poise.

Mr Bultitude stood peaceably by awhile, looking his friendly last on old Bill, who was in the final stages of dissection. Then Mr Bultitude thanked Dr Simpson again, beamed good-bye to us both, went into the mortuary yard, heaved himself on his bike and with a genial wave to us pedalled away.

"A touching little tribute of friendship," said C. K. S. "I trust my friends will do the same for me."

Such, then, were the opening months of 1944, grimmest of all those grim war years. Tragic things were happening, but there were still moments for certain wry glimpses of humour. Soon it was going to become much more difficult to see the funny side of things. Indeed, if it had not been for the stalwart Londoners around me, determined to keep smiling at all costs, I should probably have sunk hopelessly in an abyss of Gallic gloom.

203

Fortunately my friends, by their own solid example, kept my morale from sinking. "Keep your pecker up, Miss Molly, and I'll see you get a blood-orange at Christmas," said P.C. Doughty, of Shoreditch. Which is a good piece of London philosophy.

CHAPTER
NINETEEN

A Secret Weapon

June 6th, 1944, Invasion Day, found me waking dazedly in a green and silver dawn which shook with the noise of the outgoing planes streaming across the sky. Between the tremendous roaring of the planes came brief pauses of silence and then I could hear the birds singing in the garden as if they could not care less about the enormous sound above them. I lay in bed and thought, "Today must be our Invasion Day — at last." And I wish I could say that I raced out into the garden to take a look at the planes. But I didn't. I fell asleep again.

The radio at breakfast-time confirmed that the Invasion was really on, and I hurried off to work in a state of tremendous excitement and apprehension. This was the day we had all been waiting for, and working for, and praying for, during the past four long years, and we all both delighted in it and dreaded it. Everybody held their breaths, waiting for news of what was happening on the landing beaches. The entire British nation had its fingers crossed.

I met C. K. S. at King's Cross and we drove out to the eastern suburbs, where we had our first post-mortem cases for the day. When we reached Whipps Cross Corner we saw a long, very long, convoy of Red Cross field ambulances, little, square, khaki-coloured vehicles plastered with the huge red crosses on white circles, scurrying along the road to the distant Essex coast. There were so many of them. And one hoped, helplessly and no doubt foolishly, that they wouldn't *all* have to be used.

When we reached Wanstead mortuary we found Goodwin waiting for us in the little yard, for once at a loss for words. We hurried into the mortuary for our first case of the day and were greeted at once by a faint, but unmistakable, smell of bitter almonds. It meant only one thing. "A cyanide poisoning, Goodwin?" said C. K. S., not so much questioning — he had no need to question — as remarking. Goodwin came and stood by the old-fashioned slate p.m. table and nodded at the young man who lay there, in battle-dress.

"He was along with his regiment waiting in a boat at the docks, and I suppose the waiting got him down a bit, and he'd got the cyanide along with him, being a windy one, and just before they started out he was found dead in his berth."

C. K. S. turned the soldier's rather blunt-featured, cyanosed face up to the light and we all stared at him in silence. Without putting it into words we all felt that he was a blot upon our escutcheon. Nevertheless, being mere civilians, we had a delicacy about saying so. Therefore we just looked at him, without spoken comment.

When C. K. S. opened the body the smell of almonds, that unmistakable odour of cyanide, came out strongly. It is a quick death; the one, of course, which Himmler chose.

That was our first p.m. on D-Day. The young soldier who was cut up in Wanstead mortuary while his erstwhile comrades were landing in Normandy.

The rest of that day we did less topical post-mortems. In the evening came the news that the landings had been, so far, successful, and there were the voices of Churchill, Eisenhower and De Gaulle on the radio.

Chester Wilmot, in *The Struggle for Europe*, describes how Hitler's plans to launch a gigantic V.1 bombardment of Southern England and especially of London went astray. On the night of June 12th one lone bomb, out of an intended salvo of a hundred-and-twenty-eight, landed in London. It claimed only one or two victims and on the following morning, June 13th, C. K. S. was asked to do a p.m. on one of these, a woman.

The V.1 had landed in the Shoreditch neighbourhood, and Doughty, the Coroner's officer, was terribly hush-hush when he telephoned me.

"The Home Office wants Dr Keith Simpson to do a post-mortem on the victim of an incident."

"What kind of an incident?" asks the ever inquisitive Miss L.

"Enemy action, Miss Molly."

"Yes, but what sort of enemy action, Doughty?"

Doughty hummed and ha'd and at last said that so far as he could make out it had been some "sort of a rocket-bomb".

"The Secret Weapon?" I asked him.

"Don't know, Miss Molly. I suppose it might be."

As events soon proved, it was the Secret Weapon all right, but on that first morning of the offensive we didn't know any more about the matter than what Doughty had told me over the phone. The woman on the p.m. table at Shoreditch mortuary had died of a blast from a high-explosive of some kind or the other, and her injuries were ordinary blast injuries.

On the night of June 15th—16th the offensive began in earnest. A woman surgeon friend of mine in North London spent all June 16th operating on casualties brought in from a Kentish Town incident, while I sat typing in Keith Simpson's flat, listening to the explosions going off, spasmodically, around us. We were informed that we were being attacked by pilotless rocket-bombs, and a few days later one which had landed intact was put on view at Leicester Square, and I went along to look at it — I think I paid sixpence to see it. But soon I was seeing an excess of them, doodling across the sky, and I wondered why on earth I had wasted sixpence to look at a V.1.

The Londoner's pet name for them was "doodle-bombs", with less decent variations on the theme. They were, frankly, nerve-racking. They were also, I thought, so completely German; a form of death utterly mechanised, completely lacking the human touch, deriving from those master-minds that invented mobile gas-chambers for killing Jewish children, and human-soap factories. Yes, the doodle-bombs made dying a completely ignoble process. A rather ridiculous little airplane buzzing across the sky, drooling and lurching like a besotted bumble-bee, finally to cut off into silence and plunge in a top-heavy, helpless dive on to streets and houses and people, sending everything and everybody up in fragments, with a bang!

It was so inhuman it verged on the farcical. A little airplane, flying by radio, travelling so far and then automatically going off bang and killing you. What a bloody silly way to die!

We soon all got used to the business of hearing a bomb boombling nearer and nearer and wondering, "Is it going to pass over, or is it going to cut out and land on me?"

Hitler, of course, was meantime optimistically assuring his Chiefs of Staff that the war would be over in a matter of weeks, because the British civilians, under the impact of this fearful onslaught, would panic and ask for an armistice.

But although most people found the V.1s a much more gruelling ordeal than the Blitz, there was no panic, because everybody at home knew that this attack was all part of the German counter-attack against the Allied Invasion and it was as much the civilian's duty to stand up to the doodle-bombing as it was the soldier's duty to do the fighting in France. Therefore the Londoner's watchword, "Grin and bear it" once again became a battle cry, although the grinning was, by this time, somewhat dour.

The doodle-bombs seemed to have a definite time-table, and this time-table coincided wonderfully neatly with that of Dr Keith Simpson. He liked, if possible, to work south and west in the mornings and east in the afternoons. The doodle-bombs chose the same system. Mornings they plumped around Hammersmith, Wandsworth, moving towards Southwark at midday — when we too moved over to Southwark. By the time we reached Shoreditch at two o'clock or so they were also flocking down upon Shoreditch, travelling further afield to Stratford, Leyton, Walthamstow, Ilford and East Ham as we went.

I suggested, a little timidly, that we might change our routine round a bit. But C. K. S. greeted this proposal with a frigid look. "Certainly not. We really cannot allow these wretched bombs to interfere with our work, Miss L."

One afternoon, as Doughty of Shoreditch and I picked ourselves up from the floor from under his office desk, where we had been taking inadequate emergency cover while a flying-bomb exploded a few blocks away, I said, "Doughty, if I come here often enough these afternoons I know I'll cop it."

He gave me a rueful grin. "Why, Miss Molly, d'you think we've got one labelled for us here?"

"I do."

Next afternoon we didn't go to Shoreditch, but about four o'clock Doughty phoned us to say that a bomb had landed just outside the Coroner's Court, damaging the place severely — fortunately he had been in the basement of a neighbouring building — and quite destroying the funny little old Victorian mortuary and, what was infinitely worse, the wonderful old fifteenth-century weavers' houses the other side of the churchyard. As for the beautiful old church, that was still more or less standing, but blown through and through, so that it was merely a shell.

How often I had said I would go in that church some time when I had the afternoon off, to see the ancient registers with the names of Shakespeare's original players inscribed in them, and the Elizabethan plate, and the other wonderful things in there. But I hadn't hurried to visit these marvels, and now they had been blown into dust, to whirl round desolate street corners and pile on deserted bomb-sites and make the gritty pavements more gritty and more bitter.

All Londoners nurse memories of those days. The street shelters where some of the women and old folk would sit all day, talking in the sun, ready to dodge under cover when the sirens sounded. The Underground at night, crowded with people come to sleep down there, all sociable as field-mice, cheerfully retiring for the night in improvised bunks, which the occupants modestly fixed up with curtains. (My sister got a kick from peeking round these curtains at people and saying, "Hello". Some of the things said to her in return were not quite so pally.) The constant boodle-oodle-oodling and the rending crashes, every incident immediately followed by a stream of people hurrying forth on bicycles and on foot to give whatever assistance was possible at the scene of disaster. The innumerable cups of tea that were made, the narrow-squeak stories that were swapped,

211

the Union Jacks that appeared — as in the old Blitz — stuck on the piles of wreckage.

There was one afternoon in particular that I remember. It started at Stratford with a doodle-bomb which went round three times. We were all in the mortuary of Queen Mary's Hospital: C. K. S., Tiny, the giant mortuary keeper, formerly of the Guards, Cook, the Coroner's officer, the Hospital Superintendent, and myself. Suddenly we heard the thing coming and we all froze, C. K. S. with his knife in his hand, Tiny clutching the sponge he was swabbing with, Cook with an eye on the window (to see if he could see), the Superintendent holding a sheaf of notes on the post-mortem case, and myself seated at my typewriter. The doodle-bomb hum-bummed over and droned into the distance, cheered by Tiny. Then its engine started growing louder again. "It's not coming back?" shouted Tiny — I think he would have added more if I had not been there. Cook ran out to see and returned, "Yes, it's gone round in a circle. The Town Clerk's up on the roof next door, watching it." Back it came and we all froze again. Over it went and drooled away, as before. We listened. Yes, it slowly veered round and began the tedious approach for the third time. "It's ours," said Tiny. "Twice was a blooming miracle but three times is too much to hope for. Well, here goes."

"The Town Clerk's still up there watching," reported Cook.

"Thinks it's firework night, maybe," murmured Tiny. With baited breath we listened to our old gallivanting friend the doodle-bomb taking a third look down on

212

Queen Mary's Hospital, Stratford. To our astonishment he passed over once more, but crashed a short distance beyond on the railway yards. "I never want to go through an experience like that again," said Tiny, "and, by God, I've had some."

Just as we left Stratford for Leyton another doodle-bomb passed over, going in the same direction as ourselves. When we reached Leyton mortuary Miles greeted us with the news that this bomb had dropped on the bus garage at the Baker's Arms. We left Leyton for Whipps Cross Hospital and another bomb went over, apparently aiming for Whipps Cross Hospital. We had to make a detour because of the damage around the neighbourhood of the bus garage. When we reached the hospital we found the doodle-bomb had crashed a short distance from the hospital gates. A wrecked lorry lay in the roadway, trees were shattered as if by a gale, their green leaves covered the pavement as if torn down by a premature and violent autumn. We drove to the mortuary in the hospital grounds. The ambulances with the casualties from the bus garage incident were driving up to the door of the Casualty Department all the time. Stretchers were carefully lifted out and borne into the hospital building. But sometimes the stretchers were brought over to the mortuary instead.

In the mortuary already lay the driver of the wrecked lorry. The windscreen had been shattered in his face and his throat was widely cut from ear to ear, as decisively as if he had been a fanatical suicide. Goodwin was standing thoughtfully staring down at him.

Other cases were brought in, amongst them a woman, obviously a housewife, from one of the small houses near the bus garage. She was laid gently on the floor. C. K. S. fetched out his thermometer and took her temperature. Apparently there was a theory that immediately after death the temperature of the body shoots up to an unprecedented height. C. K. S. decided to put this theory to the test, and during the flying-bomb era he took several temperatures of persons just dead, but so far as I remember found nothing very remarkable about their temperatures.

While he bent over the dead housewife I stood by with my notepad, contemplating the woman who had just been killed in a Front Line which was no less a Front Line because it was in London. She was just a plain, ordinary London housewife in a shabby dress and flowered apron. Perhaps when the bomb crashed she had been peeling the potatoes for her husband's supper, I thought. And when the husband, and maybe a grown-up daughter or two, arrived home that evening it would be to find their little house a pile of laths and mucky plaster and mother taken to the mortuary. And that story was being repeated daily, all over London.

I thought of my own mother in our house in North London and wondered, for a brief moment, whether she was still intact. But what was the point of wondering that? As she herself would say, "Kismet".

Kismet was kind to me and my family. A few days later when I was at Leyton another bomb, all in key with the Simpson daily round, went off just across the road; an occasion to be remembered because, while

Miles and I heaped on top of each other for shelter under the sink — a silly place, really — Dr Simpson crouched for shelter under the p.m. table, which was complete with a body, and the sight of one who hoped to live crouching under a corpse was rather striking. It seized my imagination even though I was shaking with fright, and C. K. S. commented upon his sheltering-place with a rather crooked smile directly he had scrambled out again after the explosion. Then we went out into the street, with our ears zinging from the blast, to watch the great black coils of oily, stinking smoke undulating overhead, while what appeared to be fragments of charred paper showered down groundwards. As we watched, the inevitable stream of people came hurrying; first the A.R.P. squads, then the cyclists, and then the running neighbours, all frantically rushing to the rescue of the people in the wrecked little houses. And then came the ambulances . . .

At Whipps Cross, one morning, we obtained our best close-up view of a bomb. It was chugging along, approaching the end of its flight and C. K. S. stopped the car and we both jumped out. I began making a bee-line for some bushes, but my companion shouted at me to pull myself together. "You're perfectly safe, Miss Lefebure. It's travelling away from us. What a magnificent view of the thing! And what an extraordinary colour it is!"

Envying my pathologist's Anglo-Saxon calm I struggled to master my Gallic twitterings, meanwhile peering upwards at the little demon above us. "Oh, isn't it pretty! In a nasty sort of a way," was my feminine comment. A delicate shade of bluey-green, with a beautiful long plume of vivid scarlet and orange flame spurting out behind it like a dragon's breath in reverse. So small, so mechanical, it went into a glide and flew lower and lower, to dive suddenly over the houses of Walthamstow — landing, I afterwards discovered, on a sweet-shop I had often patronised when I was a reporter, and blowing the place to bits.

One day MacKay phoned us to say that the Home Office had an identity job for us at his mortuary. Identity and reconstruction. A special job.

We went along next morning and found MacKay waiting in the sunny little mortuary yard. He had two big trestle tables out there, too, the sort of tables one associates with Sunday-school treats, only instead of being loaded with goodies these tables were loaded with bits and pieces of people.

"A flying-bomb scored a direct hit on a brick surface shelter, Dr Simpson, in which there were some twenty people. All killed, of course, and impossible to identify in the ordinary way. Can you help sort them out a bit?"

"I'll try, MacKay," said Dr Simpson cautiously. "Have we any kind of a list of who they probably were, giving approximate ages and so on? That would help."

"The A.R.P. wardens have given me a list of suggested names, with the ages and descriptions, but it's very sketchy."

So we started work. For two mornings we worked on that hideous human jig-saw puzzle, linking this foot with that hand, this heart with that foot, going by the apparent age and physical condition of the fragments, while the sun shone, the factory next door broadcast "Music While You Work", and footsteps clacked unconcernedly along the pavement the other side of the mortuary wall.

In the end we had sorted out everything excepting one or two odd bits that proved quite impossible to catalogue.

The knowledge that the job, beastly as it was, simply had to be done by somebody or other gave one just enough strength of purpose to do it. At the end C. K. S. very nicely gave me a generous bonus, but even a generous bonus cannot dispel the memories of a job like that, I discovered.

Nevertheless, the casualty list for the flying-bomb era was remarkably low, all things considered. But the damage done to houses was very high. In due course my own home in Southgate "had a flying-bomb", although not very seriously.

One grave-digger-cum-mortuary-assistant I knew, a crablike man with sandy whiskers and a great liking for political discussion, became very fond at this time of talking over the war with me. He was very thrilled by the Russians (weren't we all?), and I particularly enjoyed the way in which he would raise an arm and exclaim, "After this war I, for one, will never lift a finger against Russia!"

He always followed the fortunes of the Russian Armies with detailed interest and was, I recall, especially concerned over the fate of Kharkov. He said to C. K. S. one day, "Well, Dr Simpson, I see Harkov has fallen at last. Or so Jerry says."

"Now that's interesting, the way you call it Harkov, instead of Kharkov," remarked C. K. S., looking up from the p.m. "Are you a student of Russian? Is that the correct pronunciation, Harkov?"

"Well, Dr Simpson, I don't speak Russian, no, I don't," said my friend, tilting back his head and leering from under his swollen lids in a particularly horrid way he had, "but Alvar Liddell, 'e says Harkov, and 'e speaks nice."

But presently the flying-bombs became the main topic of our conversations. Sandy Whiskers took a dim view of them, but remained philosophical withal. "I don't start the night in the Anderson (shelter), no, I don't. I begin it in bed and hope for at least a bit of sleep before I get disturbed. But of course, I don't get it. Well, when the warning goes we all gets into our clothes and hurries out to the shelter. Well, you can reckon I reach there in pretty quick time. But my missus, she's always last, she takes such a long time to dress. You see, she always wears one of these 'ere abominable belts and it takes quite a time to put on."

By "abominable belt" I realised he meant an abdominal belt. But, when all is said and done, abominable is, I should think, a pretty good name for them.

And so it went on. The doodle-bombs by day. The doodle-bombs by night. Those weapons that were supposed to make Britain panic and sue for armistice.

I have often tried to decide which British quality most contributed to the defeat of Hitler. Was it the determination to ignore danger and carry on at all costs? The Keith Simpsons who wouldn't have their time-tables disturbed by "wretched things" like flying-bombs? Or the astonishing national idiosyncrasy for cracking a joke at any price, so that a Tiny could talk about firework night with apparent death boombling overhead? Or philosophical resignation: "Hope for a bit of sleep, but of course I don't get it"? Or sheer British cussedness; Hitler wants to win, so we aren't going to let him?

It was the combination of all these traits, no doubt. But, upon the whole, I think the main reason for the success of the British was that they enjoyed the war. They enjoyed it not in the sense that they found it fun, but in the sense that they found it immensely satisfying. Satisfying to all their inherited instincts and traditions. It gave them the chance to do all the daring things they have excelled at throughout their long history, and a lot of new, twentieth-century daring things into the bargain. It employed their genius for voyaging and fighting all over the globe. It gave them the chance to become Commandos and raid enemy territories after the style of Drake singeing the King of Spain's beard. For six glorious years they were able to be soldiers, sailors, airmen, guerrillas, frogmen, spies, bomb experts, nurses, rescue workers, ambulance drivers, explorers, plotters, schemers, saboteurs. As a race they have thrived on adventure and this war brought them adventures galore. It gave them a feeling of great purpose for it united them in a just cause, and as a people they love just causes. It gave them a chance to

219

be great, and they have a marvellous capacity for greatness.

And, after Dunkirk, they had an unswerving faith in their ultimate victory.

As for the word, "panic", it wasn't in their language. Never has been. Never will be. Hitler produced the V.1. Hitler produced the V.2. So what? The British knew Hitler was going to go under in the end. And sure enough, when the time was ripe, under he went.

CHAPTER
TWENTY

Body in a Hole

A woman reporter, interviewing me once about my work with Dr Simpson, asked, "Is it really glamorous and exciting, working on a case with men from Scotland Yard?"

I replied that it could be exciting, but was never glamorous, and indeed was sometimes so unglamorous that even the excitement rather had the edge taken off. And, as I spoke, I thought of a certain blazing day in August when C. K. S. and I went down to Bedfordshire to assist two detectives from the Yard in a very unglamorous case indeed.

It was August 17th. The V.1s had diminished in volume a little, and the V.2s had not yet started. The first flush of the invasion had faded and life, which had been so hectic, had become somewhat turgid, so that a murder in the country seemed an attractive idea.

The train chugged along through the sun-baked countryside and I stared out of the carriage window, occupied with idle thoughts. Presently C. K. S. began talking about Chief Inspector Beveridge, the officer who had been called from the Yard to help the Bedford police unravel the case. "Beveridge is one of the Yard's leading personalities, very keen, highly efficient, perceptive," said C. K. S., adding, a trifle ominously I thought, "You'll find him rather quiet, but he notices a lot."

That meant Mr Beveridge would probably notice me if I did anything foolish. I vowed a silent vow that that afternoon I would shine as a very keen, highly efficient secretary. One of those sorts who are a hundred per cent bang on.

Unfortunately the English countryside on a hot afternoon always has a dimming effect upon me: the lazy hazy fields, the claustrophobic hedges, the somnolent trees, the tranquil milky cows. In less than no time I am well on the way to becoming a bovine yokel myself. So by the time we had exchanged the train for a car and had driven to a nice, rose-entwined little village police-station, I felt more like a nap under a shady bank than a post-mortem. I was also hot and dying of thirst. But as we got out of the car I bethought me of Chief Inspector Beveridge's eagle eye and did my best to shake myself up.

Inside the police station everything smelt of polished wood, ink, roses and dusty ledgers. The station sergeant was waiting on the doorstep to greet us and he ushered us into the office where the Chief Inspector and his Detective Sergeant assistant were waiting for us.

Chief Inspector Peter Beveridge was a large man with a fresh complexion, youthful blue eyes, a shy smile, a very firm handshake and a quiet voice which expressed great authority. Like all the Yard high-ups I ever met, he filled me with immediate respect.

Behind him, to my utmost relief, stood Detective Sergeant H. W. Hannam, whom I had met several times before and knew as an understanding ally. Always the last word in courtesy, he bowed and shook hands. Then the station sergeant fetched us cups of tea while Mr Beveridge launched into a brisk résumé of the case.

I whipped out my notebook and began taking shorthand notes. My cup of tea stood on the sergeant's desk by my elbow, steaming gently; the most seductive cup of tea I ever saw but quite untouchable. Efficient secretaries don't stop taking notes to swig tea. Alas!

The suspected murder had taken place several days previously, said Mr Beveridge, for the body, which had been lying among some bushes in the Kempston Ballast Hole, was seriously decomposed. The discovery of the body had been made on August 15th, appropriately enough by a retired police constable who had been taking his dog for a walk. The dog had drawn his master's attention to the body. The local police surgeon examined the body after it had been moved to the mortuary and found grave fractures to the skull. Murder was immediately suspected. The Yard had been asked to assist the Bedford police in their investigations early on the morning of the 17th, and now here were the four of us assembled in Kempston police station.

From time to time during this résumé of the available facts Mr Beveridge turned to Sergeant Hannam, who had taken a small sheaf of notes from his brief-case. Mr Hannam checked these notes with his chief's information. I scribbled shorthand feverishly. When Mr Beveridge had finished telling Dr Simpson about the discovery of the body he said, "I suggest we go along to the Ballast Hole first to see for ourselves where the body was found and then visit the mortuary. The car is ready to take us."

"Exactly as you wish, Mr Beveridge."

"Are we all ready?"

I swallowed two or three despairing gulps of tepid tea, Mr Hannam put his notes away, Dr Simpson picked up his bag, the station sergeant kindly took our typewriter, and out to the waiting car we went.

As we rode along the dusty lanes to the Ballast Hole, Chief Inspector Beveridge said, "If the body is very decomposed it may prove difficult to identify."

"The teeth should help us there," observed C. K. S.

"Yes, I was thinking we might have to resort to the teeth."

The local mortuary was not far from the Ballast Hole. From inside the little brick mortuary itself came the buzzing of flies, the sound of water running and a reek of rotting body and disinfectant. In the mortuary yard a group of police officers and young detectives were gathered rather anxiously round a drain, at which they were all peering. Mr Beveridge greeted them briskly and was informed, nervously, that some of the dead man's teeth had accidentally been washed down this drain. Mr Beveridge replied, "Get them out. We must have those teeth."

Leaving this worried company to retrieve the teeth, the Chief Inspector headed our little party in the direction of the Ballast Hole. Two Bedford police officers accompanied us. We climbed a five-barred gate which was secured with a padlock against all comers, even the C.I.D., and marched down a very long, hot, crunchy cinder track.

The Kempston Ballast Hole was the kind of place criminals seem to be particularly devoted to. It was an area of shrubby waste land amongst rusty railway sidings, old railway sleepers and derelict trucks. It was painfully reminiscent of T. S. Eliot. I lurched along the cinder track inwardly reciting:

"What are the roots that clutch, what branches grow
Out of this stony rubbish? . . ."

Nothing could have been more pat.

Another five-barred gate, this one decorated with a large notice, "Strictly Private. Keep Out" and festoons of barbed wire. We climbed it gingerly, Sergeant Hannam offering me assistance. Then came a stretch of old railway track. Railway track, in my opinion, is the most awkward thing in the world to walk along. You cannot step from sleeper to sleeper because they are just that much too far apart, and for the same reason you cannot stride along between them. You have to teeter up and teeter down and run great risk of twisting your ankle. And the strange thing about criminals is that they adore railway tracks.

Finally we reached the end of the track and stepped into a wilderness of tangled grass and scrubby bushes, illuminated with lovely patches of willowherb which blazed, crimson, in the sunshine. To make you watch your step were brambles, long-abandoned tins, remnants of broken zinc baths and the like. As we walked the grasshoppers sprang up, whirring, from our feet. The sun beat down on us mercilessly. I began to think of Bethnal Green with nostalgia.

This was Kempston Ballast Hole, and it was not a beauty spot. At least, not to my mind.

Presently we reached a particularly dense thicket of elder bushes. It was here that the body had been found, concealed by the bushes and also by a branch over which had been arranged a screen of willowherb. Dr Simpson and the detectives carefully examined this spot. Then they turned their attention to the ground around.

We all searched slowly through the long, tatty grass for possible clues. Mr Beveridge was very intent upon collecting and examining all the scraps of paper which lay scattered about; for in such places there are always plenty of stray pieces of paper. Most of the fragments we found were merely old bits of newspaper, dated well before the estimated time of the assault, but about twenty feet from where the body had been hidden we found the torn-up photograph of a girl, and the torn-off loop of a man's trouser brace.

This searching through the grass and bushes took quite a while, with the sun burning down and the grasshoppers whirring and skipping. At last Mr Beveridge decided we had searched enough for that session; we must now get back to the mortuary so that Dr Simpson might take a look at the body. Accordingly we picked our way over the sleepers, climbed the wired gate, crunched along the cinder track, climbed the padlocked gate and went, all rather wearily, into the mortuary yard.

Here the wretched police officers and C.I.D. men were crouching on all fours, wrestling with the drain. Their faces were scarlet with heat and exertion. "It looks as if we'll have to have the yard up to get at the drain, sir."

"Then we'll have the yard up," replied Mr Beveridge. "If it means taking up the road I'm going to get those teeth."

The mortuary yard, the mortuary, was puddled with disinfectant and reeked horribly.

Disinfectant and body combined to make an astonishingly hideous smell. Outside in the yard the desperate subordinates struggled with the drain. The detectives from Scotland Yard divided their attention between the drain and the post-mortem table, both men with admirably impassive faces, while the Home Office pathologist examined the remains in a manner also detached and unperturbed. Nevertheless I knew him well enough to sense a raging interior behind the mask of calm. The individual, who was the cause of the raging interior, having done his wild but ineffective best at cleaning the mortuary, now evidently considered his task finished, for he stood silently by, his arms folded on his chest, watching first Chief Inspector Beveridge and then Dr Simpson with an absorbed, yet remote, expression; as a zoologist might observe two very interesting but excessively rare species. He did not lift a finger to help, either with the drain or the post-mortem. When Mr Beveridge threatened that the entire drain would have to be taken up, he stared into the yard, and when Dr Simpson, finally utterly disgusted by the state of the mortuary, started filling buckets with water and disinfectant and sloshing them furiously in all directions, he turned and stared at him as if asking himself, "Did you ever see such a berserk pathologist in all your life?"

Under these circumstances it was impossible for C. K. S. to examine the body in detail, and so he decided to have it taken to Guy's where he could study it properly.

We left the mortuary with Chief Inspector Beveridge and Sergeant Hannam and went back to the pretty little police station from which we had started out. The afternoon was still very hot and our last view of the mortuary was one of purple-faced men still struggling around the wretched drain. Mr Beveridge called that he would be back presently to see if they had found those teeth.

When we reached the police station we went into the sunny little yard there, where beautiful rambling roses bloomed and where spread on the ground were the filthy, slimy, stinking clothes that had been removed from the body. Mr Beveridge, Mr Hannam and C. K. S., together with the station sergeant, squatted down beside these clothes and began examining them.

C. K. S. had already told Mr Beveridge that the assault must have taken place some ten to fourteen days previously, judging by the condition of decomposition, the hot weather and the exposed way in which the body had been lying. The clothing of the dead man now showed that his body had been dragged to its hiding-place under the bushes. The seat of the trousers had been pulled away from the rear brace attachments, as though the body had been pulled by the arms or shoulders, the feet trailing on the ground. The brace attachment which we had found earlier that afternoon at the Ballast Hole clearly belonged to the torn braces which were still attached to the deceased's trousers.

Besides the trousers there were filthy socks, a crumpled sports shirt. The shoes were missing.

Mr Beveridge and C. K. S. pored lengthily over these things, discussing together, occasionally dictating to Mr Hannam and me. At last, however, it was time for C. K. S. to catch his train back to London. We had left our departure to the last minute and we therefore had a very helter-skelter trip to the railway station. Cups of tea were brought to us as we were about to leave but we didn't have time to drink them. Mr Hannam gave me a sympathetic grin as I gloomily by-passed my second cup of tea that afternoon. Calling good-bye and waving, C. K. S. and I dived into the car and were raced away to the station, which we reached in the final nick of time, tumbling head first into the train, which was just sliding from the platform as we chased and gasped past the ticket inspector.

Collapsed in a hot carriage of strangely Victorian aspect, all black horse-hair upholstery and drab carpet, we mopped our brows and spread ourselves out. We had the carriage to ourselves. Dr Simpson confessed he was feeling rotten with a migraine and attempted to revive himself with a few acid-drops he had been carrying around for his small daughters. He also let

229

escape a blast of reasonably mild invective concerning the mortuary and the disinfectant. Thus relieved he soon felt much better.

I discovered, and squashed, a very large louse crawling up my leg.

Back in London a good dinner at Simpson's in the Strand restored us pretty well to normal health and spirits. All the same I remember our visit to the Ballast Hole at Kempston as a trying experience.

The last thing I remember about that day was arriving home at Southgate to find the house smelling exceptionally ripe, so that for a moment or two I thought it must be me carrying the smell of Kempston around with me. But it turned out to be a very fine Camembert cheese which Basil Dean had brought back from an E.N.S.A. trip to France as a present for my father. It was the first Camembert cheese I had seen for five years and under any other circumstances I would have fallen on it with whoops of joy, but now I turned away from it with a shudder . . .

The Kempston body arrived at Guy's next morning and C. K. S. demonstrated it to his students, who all turned up in swarms when they heard the details, but didn't look quite so thrilled when they discovered what the body was like. Nevertheless, they all stuck the demonstration out. Gibb trotted round the mortuary meanwhile looking a wee bit miffed and armed with a fly-spray. He confided to me that the body was "a nasty dirty thing, a pity to have it in here, really. More suitable for the anatomy department than my mortuary." However, it was a Scotland Yard case, and as such carried unmistakable prestige. And pretty soon it was put in a carbolic tank upstairs where Dr Simpson could examine it "in his spare time".

Meanwhile, at Kempston the teeth had been retrieved from the drain-pipe and more back-aching searching had gone on amongst the grass and bushes of the Ballast Hole. Nothing of importance was found there. But enquiries had already been made about the girl whose torn-up portrait had been found near the body's hiding-place and these enquiries proved fruitful.

A woman police officer who saw the photo said she recognised it as the portrait of a girl who frequented a local dance hall. So detectives went to the dance hall and picked up the girl. She was shown the dead man's clothes and said they undoubtedly belonged to her cousin, Robert Smith, a youth of twenty-two who had been working for a firewood merchant named Gribble. But, said the girl, she hadn't seen her cousin Robert since Sunday, August 6th, and she supposed he had given up the firewood round for the time and gone harvesting.

She added that Smith had been very friendly with Gribble, his employer, and particularly friendly with Kenneth Gribble, the firewood merchant's son, a boy of sixteen. If anybody knew about Robert's movements Kenneth Gribble certainly would.

So round to Gribble's house went Chief Inspector Beveridge and Sergeant Hannam. Kenneth Gribble proved reasonably helpful and was apparently sincere. He said he had last seen Robert Smith on the afternoon of August 6th, when he had paid him his wages, in a field about midday. When questioned about the Ballast Hole, Gribble said he knew the place well, but had never visited it at any time with Smith and had not been to the place himself for over six months.

Sincere? Apparently. But Kenneth Gribble was no match for the men from Scotland Yard. The astute Mr Beveridge had already interviewed another youth, a pal of Gribble's, who said he had heard a conversation between Kenneth and Robert in which they had arranged to meet at the Kempston Ballast Hole at three o'clock on Sunday afternoon, August 6th. This youth added that at the time of making this date Kenneth and Robert had had "words" about money paid to Robert Smith by Mr Gribble, senior.

Now, despite his air of sincerity, Kenneth Gribble had been very careful to tell Mr Beveridge that he had never been to the Ballast Hole with Smith.

Mr Beveridge confronted Kenneth with this omission. Kenneth said ah yes, that was right, he had made a date to meet Bob at the Ballast Hole that Sunday afternoon, but he'd forgotten to mention this appointment to the Inspector. Mr Beveridge said he would like to hear about the meeting. Well, said Kenneth, there hadn't actually been any meeting. He'd gone to the Ballast Hole at three o'clock to meet Bob as arranged, but Bob hadn't turned up, and after waiting around for him for ten minutes he had decided to go home. He hadn't seen Bob at all that afternoon, at the Ballast Hole or anywhere, and what was more he hadn't seen him since, either.

All said, as before, with an air of sincerity. But Kenneth Gribble did not make a very good impression upon Mr Beveridge. And Mr Beveridge was well used to judging people correctly. So the detective continued with discreet enquiries round and about Kempston.

Then he learned that the caretaker of the little church opposite the public entrance to the Ballast Hole had taken to the local police station a bike which he reported having found propped against the church wall on the afternoon of August 6th. The caretaker had first found it there at half-past three that Sunday and at midday, next day, it was still standing there. Finally, the caretaker took the bike to the police as "Lost Property". It was identified as Robert Smith's bike.

Mr Beveridge showed the bike to Kenneth Gribble. Kenneth said he didn't recognise it as Bob's bike. To this the Chief Inspector said nothing. He did, however, instruct the detectives under his command to search the ground of the Kempston Ballast Hole afresh, inch by inch, missing nothing.

For by this time Mr Beveridge had reason to suspect that somewhere amongst the tangled grass and bushes lay the weapon, probably a large and heavy wooden weapon, a club or something similar, with which Smith had been struck down and killed.

Dr Simpson had concluded his examination of Smith's body and had sent Mr Beveridge a copy of his report, in which he strongly suggested that such a weapon had been used. Dr Simpson said that Smith had been killed ten to fourteen days before his body was found. If he had disappeared on August 6th, as everybody said he had, then that was eleven days before his body was discovered. He had been killed, Keith Simpson said, and dragged along the ground afterwards to the bushes where he had been concealed. He had not been involved in much of a fight before he was killed, for although he had been a strong, sturdy young man, well capable of defending himself in a brawl, his hands did not suggest that he had done any serious fighting before he was overpowered and killed.

It seemed rather, Dr Simpson said, that Smith had been attacked suddenly from in front while he was standing upright and had been struck a violent blow from some blunt heavy weapon to the left side of the face. This blow had been followed by a second one to the mouth; very vicious, knocking out eight front teeth. Smith had probably tried to ward off these two blows by raising his left arm, which bore signs of injury. A third blow, however, had caught him on the jaw and felled him to the ground, unconscious. Then, while Smith lay senseless and helpless on the ground, his assailant dealt him another violent blow to the head, which killed him.

The intense searching of the ground of the Ballast Hole continued without result until August 21st, and then, amongst the thickest bushes in the Ballast Hole, about a hundred feet from where the body had been hidden, was found a heavy sawn-off bough. It was blood-stained and to it adhered several hairs.

It was taken up to London to the police laboratory and examined. The bloodstains were definitely human. One of the hairs — seven inches long — was a human head hair, while six further short hairs were eyebrow hairs. All these hairs corresponded with samples taken from Smith's body. (It had been impossible, of course, to take a specimen of Smith's blood for grouping because of the advanced decomposition.) Undoubtedly here was the weapon the assailant had used.

Meanwhile more discoveries were being made at the Ballast Hole. Smith's shoes were found; the right shoe in a disused railway truck and the left shoe a little farther away, nearer to the public entrance to the Ballast Hole. His brown jacket, roughly folded, was lying under a blackberry bush and his hat was discovered some distance from the jacket. All these were identified as clothes Smith had been seen wearing on that Sunday afternoon he disappeared.

Armed with this fresh evidence Chief Inspector Beveridge went again to visit Kenneth Gribble. The youth had an alibi ready; he said he had spent the afternoon of August 6th in the company of a woman friend. But what is the use of putting up false alibis to the police? Especially, what hope is there in putting up a false alibi to a Chief Inspector from the Yard? Mr Beveridge immediately interviewed the woman concerned and satisfied himself very quickly that young Gribble was lying in his account of the afternoon.

Now, nothing makes a detective more deeply suspicious than a false alibi. Mr Beveridge didn't go back to interview Kenneth Gribble at that stage, he issued instead instructions that the young man should be watched.

So a month passed. A month of watching, and waiting. The grass in Kempston Ballast Hole grew drier and browner, the leaves on the bushes withered and started dropping. And it was reported to the Chief Inspector that Gribble was beginning to talk freely about the crime; far too freely. He seemed quite unable to leave the subject alone, and although he never actually boasted of being the assailant he talked so injudiciously that it was clear he knew far more than he should of the inside story of the crime.

So, on September 20th, Chief Inspector Beveridge, Detective Inspector Sandell of the Bedfordshire Police, and Sergeant Hannam all went round to Gribble's home. Their arrival, late in the evening, caused a family scene. Mr Hannam described it afterwards in conversation with us: "The whole family was in an uproar, and Gribble's poor old parents terribly upset, everybody weeping and clutching one another . . . well, you can imagine it."

Mr Beveridge sternly told Kenneth Gribble that he had reason to believe that the youth knew more about the crime than he had hitherto confessed. Gribble began bluffing and lying again, denying he knew anything. But his father, who was present at this interview, suddenly intervened, tearfully imploring the boy to make a clean breast of things if he were really guilty of the crime. Kenneth then broke down.

"Yes, I did meet Bob Smith three o'clock on August Sunday afternoon and we had a fight in the Ballast Hole. He threw a piece of tree at me and I hit him with it."

He was cautioned and then he made a long statement. He described how he and Smith went to the Ballast Hole for "a lay down". As they strolled there, Gribble said, he told Smith that he needn't bother to come to work for Mr Gribble, senior, any more, "for," said Kenneth Gribble, "you know you have been doing me out of money on the round".

That, then, was how the quarrel started. Gribble continued his account of it, "We got to high words . . . and Bob took off his jacket and came for me. There was a fight and Bob fell over a large piece of tree wood. He picked up the bit of wood and threw it at me. I dodged the piece of tree but picked it up and as Bob come at me I struck him with it. I first struck him on the side of the face. He hit me in the stomach and I hit him again with the piece of tree on the head. He was bleeding but continued to fight me, so I hit him twice more with the piece of wood on his head. He fell down then and whilst he was lying on the ground I hit him twice on the head with the same piece of wood. I then threw the piece of wood as hard as I could into some bushes because there was some blood on it. I then picked up Bob's feet and dragged him into some bushes in the middle of the spinney."

He went on to say he stayed with Smith "for about ten minutes", trying to bring him round. He then covered up the entrance to the thicket with the branch of a tree and a screen of willowherb. He took up Smith's jacket, hat and shoes — these last had come off as the body was dragged to the bushes. From the pocket of the jacket fell the photograph of a girl. "I just tore it up and threw it back on the grass near the bush where Bob was lying."

Gribble, as he walked back to the entrance of the Ballast Hole, discarded the shoes, the jacket and the hat. From the jacket pocket he took Smith's wallet, which he burned when he got home, without having examined its contents.

Gribble was charged with murder and appeared for trial at Leicester Assizes. The case for murder was, of course, that he had attacked an unarmed opponent with a heavy weapon with far more force than was necessary for self-protection and had, what was much worse, struck this opponent two violent blows after he, the opponent, was lying unconscious on the ground. The case for a reduced verdict of manslaughter was Gribble's own account of the quarrel whereby he insisted that Smith had attacked him and continued to attack him in spite of being injured. This evidence of Gribble's, combined perhaps with his youth, persuaded the jury to find a verdict of manslaughter.

This then was the final chapter in a sordid little story; sordid from every angle. Yet, as a case, it provides an excellent example of typical detective work. Sordid details, dirty scraps of old newspaper and torn odds and ends, a drain to be delved into, a patch of waste land to be searched again and again under a gruelling sun, much questioning, the wearisome taking of repetitive statements, discreet enquiries from all and sundry, more searching of the waste land, more enquiries, a long and patient watch kept on a suspect, finally the closing of the trap, painful scenes, tears, admission.

All part of the day's work. All part of a detective's job. Not in the least glamorous. Not, really, all that much exciting. Indeed often just a grind of a job, requiring immense patience and determined application.

Most criminal investigations consist largely of such grind and dogged sweat. These two unspectacular ingredients are the cornerstones of a successful detective's career. Most murder investigations are sordid and mucky. A detective needs strong nerves and a steady stomach.

Shortly after this case at Kempston Mr Beveridge became an Area Superintendent and he is now Chief Superintendent Peter Beveridge, a very high "high-up" indeed. As for my old friend Detective Sergeant Hannam, at the time I am typing this he is a mere few miles away from me, down the river at Richmond; Supt Hannam, conducting enquiries into the double murder of two young girls on the towpath there. He and his detectives have been dragging the river, searching through undergrowth for a weapon, combing London for a maroon-coloured bicycle. With Mr Hannam is some Detective Sergeant — I don't know his name — who is wallowing in the Thames mud, sweating and searching through the dusty summer grass, muttering a few unholy somethings under his breath, no doubt, and learning in the course of it all how to be a Chief Superintendent himself some fine day.

CHAPTER
TWENTY-ONE

Private Diary

I am one of those tiresome people who keep diaries; pages and pages of scribble on my daily doings and daily thoughts. From time to time I read over what I have written and am overcome with shame. What an obnoxious and stupid person I find myself to be! And I stoke up the boiler and burn the diary, vigorously stirring it into the flames.

But even so not all the diaries have been burned. Quite a lot of them lie at the bottom of an old cupboard. I never got around to burning every one of my blush-making volumes; just shoved them into the cupboard and shut the door on them.

Recently I lugged them out and looked at them to see if they contained anything interesting to include in this book. Some of the entries gave quite a good idea of what life was like with Dr Simpson. Let me quote a little:

"*August 24th, 1944.*

"Yesterday Paris was liberated. I've always vowed that when Paris became freed from the Nazis I'd celebrate wildly, but of course I did nothing of the sort.

The day simply didn't pan out that way. On August 23rd, Day of Liberation, C. K. S. and I travelled down to Ashford in Kent on a murder job. The morning was an awful rush and lunch for me consisted of two sardine sandwiches eaten in a cloakroom at Guy's. We just managed to catch our train.

"This train was a hoppers' train from London Bridge and it was chock-a-block with fat old mother hoppers from Lambeth, Southwark, Bermondsey, loaded with bundles and folding prams and bulging bags, and each one accompanied by cohorts of yelling children, who all passed the journey by scuttling backwards and forwards to the lavatory.

"Passing through South London was sad, although interesting. Heavens, the terrible damage done by the doodle-bombs! It was rather thrilling passing through the vast balloon barrage outside London, which extends coastwards — that is, south as far as Maidstone — and which I have been told contains as many as ten thousand balloons. They all looked very beautiful, floating silver and serene in the blue sky over the low Kent hills. Others were on the ground, and they stood around the fields like monster silver cows.

"While our train was waiting at Tonbridge station I heard a soldier on the platform remark to another that Paris had fallen. I felt an inclination to stand on my head on the carriage seat and sing the 'Marseillaise', but refrained because of Keith Simpson. Felt certain he would not approve of upended secretary publicly singing French National Anthem. So squelched down

241

my excitement and tried to continue looking cool, efficient, secretarial.

"Poor Keith Simpson! Becoming distinctly peeved with the hoppers! At each station the good old hoppers had terrific struggles with their baggage; mainly goods wrapped up in tablecloths. These unwieldy bales would be finally packed into a pram, along with antique trunks dating back to the days of Pickwick, together with loose saucepans, kettles, frying-pans, canvas bags, string hold-alls, etc., and each adult accompanied by swarms of children, mostly little girls, all eating sandwiches, shrieking and yelling with their mouths full, and enjoying themselves hugely. And of course each family had its respective dog or cat.

"Most of these people seemed to quit the train via our carriage. It was quite an experience.

"So, as a result of all this chaos at each station, by the time we arrived at Ashford our train was half an hour late. C. K. S. all worked up, kept taking out his watch and muttering, like the White Rabbit.

"The murder was not very interesting; a girl of fifteen-and-a-half who had already given much trouble by running around with men. Post-mortem showed her to be — even at that tender age — well accustomed to sexual intercourse. She had been found at seven o'clock that morning lying strangled on a cricket ground near the railway. She had been strangled during intercourse.

"Such a case is, really, more a matter of sordid accident rather than murder. There seemed to be no murderous intention behind it. It seems to me a bit much to hang a man under such circumstances.

"All the time we were at Ashford fighter planes were cruising overhead, ready to chase and shoot down doodle-bombs.

"A great many people are now saying the war will be over in two weeks. I just don't think so. The Germans are fighting frantically. At one place in France, the news says, a German Youth Unit fought tanks at a twenty-five-yard range with rifles and, refusing to surrender, was simply slaughtered. It will take more than two weeks to vanquish people like that.

"The Maquis are going great guns all over France. Our old house-painter has a lovely one. He said to mother the other day, 'I've just had a good read of the papers and it's all most interesting news, but this here Marquis who's fighting in France, he seems to be everywhere at once and I'd like to know, is he an individual fellow?' "

Two American soldiers were arrested for the Ashford murder. They were identified by hairs they had left on the girl's body.

"*Sunday, October 1st.*
"Last Friday, alas, I lost my little scarlet tartan umbrella of which I was very fond. Lost it struggling in a crowd of home-coming hoppers at London Bridge. The Station Approach was thronged with little coster carts and coster-mongers come to collect the returning families and the baggage; the eternal large mammas with their screaming, excited children, ranging from little devils of twelve or so to babies in arms. They all

243

piled on to the carts, on top of their luggage, and then father drove them home. The fathers don't go hopping. Reckon they're sorry when the hopping season is over.

"Most of the women hoppers wore fur coats.

"When I got on a bus, my, that was crowded with hoppers, too! One large lady had a bottle she took constant swigs from and she kept singing, 'Take me back to dear old Blighty'.

"On Friday, too, we did a p.m. on the original Fat Boy of Peckham. His real name was Traddle, or Truddle, or somesuch. Afraid I've forgotten. He had a very dull face. When he was in his prime, the Coroner's officer told us, he weighed thirty-five stone and at school he had to have a special desk made for him. He also had a special little donkey-cart. But at the time of his death he only weighed a meagre sixteen stone or so. Poor man, he had T.B. and he collapsed in the street. He was a watch-maker by trade. I felt sorry for him. What a weird life! To be a sensational Fat Boy of thirty-five stone, finally whittling away to a mere tuberculous sixteen stone.

"I always remember my grandfather laughing and talking about the Fat Boy of Peckham. Funny to think I've at last seen him — on the p.m. table!

"West was highly interested in this p.m. and so were all the Coroner's officers. They all came in to take a look at the unhappy celebrity. Poor old Fat Boy of Peckham!"

The diary remarks rather nicely upon the newly arrived V.2s that "they aren't so bad as the V.1s because you don't hear them coming and so you know nothing about them until you are actually being blown up". I might add that I never got blown up, else I might not have thought so kindly of them.

On October 4th we went to Ashford on another murder, but this the diary didn't comment upon, which was natural, as I remember the episode was a very muddy, chilling one, best quickly forgotten. The victim was a girl of thirteen who had been strangled in a ditch by a species of village idiot. We had to cross some very muddy fields to reach the scene of the crime and once again I found myself taking a dim view of Kent. The murderer was soon arrested and found guilty but insane.

Apart from this murder and the rocket-bombs life went on tranquilly, it would appear from the diary, with a great deal of ballet-going and occasional entries such as:

"I really must diet and give up alcohol, but every time I swear to devote myself to Health and Beauty and not to touch another drop for six months I immediately receive an invitation to a party and find myself having some more."

Or:

"My financial position is still worrying. I don't save nearly enough. I go out and about far too often, I buy too many books. It is most distressing. I should check myself and live like a hermit."

★ ★ ★

It was at this moment that MacKay of Hammersmith lent me Thoreau's *Walden*. I regret to say it bored me profoundly and left me with an utter distaste for hermits.

"*November 9th.*

"Dr Keith Simpson said he had some needlework for me to do in the Museum, so I went down there and found he had four little embryos, in varying sizes, which he wanted me to sew on a piece of mica to put in a pickle jar. They were fascinating little things, ugly, but beautifully made. I had a good opportunity to examine them as I stitched them on to the card. Both Dr Simpson and Ireland complimented me on the neatness with which I did the job.

"I had thought at first C. K. S. wanted me to darn a sock or something."

"*November 11th.*

"Last night C. K. S. had a call to a murder, a country job, but as the weather was bad and I am down with a cold he went without me. The trip was to Beccles, in Suffolk, with Chief Inspector Greeno. This morning my Boss tottered home, very pink in the nose and blue in the face, indeed looking thoroughly frozen, rather as if he had returned from the Russian Front. He assured me that I had missed nothing. Apparently he spent the midnight hours crouching in a ditch, in the snow, together with Mr Greeno and the body of a murdered W.A.A.F. This was followed by an autopsy on the said W.A.A.F. at two in the morning in Beccles mortuary.

"He kept saying to me, 'You didn't miss a thing, Miss L., just a horrible night freezing in the snow.'

"'Apparently the wretched girl was murdered after a dance. It'll be a job with a great deal of work in it for Mr Greeno.'"

This Beccles case proved to be a very interesting one indeed, and before it was over I had heard a great deal about it. The victim was a twenty-seven-year-old W.A.A.F. called Winifred Evans. She had been found lying in a ditch, as described, wearing a full outdoor W.A.A.F. uniform that was considerably disarranged.

Typing C. K. S.'s post-mortem report I learned that she had been a respectable young woman, completely healthy. She had been knocked on to her face and dragged along the ground, had been rolled, or turned, on to her face and thus heavily pinned down by somebody violently kneeling on her (with such violence indeed that her liver was ruptured), after which she had been subjected to a most savage sexual assault.

The effect of being knelt upon with the face pinned to the ground was suffocation. Her death, therefore, was due to asphyxia.

There were no foreign hairs found upon the girl's body. Indeed there were at first no clues at all to the identity of her killer.

Near the aerodrome where the girl was stationed there was an Italian P.O.W. camp and Chief Inspector Greeno interviewed two hundred of the men there. But meanwhile one of the dead girl's W.A.A.F. colleagues had come forward with some interesting and important information.

She said that on November 8th Winifred Evans went to a dance at Norwich. She returned at midnight. She was due to go on duty and she changed from her dance things into working-kit. Then the unlucky girl walked away to the working-site where she was due to report. She was followed by an L.A.C. Heys.

Heys, according to Evans' colleague, had appeared on the scene shortly after midnight. He was drunk and asked to be directed to Number One site. The W.A.A.F. colleague directed him and he then said, "Can I thank you?" She replied briskly, "No. Get down the road." He went away then, walking off along the road which Evans had just taken . . .

At 1a.m. Heys returned to his billet. His shoes were noticed to be very muddy, he had long scratches on his hands. No comment was made at the time.

When Mr Greeno was told all this he went straight away to interview Heys. He found that Heys' uniform jacket had very recently been sponged and brushed, but despite this it had several large faded brown stains on it; they looked very much like bloodstains which somebody had unsuccessfully tried to remove. There were similar residual stains on Heys' trousers, which had also been recently sponged and pressed. These clothes were sent to the police laboratory and the stains were shown to be human bloodstains, but they were unfortunately too weak to give positive results for blood grouping.

248

Nevertheless, they showed, without any doubt, that Heys had recently got his uniform very heavily stained with human blood and that he had made energetic attempts to remove these stains from his clothes.

Chief Inspector Greeno charged Heys with the murder. Heys said, on being charged, "I didn't do it . . . I can't think what to say to my wife."

It did not really matter very much what he said to his wife. He was found guilty in due course, and hanged. But it was a very interesting example of how a murderer leaves the scene of his crime with "Murder" written all over him and how, try as he might, he cannot efface this inscription, "Murder".

CHAPTER
TWENTY-TWO

Boys of the New Brigade

Lunch hour in the City on December 8th, 1944. A muddy, cold day, people hurrying everywhere, already thinking of Christmas, trying to do a little shopping in between snatching a jostling, crowded lunch-time snack and getting back to the office. Traffic teeming in the roadways, people teeming on the pavements. The usual, chock-a-block, scampering, high-blood-pressure City lunch hour.

The usual? No, not quite the usual. For on this day a new page of London's criminal history was commenced. The page which tells the story of her young post-war gangster boys: the Jenkinses, the Geraghtys, the Ginger Kings and Craigs and Colemans.

Even today the nation is still shocked and bewildered by the exploits of its youthful thugs, whose very youth seems to add to their complete callousness. But in December 1944 these monstrous little juveniles were an entirely new experience for London and people were completely dazed by what happened in that City lunch hour . . .

It was just on two o'clock and the hordes of office workers were hurrying back to their offices. People going along Birchin Lane, one of those narrow City streets, saw a car draw up outside a jeweller's. Nothing very unusual about that. In the car were two youths, one of whom leapt from the car, carrying an axe, rushed to the shop window, smashed the glass with his axe, snatched a tray of rings and a pearl necklace and then dashed back to the car, leapt into his seat and slammed the door shut as the driver started the car. The many people who saw this smash-and-grab raid taking place so audaciously under their very noses were too astonished to do anything, all save one, a retired naval captain, fifty-six-year-old Ralph Douglas Binney. He, in true naval tradition, placed himself fair and square in the roadway before the accelerating car, his arms stretched out in a human barrier.

The driver drove straight into Captain Binney, knocking him down, then passing full over him, then passing back over him as the young brute at the wheel put the car into reverse and backed at rapid speed down the street for several yards until he gained Lombard Street and accelerated into a frenzied dash for freedom.

Captain Binney was trapped by the undercarriage and was borne away, shouting wildly for help. The crowds on the pavement shouted too, with horror and fury. Women screamed. But the car didn't stop. Along Lombard Street it was chased by another car, but to no avail. Over London Bridge sped the car, up the Borough, swerving perilously into Tooley Street, with Captain Binney shouting, "Help! Help!" and appalled onlookers able to do nothing. As the car swerved round the corner into St Thomas's Street Captain Binney was flung forth from under the car and rolled against the kerb. The car disappeared round another corner.

The sickened people on the pavement ran to Captain Binney and he was carried across the street into Guy's Hospital. But he had been terribly injured, and in spite of the speedy medical aid he received he died within a few hours.

In all, he had been dragged along the roads for a mile and sixty-six yards.

The City Police were in charge of this case and immediately began searching for the car. It was soon found, abandoned in an unfrequented alley near the Elephant and Castle. It was a stolen car and provided some useful clues. The people in Birchin Street who had witnessed the smash-and-grab were able to furnish full descriptions of the two young men, especially the one who had actually smashed the shop window. The police began combing the Elephant and Castle area and it was not long before the two young men had been identified and arrested.

They were a twenty-four-year-old welder, of Rotherhithe, named Thomas Jenkins, and one Ronald Hedley, a labourer, aged twenty-six, of no fixed abode. Hedley was the driver of the car, Jenkins had been the man of action; the axe-wielding smasher-and-grabber. Both of them were well-known "Elephant Boys".

These "Elephant Boys" were a group of young toughs from the Elephant and Castle area who posed in the role of juvenile gangsters and who had already caused a good deal of trouble in the Elephant area —

hence the name, "Elephant Boys". The attention of the police had become drawn to them some time before the Binney murder. Several of the "Elephant Boys" were already gracing Borstal institutions; others of their company, the senior members as it were, had graduated from thence back to Elephant Land, there to become the lords and leaders of all the aspiring hoodlums in the locality.

Now juvenile "street gangs" had once flourished all over working-class London, particularly in such salubrious neighbourhoods as Hoxton, Whitechapel, Limehouse, Bethnal Green and the like. They had given the police and social reformers of the Victorian era many headaches. But as the worst slums of London were "cleaned up" and working-class conditions improved, the street gangs disappeared, or at the least became harmless play gangs rather than dangerous groups of young street marauders and budding criminals. The 1939 War, however, revived the street gangs. The London children, at the start of the war, were evacuated en masse to the country, but many of them returned to London as the months passed, especially those who came from the less responsible, slap-happy, neglectful homes. Parents with little sense of duty allowed their children to come back to bomb-rocked London: "Our Albert's come 'ome. Couldn't stand it in the country. Rather have him 'ere with us and take the risk." I've heard several mothers saying it to me. What a London for the children to come "home" to! Often "home" had been blasted sky-high and the family lived in shelters, or Rest

Centres. Anyway, whether home was standing or not, nights were invariably spent down the shelters, or on the platforms of the Underground, in a hugger-mugger of humanity. The schools were closed, so during the day the children ran wild in the streets. Lacking any authoritative supervision and coming from the "homes" they came from it should not surprise anybody that they were soon developing into young gangsters; for although school education had ceased, the cinema was still open to them and they learned a good deal there. Nobody bothered about these children, nobody checked them. Young Londoners are by nature daring and full of enterprise and individuality; characteristics that can be developed for good or bad. These children lived in a world shattered by bombs and rockets, the very background of their lives was violence, the newspapers were full of "heroic" war stories; tales of daring and desperation. Their only culture, if culture it could be called, derived from comics and films. The children got the rest of their specialist education from the streets themselves; first-hand education from the wide boys, the spivs, the boys on the Black, the young crooks who had been to the Borstals and who returned covered with glory to impart their cynical philosophy and squalid experiences to admiring and eager juniors.

Street gangs were soon flourishing everywhere. Toughest among them were the "Elephant Boys" and their rivals the "Brick Boys" of Brixton. Jenkins and Hedley were two of the seniors the "Elephant Boys" particularly cared to emulate.

But Jenkins and Hedley themselves cannot be explained as products of the war years. Jenkins was nineteen when the war broke out, Hedley twenty-one. No doubt the war encouraged their tendencies towards lawlessness and provided them with unusually favourable opportunities to become callous young criminals, but it cannot be said in extenuation of these two that they did not go to school because all the London schools were closed, or that their home life had been disrupted by the bombing. They both went to school, they both had "homes" of a sort. The truth is they were the products of the 'thirties. The decade of unemployment, chips on shoulders and sloppy thinking. Religious conviction waned, the old values declined. Emphasis was on rationalism and intelligence. But most people are neither rational nor very intelligent. Hence all the muddle.

I think it was Bernard Shaw who once remarked that it requires far more self-discipline to be a free-loving atheist than a God-fearing conservative. Jenkins and Hedley were two of the very many who simply weren't up to being self-disciplined atheists, and nobody had taught them to be God-fearing conservatives, because that would have been old-fashioned. So they followed their own inclinations and took to being good plain cave-men, in an up-to-date Chicago style. Thus they combined the old and the new.

Dr Simpson and I had our first glance of the Captain's killers in the dock of Mansion House Court, presided over by the Lord Mayor of London, an awe-inspiring "beak" if ever there was one, but who apparently made little impression on the two young thugs, who stared brashly round them and leered from time to time with an apparent sense of something they considered humour.

So there they stood, side by side in the dock, rather undersized, with the pale, thin faces of young Londoners. Their hair was a trifle too long and their ties a trifle too gaudy. Their eyes were cynical, hard and cold, and the expression in them both shrewd and stupid; the eyes of those who have learned to observe much but who comprehend singularly little of what they observe. Their minds moved within tight little boundaries, shut in by four ready-made fences labelled respectively, "I'm a Have-Not"; "Nobody's Going to Exploit Me"; "Don't Try to Come That on Me"; and "Never Heard of It".

The Jenkinses and Hedleys of this world won't accept anything they've never heard of, and as they've heard of little outside their slum alley and small-time criminals' sphere they are necessarily very limited people. Their chief response to anything and everything is "Couldn't Care Less".

Basically, the two young men in the dock had had their sensibilities stultified and shrivelled by the great, great big chip each of them carried, one almost might say flaunted, on his shoulder.

The corners of their mouths drooped in sullen lines of perpetual discontent and boredom. (For another basic factor in the lives of these wretched juveniles is that despite their constant attempts to seek out excitement they are always, always bored.) They smouldered with resentment and stared at us all as if we had committed an unspeakable crime against them, for which they could never forgive us. (Which no doubt they both firmly believed.) Although they were both very young they gave a spine-chilling impression that they were already habitually criminal and that all the help in the world would be too late. It certainly was likely, I thought, that they'd never had a decent chance from the start, but one realised equally well that any helping hand held out to them would be promptly bitten. They were quite the most petrifyingly depressing couple I had ever set eyes on.

In their Birchin Street bid to get rich quick they had stolen jewellery valued at £3,795, but nobody was really very worried about this. (Excepting, very probably, the jeweller from whom the things had been stolen!) They were charged with the murder of Captain Binney and the callous details of this murder, or more, properly, killing, were red-hot in everybody's mind.

One of the counsel representing them was a gentleman of whom it might be said that "he was a real character from Dickens". (One of the unattractive ones.) The fact is of course that Dickens took his characters from life — excepting his heroines — and this counsel was an obvious descendant of a Dickens prototype; one of those legal portraits the author so loved to draw. He bore a peculiar and even alarming resemblance to a carrion crow, standing with his big voracious head sunk between his humped shoulders and his beaky nose thrust forward. When he spoke he rasped and croaked. He was determined to get us all ruffled and uneasy, like scared little birds in a hedge. Directly C. K. S. got into the witness-box to give evidence, for example, the carrion crow tried to ruffle him by attempting to get *me* turned out of court.

The carrion crow did this by complaining that I was taking up too much room in the bench reserved for lawyers and professional witnesses. He said that because I was taking up too much room his clerk was obliged to squeeze in a seat in a back bench where he couldn't hear properly. The carrion crow wanted to know who I was and what business I had in the court.

C. K. S. replied I was his secretary and I always accompanied him into court in order to take shorthand notes of his evidence.

The carrion crow responded I was still taking up too much room and he must insist I move to another seat.

One of the representatives of the Director of Public Prosecutions rose in the bench behind me and said politely that there was plenty of room in his bench if I would care to move there.

The carrion crow replied leeringly and sneeringly with nasty intimations that one could understand perfectly well the gentleman's eagerness to have the young lady beside him, but she would still be taking up valuable room to which she was not entitled.

The young lady went puce in the face with rage and embarrassment, and so did the gallant from the D.P.P.'s office. Dr Simpson had also assumed a very angry tint. However, dignity and restraint triumphed. After being moved for a few moments from seat to seat, each move being objected to by the carrion crow, I came to rest in a seat from which all his croaking and cawing could not dislodge me. His wretched clerk moved downstage to the place where I had originally been sitting and huddled there clutching a tatty little notebook and a stump pencil. The Lord Mayor surveyed the scene for a moment and then, bowing his head politely towards me, said, "And now, I trust, the young lady is comfortably installed?"

The young lady, by this time the shade of a peony, murmured rather inaudibly that she was comfortably installed, thank you.

This little pantomime gave great satisfaction to Jenkins and Hedley, indeed I think they thought such clever manoeuvring would ensure an ultimate verdict of Not Guilty. The carrion crow looked pleased too. But everybody else, apart from the carrion crow's clerk, who looked scared, appeared furious and fed-up; and this was unfortunate, for Jenkins and Hedley had infuriated everyone sufficiently already, without the assistance of the carrion crow.

His objection to me, however, was but the first of a long series of objections, which he carried over from Mansion House to the Old Bailey, where he objected to evidence, statements, jurymen, witnesses, merely for the sake of objecting and causing trouble. Perhaps there was nothing else for him to do. The position of the defence in this case was very weak. The evidence against Jenkins and Hedley was of a nature that condemned them from the start.

However, only one of them had been at the actual wheel of the car, knocking the Captain down, running forwards over him, then reversing over him and finally driving for over a mile with him caught underneath the vehicle. Jenkins, seated next to the driver, never at any time appeared to have protested violently against Hedley's decision to make a getaway at all costs, but his plea that he had not been driving and was not therefore directly responsible for Captain Binney's death could scarcely be refuted. The result of the trial was that Hedley was sentenced to death and was hanged, while Jenkins received eight years' penal servitude.

But this story, alas, doesn't stop here. It had a sequel, every jot as brutal as the killing of Captain Binney.

Early one afternoon in April 1947 three young men, their faces masked with scarves, drove into Charlotte Street, off the Tottenham Court Road, and staged a hold-up in a jeweller's shop. But the hold-up, owing to the inexperience and impetuosity of the youngest member of the trio, was bungled. A member of the shop staff pressed a warning buzzer, a revolver was fired in panic by one of the bandits and next moment all three desperadoes were racing from the shop to their car. But at that very moment a large lorry parked itself in front of their car. The three, panic-stricken now, began running wildly up the street and it was then that a passing motor-cyclist made an attempt to stop them. There was the report of a revolver again and the motor-cyclist fell, dying, to the pavement. The three young men fled on. One of them jumped on to the running-board of a passing taxi, but was turned off again as the driver already had a fare. This youth and another then ran into a nearby block of offices. The third disappeared down a side turning.

There was so much confusion in Charlotte Street that none of the spectators of the crime noticed the two youths vanish into the offices and as the taxi-driver hadn't witnessed the shooting he didn't realise he had just had a murderer ask him for a lift. He placidly continued on his way with his fare.

Therefore the three young bandits and killers made a get-away.

Within an hour or two the newspapers were splashed with huge headlines describing the murder of the motor-cyclist, Alec de Antiquis. The story of his killing shocked the nation and threw London's usually hard-boiled underworld into a state of agitation too, for gunmen are not approved of by the British underworld, any more than they are approved of by Whitehall or by suburbia; although the underworld disapproves for different reasons. A gunman not only brings down dire trouble on to his own head, but he stirs up the police and public to a degree that gets everybody uncomfortable all the way round. There is a public clamouring for the police to be armed, judges call for stiffer sentences, people declare that flogging should be brought back; in short, everyone toughens up. Besides, there are definite professional standards among crooks. Skilled criminals take a dim view of gangster rough-stuff. Any clod can run round shouting, "Stick 'em up." Professional criminals have scornful things to say about hoodlums. Gunmen are beyond the pale, and the Antiquis shooting was therefore considered an outrage in all strata of society.

The detective put in charge of this case by Scotland Yard was the debonair but dangerous Robert Fabian, by this time a Chief Inspector, of reputed flair.

The Antiquis case followed only shortly upon a similarly outrageous shooting in Winchmore Hill, when a young gunman named Thomas fired at and killed a detective-constable. Thomas, found guilty of murder, had not been hanged, as capital punishment had been experimentally suspended. Public opinion, divided on the great problem of the death sentence, now hardened. Hanging was reintroduced and the nation awaited not only the arrest of the Antiquis killers but also their execution.

But the killers weren't all that easy to catch.

Although several people had seen Antiquis shot, descriptions of the youths concerned were unreliable and vague. All three of them had been effectively masked, all three of them had been moving quickly, and the raid on the jeweller's, the shooting, the shouting, the general confusion and horror, had made it difficult for spectators to register any clear impressions of the bandits. Clues consisted of a discarded and unfired revolver, without fingerprints, however, and the bandits' car, which was a stolen one as is usual in such cases, but which afforded little information. A .45 bullet was found embedded in the woodwork of the jeweller's shop, and Sir Bernard Spilsbury removed a .320 bullet from Antiquis' body at the post-mortem.

Chief Inspector Fabian had but little to go on, therefore, when he started his investigations.

A check was begun on all young men recently released from Borstal. Detectives began combing London's underworld. Mr Fabian rounded up and interviewed everybody who had been near or in Charlotte Street at the time of the crime, among these the taxi-driver. As a result of his interview with this driver Mr Fabian and his men were soon exploring the offices into which the taxi-driver had seen the two young men run.

An office boy had also seen two men, in a hurry, going up in the office lift about the time of the shooting, and had later noticed one of them lounging against a window-sill in an empty room while the other leaned idly against a banister. The lad was able to describe both of them fully to Mr Fabian.

A lorry-driver had also noticed them go into the building, although he had not realised that they were involved in the shooting. Presently he had also seen them coming out of the offices. He remarked that one of them had been wearing a raincoat when he hurried into the building but was without it when he came out.

A raincoat. Just a dirty, shabby, cheap raincoat.

Mr Fabian began combing the office premises for this raincoat. At length it was found in a lumber-room, tucked underneath a counter. It was a stained, crumpled garment; in its pockets were a cap, a pair of gloves and a piece of white cloth such as the bandits were said to have masked their faces with.

The police routine procedure of taking a garment to pieces was followed, and stitched under the lining of the arm-pit Chief Inspector Fabian found a manufacturer's stock ticket. This was painstakingly traced and led to a factory in Leeds and from thence the trail led to South-East London. In a shop in Bermondsey the raincoat was traced to a purchaser, a youth who was already known by Mr Fabian to be a relative of a certain Charles Henry Jenkins.

Now Charles Henry Jenkins held considerable interest for Mr Fabian. Although he was only twenty-three he had eight convictions already marked up against him. The last had been two years previously when he had seriously assaulted a police constable. For this assault Jenkins had been sent to Borstal, and he had come out of Borstal, Mr Fabian discovered, six days before the Charlotte Street crime. This meant that he would be broke and anxious to do a job as soon as possible after his return from the institution of correction. And, knowing Jenkins as he did, Mr Fabian guessed this job wouldn't be one that Borstal would approve of.

Charles Henry Jenkins was the brother of Thomas James Jenkins, still inside, serving the eight years the judge had given him for his part in the Binney murder.

Charles Henry, at the time of the Antiquis case, was, as I have said, twenty-three. Thomas James, at the time of the Binney case, had been twenty-four. Charles Henry, like his brother, was tough, cynical and highly experienced in certain ways of this unhappy world. When Chief Inspector Fabian had him brought to the Yard for questioning he remained very cool, even sardonic. He said he had borrowed the raincoat from his relative but had a day or so later loaned it to another man in the Tottenham Court Road district. He refused to give the name of this person. "I'm not the sort who squeals," he declared, indignantly.

Mr Fabian let Jenkins go but issued strict orders he was to be watched. Then he began checking up on Jenkins' associates and soon found two who answered to the description of the bandits. One was twenty-year-old Christopher James Geraghty, already a desperate young thug. At eleven Geraghty had stolen a car. Later he was convicted of assault and sent to Borstal. On coming out of Borstal he had taken part in a six-thousand-pound jewel hold-up and had struck a shop-assistant on the head with a revolver, very seriously injuring him. For this he had been sent to prison. He had returned to liberty a month or so before the Antiquis shooting.

The second youth was Terence Peter Rolt, aged seventeen. He had only two petty offences against his name so far, but he was not an impressive character and Chief Inspector Fabian had him brought in with Geraghty for questioning.

Both had alibis for the day of the Charlotte Street shooting.

Jenkins, Geraghty and Rolt were all let at large again, and all were trailed assiduously by the police. Foolishly the trio fixed a meeting at a Clerkenwell public-house. At this meeting, which was also, unbeknown to the bandits, attended by detectives, Jenkins, Geraghty and Rolt were plainly very nervous and on edge. They held a brief consultation together and then parted.

Mr Fabian decided he knew enough by this time to arrest them. Once they were safely shut away informants from the underworld came forward, ready to tell the inside story of the Antiquis case. This is what Chief Inspector Fabian learned:

When Jenkins came home from Borstal his friends staged a party for him at the public-house in Clerkenwell. Geraghty and Rolt were the hosts. At this party possible jobs for the future were discussed — the immediate future, for Jenkins was flat broke and needed money in a hurry. He finally made some plans, but Geraghty and Rolt were not implicated in them. However, three days after the party Jenkins got into touch with Geraghty. He was in a furious temper. He had, he said, taken part in an armed hold-up in a Queensway jeweller's and had afterwards been tricked out of his share of the loot by his partner in the hold-up. He was now even more completely broke than he had been before, if such a thing were possible, and he urged Geraghty to do a job with him without delay.

They had, at the party, tentatively discussed the Charlotte Street raid, and now they drew up a hasty scheme to put this plan into action the very next day. Rolt was called in to drive the car. He was also to help grab some of the stuff from the shop while the other two held up the staff with their guns.

These plans were hastily made, too hastily. Rolt, in his inexperience and excitement, entered the shop too soon, mistaking a signal. As a result chaos ensued. Instead of getting rich quick the three found themselves in the dock at the Old Bailey, watching Mr Fabian exhibit to the court the "murder" gun, which had finally been found by a small child on the Thames foreshore.

Jenkins, standing there scowling at the jury, no doubt thought of his brother who had stood there three years previously, charged with murdering Captain Binney. But Thomas James had managed to escape the gallows. There were no mitigating circumstances to save Charles Henry. Along with his pal Geraghty he was sentenced to death.

Rolt was too young to hang. He went to penal servitude instead.

Jenkins and Geraghty remained completely cynical and hard-boiled to the end.

Is this the close, then, of the Jenkins story, which began with the death of Captain Binney and developed a second chapter three years later with the death of Antiquis? Not really. For the other evening I saw in the paper that Thomas James Jenkins, only recently released from his imprisonment for the Binney case, had just been sentenced at the Old Bailey to another long term of imprisonment on a charge of robbery with violence. Here, therefore, society faces a truly violent and hardened criminal.

The Jenkins brothers and those like them have provided post-war Britain with a brigade of thugs who do not hesitate to cosh, slash and shoot. Most of them are to all intents and purposes illiterate. They are fundamentally cowardly, which is why they carry guns (not to mention knuckle-dusters, razors and sheath-knives). They suffer terribly from boredom, and their minds and conversation are dry as dust, save for occasional gleams of a brutal and sardonic sense of humour. (I have discovered they can appreciate the humour of Continental X films more quickly and subtly than educated, refined audiences! How, for example, they enjoyed "Le Garcon Sauvage", when it was shown at Kingston.)

They are the children of the age of Hitler's secret weapons. Perhaps they and the rest of their kind, in whatever country they may be, are the Nazis' real secret weapons; horrible germs left behind to impregnate the future. Cosh, slash, stab, shoot, and don't give a damn for anyone or anything.

For their juvenile admirers they possess glamour. For the more perceptive they are as repugnant and abortive as any of the little monsters put up in pickling jars in the Gordon Museum . . .

One last word in this story, but not a dismal word this time. To commemorate the courageous and public-spirited Captain Binney his relatives have created a Binney Medal, which is given annually to the member of the public who displays the greatest bravery and resolution in trying to prevent a crime. In this way the memory of a very gallant man is kept alive and honour is paid to other citizens who do not hesitate to stand up to violence; the ordinary people who refuse to knuckle under to thugs and who, by their courage and spirited devotion to the laws of decency, help to prevent Britain from turning into a Chicago, or a Nazi Germany.

CHAPTER
TWENTY-THREE

"'Tis Love, 'Tis Love that Makes the World Go Round..."

Early in the New Year of 1945 I learned I had won fourth place in a novel competition. It wasn't a very important competition, and fourth place is certainly not first, but it served to give me a sense of some slight literary achievement and I decided the time had come to adopt a more dignified approach to my work. I considered the matter and decided the first step towards dignity was to buy myself a proper blotter. Hitherto I had contented myself with small, odd pieces of blotting-paper, mostly, I regret to say, gleaned from Court Number One at the Old Bailey, but now that I was truly a budding author I would invest in a proper blotter.

The kind of thing I really fancied, of course, was in hand-tooled scarlet leather. But it was 1945, austerity prices had reached a fantastic high, and I was obliged to buy something less grandiose, made of black American cloth posing as leather and, I must admit, very nearly succeeding. Very nearly, alas, not quite! Shams distress my aesthetic principles, but there was a war on. So I bought the American cloth article, but to compensate for its American clothness I chose the largest blotter possible, it was almost the size of the top of a card-table, and when I stepped from the shop, complete not only with outsize blotter but also plenty of magenta blotting-paper to go with it, I felt like Henry James, Thomas Hardy and Arnold Bennett all rolled into one.

The journey home by Underground in the rush hour was not too easy. The blotter was desperately awkward and earned me many hard looks, but I ignored these and dreamed of the masterpieces I was going to blot dry on my blotter. When I emerged from the Underground I strode off feeling on top of the world; a Nobel prizewinner for literature wasn't in it. But presently dignity gave way to sheer exuberance and I began to run simply from *joie de vivre*. I was prancing up the hill, full steam ahead, when somehow or other I managed to get the giant blotter wedged between my legs and down I fell slap! full length on my face. I struggled up slowly, with two damaged knees, my hair all falling down and the *soignée* little chignon I wore in those days dangling over my right ear. At this point a youth rode by on a bicycle, shouting as he rode, to a pal, "Do you see green in my eyes?" For some reason I thought he was addressing me and I yelled furiously at him, "No, I certainly do not!" (My fall had thoroughly rattled me.) He looked absolutely startled, then said, soothingly, as to a mad person, "That's all right, ma'am, that's all right."

I felt quite idiotic and thoroughly fed-up with the wretched blotter. Picking it from the pavement I gave it a first-class cursing, using all the expressions I had learned, as a reporter, from my chief sub-editor. Then I limped home, no longer feeling in the least like Henry James, Thomas Hardy or Arnold Bennett.

The blotter, as a result of this episode, bore several scratches and was dog-eared in one corner. But I was soon too busy scribbling away to bother much. And after I had once or twice knocked the ink-bottle over it and burned a hole in it with a cigarette and got nail-varnish on it I was thanking my stars it wasn't scarlet hand-tooled leather.

So time passed, very pleasantly. Mortuaries by day, scribbling by night. The cold weather began easing off and spring started to peek at us again, in a coy and fitful manner at first and then more boldly. In mid-March we had a call to Portsmouth on a suspected murder. It was a very blustery day and when we arrived we found our old friend Superintendent Fuggle blowing about in his vast overcoat even more astonishingly than on our previous visits.

He told us that the body of the queried murder victim was already in the public mortuary. It was the body of a man, strongly bound, and he had been found floating in the waters of the dockyard.

We all went along to the mortuary. There on the p.m. table was the body of a partially clad man, bound very securely with strong cord. He was quite trussed up, in a most complicated fashion, rather like one of those street buskers who get a partner to rope them up and then, apparently in the face of all possibility, free themselves from their bonds. Somebody had had a busy time knotting up this wretched man. But after C. K. S. had examined him carefully he announced, much to everyone's amazement, that the man was a suicide. He had sustained no violent injuries of any kind, he had died of drowning, and the trussing and tying, as C. K. S. demonstrated to the detectives, was most ingeniously, but clearly, done by the man himself.

"The most determined suicide I ever saw in my life," said Mr Fuggle. "He'd certainly made up his mind to drown all right."

Subsequent investigations proved that the man had been a very strong swimmer and had tied himself up in this fantastic manner because he hadn't wanted to spoil his chances of drowning by striking out for the shore automatically when he found himself going under.

We returned to London, therefore, without a murder investigation to keep us busy, but feeling cheerful all the same because the hospitality of Portsmouth police had proved as delightful as ever and we had enjoyed an excellent tea and conversation with the Chief Constable and his elegant *aide*. (I particularly recall the sardine sandwiches. One would have liked to ask for the recipe of the mixture.)

Next day, while we were doing a p.m. at Southwark, P.C. Griffin, the then Coroner's officer for Brixton, poked his head round the mortuary door, saying, "Dr Simpson, you're wanted by the CI.D."

"What have they got this time, Griffin?"

"Any more old bones?" chimed in West, who had not yet forgotten the Dobkin case.

272

"They've got a very nice murder at Brixton, Dr Simpson. Well-known prostitute, living in 'Little Heaven', sir, thought she'd like to spread her wings and try the other Heaven for a change."

"Surprised she thought she'd get there," said West.

"'Little Heaven', where is that?" I asked.

"It's the name of a locality in Brixton that used to be very popular at one time with top theatre people, and especially variety people. Marie Lloyd lived there, one time. It's a district of big houses, most of them are now divided into flats. This prostitute worked in the West End, sir, but she's been and picked a customer who's given her something she wasn't expecting and cracked her head open for her. Chief Superintendent Beveridge and the D.D.I. will be round there after lunch, sir, two o'clock. Shall I tell them you'll be there, too?"

"Please, Griffin."

Griffin returned to the telephone and we finished the post-mortem while West told us anecdotes about Little Heaven and about Marie Lloyd, whom he claimed to have known in his early days, and who had been a wonderful woman, he said, and a great Cockney. "You don't get Cockneys like that now. She talked real Cockney and thought real Cockney. These people on the wireless that call themselves Cockneys, why, they don't know what real Cockney sounds like. I can hear her calling me now, when she saw me going along the street, ''Arry boy!'" West produced the ear-splitting, lemon-sharp, piercing cry of greeting of the genuine lady Cockney. "Trying to turn refined is ruining the

Cockneys," concluded West. "But I'm proud of talking Cockney."

Personally I could have listened to him all day.

After lunch we collected Griffin and drove to Little Heaven. It was a shabby old suburb with rambling brick houses which still clung to the shreds of respectability and a sad air of hasbeenness. We found the flat we wanted without any trouble, for it was in an old brown house outside which stood a formidable array of unmistakable C.I.D. cars. One of them had just brought the D.D.I., Mr F. Narborough, to the scene and it was he who opened the front door of the flat to us.

Mr Narborough, who has since retired from being a detective to run a successful hostelry instead, was a very cheerful, stocky man who was something of a gourmet. We had met him lunching, once or twice, at La Coquille and he confessed to us, this afternoon at Brixton, that he had a date to meet his wife and two friends at Frascati's that evening. "But there it is. If I ever arrange to meet my wife anywhere somebody gets murdered and I either keep her waiting for hours or have to cancel the whole thing."

The flat in Little Heaven was a very neat, tidy place. It looked rather small and overcrowded when we walked in because it already contained Mr Beveridge, recently appointed a Chief Superintendent, Mr Cherrill and his fingerprint apparatus and Yard photographer Percy Law with all *his* apparatus. There were also several other detective officers, mostly strangers to me, who were hurrying around with intent expressions doing a variety of things at once. The telephone was ringing, people were giving and carrying out instructions, flashlights were flashing.

Mr Narborough led us into a tiny sitting-room and gave us an outline of the case. While he was talking we were joined by Mr Beveridge. The victim of the murder, Mr Narborough explained, was a forty-four-year-old prostitute named Gertrude, alias Maisie, Rose. "She had been in the big money in her time," said Mr Narborough. "Had a beat in the Leicester Square area, near the Hippodrome. Very smart and quite a good-looker, but of course she was beginning to show signs of wear, and times for her weren't what they had been. Still got plenty of clients, but not the old class. Most of her clients for the past two years have been Yanks. Used to pick them up in Town and then bring them back here by taxi.

"She had a woman who came in every morning to clean and do the chores. When she arrived this morning — had a key to let herself in — she found Miss Rose wasn't up, but thought she was merely taking a lie-in, as she did sometimes, and decided to let her sleep. However, it grew late, the charlady knocked on Miss Rose's door once or twice to rouse her, but there were no sounds of Miss Rose getting up, and finally she went into the bedroom. There she found Miss Rose lying battered to death in a bed full of blood. Apparently she'd been beaten-up with the shillelagh she always used to keep beside her bed to defend herself with against clients who turned nasty. It's a real Irish shillelagh, Dr Simpson."

"I shall like to see that," said Dr Simpson.

"Mr Cherrill's looking for fingerprints in the bedroom at the moment and the photographers are busy too; I think we'll have to wait until there is a little more room in there," observed Mr Beveridge.

While we waited to go into the room where Maisie Rose lay murdered by her own shillelagh I spent a quiet little time prowling round the flat on my own behalf. One of the disadvantages of being a woman is that you never get the chance to see half the things in this world. What chance would I normally have of poking round a prostitute's flat? None. If I ever wished to write about a prostitute I would have to draw upon my imagination for the details of her home. Now here I was in the flat of a well-known member of the profession, so I lost no time in collecting a little data. I trotted quietly round with my own notebook, peeping here and poking there and smiling big sweet smiles at Mr Beveridge whenever he cocked an eyebrow at me, wondering what I was up to.

It was all very clean, tidy and respectable; an example to many of the homes we went into in the course of our work. Everything had just been redecorated, too, and not many homes got redecorated during the war. The little hall was papered with brand new yellowy-orange paper scattered with a design of yellowy-orange berries. There was an empty umbrella-stand and a little round occasional table with a snowy white crochet mat in the middle of it, and in the middle of the mat a gaudy glass vase, the sort of vase people win as prizes at fairs. This had a chip out of it. This vase, and its owner, were the only two things in the flat that had been chipped. Everything else was in excellent order.

I peeked into the bathroom, which had an eau-de-nil *décor*, and was very neat excepting for the window-sill, which was crowded with a variety of things, ranging from toilet-paper and cosmetics to a large selection of douche preparations.

Dr Simpson, Mr Narborough and Superintendent Beveridge were sitting talking in the little lounge which Miss Rose's clients had obviously used as a waiting-room. Indeed, it bore that waiting-room look and could have belonged to a doctor, a dentist or a fortune-teller with equal propriety. There was the inevitable suite of sofa and easy-chairs, covered in the equally inevitable rexine, and in the middle of the carpet was another little table with another crochet mat, but with an ash-tray instead of a vase. The curtains were a depressing blue decorated with orange cape-gooseberry motif and on the mantelpiece stood a pair of uninspiring china figures. An oval mirror hung between them, dead centre. The lady, I noticed, didn't provide magazines, but perhaps, I thought, she made a point of not keeping her clients waiting very long.

It was an impersonal, cheerless room and Maisie Rose had obviously never gone in there. Her room was the kitchen. Here was her sanctuary, the room where she ceased to be Maisie Rose, a highly professional West End prostitute and became Gertrude Rose, a cosy, domesticated, cheerful, sentimental soul. Here everything was in glistening cream and turquoise-blue paint, with spotless china and glass on the little dresser, together with a highly coloured Oriental tea-set which would have gladdened any housewife's proud heart. There was — because it was 1945 — a tin of "Poison Gas Ointment Number 1", ready for an emergency which never came, but for which all good fighting citizens, including Maisie Rose, were bravely prepared. There was also a big box of "Bienaimée" face powder, a neat little sewing-basket, an American candy bar, a pink comb, and a packet of cheap cigarettes.

By the table was a very cosy little green arm-chair. On the table was a fresh black-yellow-and-white check tablecloth, a pair of reading glasses and a black handbag. Somebody had had a drink from a milk bottle; a half-full glass stood by the bottle. Mr Narborough, who was pottering round the kitchen too, went through the handbag and announced there was no wallet, neither could he find one anywhere else in the flat, and it looked as though the murderer had had sufficient presence of mind to take this with him.

I was scrupulously careful, of course, not to touch anything as I looked around. Mr Cherrill would not have thanked me if he had discovered my fingerprints scattered about.

The scullery was not so spick-and-span as the kitchen. The charlady had not completed her morning's chores before discovering the body. There was a basin of dirty washing in the sink. Some underclothes dangled on a little line outside the scullery window.

Back in the kitchen I contemplated a very highly-coloured calendar depicting Christ arrayed in gorgeous attire with a prayer printed underneath asking Sweet Jesus to have mercy on us and remember us. Mr Narborough came and looked at this with me, muttered "Umph" and went back to sorting out some papers. Over the mantelshelf were several snapshots of babies and little children — evidently young nephews and nieces of the deceased. There was also a small photograph of Maisie Rose herself, clearly taken some years previously. It was not a good photograph, however, being speckled and under-exposed, and gave little idea of how she had really looked. There was a funeral card propped beside it, "In Ever Loving Memory" — with ivy and a cross. And there was a Free French Christmas card, showing a *poilu* sitting on a hillock gazing pensively at a distant Eiffel Tower and murmuring "*Bon Noël.*" This card had been coloured in by crayon, by hand.

I was musing upon all these clues to a rather confusing personality and thinking over what Henry Miller has written about prostitutes — their incurable sentimentality, good nature, thriftiness, domestic virtues and so on — but I couldn't recall if he had ever mentioned *devout* prostitutes. Henry Miller is by far the best writer on prostitutes. He is never sentimental about them, and some of his stories are truly very funny. I was thinking of one particularly funny one when C. K. S. popped his head round the kitchen door and said, "Oh, there you are, Miss L. Come along, we're getting to work."

I trotted after C. K. S. and the D.D.I. down the little passage into the bedroom, which was crowded with burly gentlemen from the Yard and all Inspector Law's paraphernalia of cameras, flashlights and tripods. Mr Cherrill gave me what is known as a Big Hello, and Dr Simpson instructed me to stand by the fireplace to be out of the way.

The bedroom had been just as neat and tidy as the rest of the flat. There was a big double bed, a chest of drawers and a dressing-table, just as nice a mahogany suite as anybody could want. There were one or two little items perhaps not quite *comme il faut*: a box of contraceptives on the bedside table and a pair of ladies' shoes dropped, spontaneously as it were, on their sides by the bed, as if kicked off in a moment of abandon. But there were some more very nice photos of the little nephews and nieces over the mantelpiece, and a portrait of Maisie Rose taken several years earlier, showing her to be a handsome brunette with a lively, pleasant face and wearing a cute little cap and a coat with an enormous fur collar.

On the whole it was a bourgeois, orderly, respectable room enough, not at all what the aspiring novelist would have conjured up. But on that March afternoon the scene in that room would have defied all powers of fiction, however imaginative the writer. That room that afternoon had to be seen to be believed.

The bed was tossed, disordered and sodden with blood. Lying obliquely across it on her left side lay Maisie Rose, clad in a blue satin night-gown, her bloodstained hands raised to her breast and a cloth placed over her head. This was exactly how the charlady had found her, so the murderer must have put the cloth there; perhaps he didn't like to see what he had done.

Dr Simpson now gently removed the cloth. The murdered woman's head and face had been shattered by blow upon blow of the shillelagh. She really had been "battered to death".

Upon the floor by the dressing-table lay the shillelagh; a wooden club like a polished tree root. It was heavily bloodstained and had a long dark hair sticking to it, no doubt the dead woman's.

Dr Simpson, Mr Beveridge and Mr Narborough now made a thorough examination of the room, and of the body as it lay on the bed. Some short hairs were removed from the dead woman's body; they were proved subsequently to be hairs from off a man and were an important clue. The temperature of the body showed that death had taken place during the early hours of that morning. The injuries to the woman's hands and forearms indicated she had put up a violent struggle to protect herself.

The body was presently removed to Southwark mortuary, and here a detailed autopsy was made on the remains of Maisie Rose. Although she had lived in such a clean little flat and had dressed so neatly and smartly she concealed behind this façade an active gonorrhoea and old syphilis. (I suppose one might refer to them in her case as mere occupational diseases.) Of course, dead and without any make-up she didn't look in the least like her attractive photograph. Her skin was sallow, lined and coarse and she looked considerably more than the forty-four she had admitted to. In her favour, she had well-marked, strong eyebrows and a nose suggestive of humour. But otherwise there seemed little to say for her.

Of course, dead people never are attractive. The lovely waxen corpse, as C. K. S. would sometimes observe to me, is purely a creation of fiction. The dead may occasionally be impressive, but never beautiful. Even little babies look like weary imitation flowers. As for murdered people, they invariably look dreadful, so perhaps I was altogether wrong to judge Maisie Rose now as she lay on the p.m. table. Dressed up in Leicester Square, well made-up, under the brilliant electric lights, she no doubt looked a very different proposition. Or even sitting in her cosy kitchen, mending her stockings and thinking of her nephews and nieces.

On her rather coarse, thick, short fingers she wore a wedding ring and an engagement ring, and a solitaire on the middle finger of her right hand. Mr Narborough said he had heard she had had a husband some time in her life, but the story of her life was very vague.

The story of her life was very vague . . . . There she lay, this well-known West End prostitute, Irish born, of forty-odd years, unglamorous and diseased, one who had once been in the big money, but who "wasn't very expensive or exclusive these last few years" as D.D.I. Narborough put it. She had had a tidy flat and a cosy kitchen full of family snapshots and a religious calendar and a funeral card. And she had been battered to death by a sensitive gentleman who had covered her bleeding and broken face with a cloth in order to mitigate the horror of the scene . . .

While C. K. S. completed the post-mortem Mr Narborough and I wrapped the shillelagh up in cellophane paper, a delicate operation, for we had to handle it very gingerly in order not to dislodge the long dark hair or leave fingerprints of our own on it. It was to be taken to the police laboratory for examination, together with the small hairs found on the deceased's body.

The case looked a promising one. Investigations at first went well. We learned that the Yard had two suspects; both American servicemen. They were almost without doubt responsible for Maisie Rose's death, but before the police had collected enough evidence to arrest them — but only just before — the two men crossed the Channel to fight the foe. Nothing could be done. They could not be traced and brought back to London and so the word UNSOLVED had to be written against the murder of Maisie Rose.

What happened to her murderers nobody will ever know. Perhaps they met their deserts in the form of German bullets. Maybe they were lucky and finally returned home as two worthy American veterans, to be welcomed royally and proudly toasted by some small town. Nobody will ever know.

Just as I shall never know about Maisie Rose, with her nice little flat in Little Heaven, her ancient but abysmal profession, her family snaps, her calendar with its prayer, "Sweet Jesus have mercy on us and remember us". A Graham Greene character, in every respect. Impossible for me, with my unsubtle Protestant background, to understand. Or is that so? Maybe we

283

like to think too much. Maybe faith is indeed sufficient. In which case I need not bother my so-called brain with Maisie Rose, but merely breathe the prayer which somebody slipped into my hand once as I came out of a church in Montmartre, "*Sacré Cœur de Jésus, ayez pitié de nous*".

CHAPTER
TWENTY-FOUR

Murder at "Charley Brown's"

Poplar Coroner's Court and mortuary stand in Poplar High Street, just past the bowling-green. To find them you drive along Commercial Road into dockland, along the West India Dock Road into Chinatown — or what the Luftwaffe left of Chinatown — and turn left at Pennyfields and thence into the High Street. Here new blocks of fine flats and little prefabricated houses jostle with old, slummy, sooty buildings between which blow winds tangy with dockyard water.

The name Chinatown is still one which journalists like to write with a shudder and detective-writers mouth with glee. Chinatown — it conjures up everything that is murky and mysterious, and vicious. But Chinatown today is really very mild. Most of it was bombed out of existence and the parts that are left, although still definitely Chinese, are most respectable.

You still see notices and posters in Chinese on the street walls, and Chinese signs outside the little shops and laundries, while the small, yellow people with their quiet, deft movements and bright dark eyes glide about the narrow roadways and flicker in front of cars in an inconsequential fashion. There are many Chinese restaurants, one or two of them famous among Chinese gourmets, and there are little Chinese seamen's hostels, very clean and well kept, and Chinese seamen's missions, and small, dark houses with broken-down backyards where you may espy through the cracks in the fences rather oriental-looking ducks and fowls squatting around in interesting Chee Yang attitudes. But all this is a mere shadow of what Chinatown once was, and the shadow is fading and may well one day be gone. For, I am told on excellent authority, the Chinese of Chinatown in recent years have indulged greatly in intermarriage and now there is only one pure Chinese family left in the district; the family of a famous restaurateur.

Nevertheless, when Chinese witnesses turn up in court they still insist upon taking the oath in Chinese fashion, with a little pile of saucers to break and much rigmarole. (The Coroner's officer used to complain that, with saucers getting to be the price they were, Chinese witnesses were becoming an expensive luxury.) And still, as you go through Chinatown, Chinese voices come from doorways and courtyards, sing-song, light and strange; the language which has sounded for so long in this peculiar little corner of London, a corner once so fabulous and fearsome, and still full of memories.

It is interesting that during all the years I was with C. K. S. we did only one post-mortem on a Chinese. This was a man found hanging in a bombed-out house in Chinatown. He had been hanging there some months before anybody discovered him and he had become quite mummified. He was plainly a suicide, but the police were unable to learn anything about him. Was he some tragic sailor who had returned to find his home and family blown to dust and had decided that life was no longer worth living without them? Nobody will ever know. An inscrutable Oriental, indeed.

The Coroner's Court and mortuary were built just before the war to replace out-of-date premises. By a miracle they escaped any grave damage by bombs, which dropped all around in a charmed circle, but always just missed the domain of H. M. Coroner, Mr W. H. Heddy.

The Coroner's Court is Tudor in design, with much olde oak panelling and heavy beams. The mortuary is startlingly contemporary in design, a bit like the South Bank Exhibition. The p.m. room is mainly of glass and porcelain tiling; the walls are mostly vast windows and there is subtle strip-lighting in the ceiling. It might well be a chic Paris *atelier.* An excellent idea in a less hectic era, but during the war years this mortuary was either wide to the winds of heaven or windowed with thick black-out paper. From time to time it would be boldly equipped with new glass; "All shipshape again, Dr Simpson," the mortuary keeper would proudly announce. Next morning there he would be, sweeping up the glass . . .

The grey and pale-blue *décor* of the p.m. room is tasteful and restrained. There is an office for the doctors, panelled and furnished in light oak, business-like and dignified, but in those war years very draughty and dusty because it too had no window-panes left.

There is a fine, glittering cold-storage room with vast, smooth-humming refrigerators. But the *pièce de résistance* of the mortuary is the viewing-room, the little room to which relatives go to view and identify their dead.

Imagine an ornate alcove, rather than an actual room, with a big window for the said relatives to look through at . . . ah, yes, at poor old Joe, or Liza, or Harry, stretched out on a magnificent bier between two giant standard lamps, against an exotic backcloth reminiscent of Bakst. Dramatic concealed lighting heightens the effect. It is certain that Joe, Liza and Harry never lay in such splendour all their lives; rickety old beds, seedy bedrooms, were no doubt their lot, drab and uncomfortable. But now that death has robbed them of all feeling and all pride here they lie, in the most sumptuous style imaginable.

The relatives of the deceased invariably express immense gratification.

Opposite the viewing-room is a little room for the Jewish watcher.

Jewish custom demands that the dead must be watched; the body, until burial, must be attended by a guardian, a mourner. This body watcher must not, under Jewish religious law, be a relative of the deceased. So a professional body-watcher is hired.

These watchers are often repulsive and hideous old women, either very stout or very skinny, dressed in a collection of shabby garments apparently collected over the course of years and donned in bulky layers. They sit in their little rooms in the mortuaries, if not actually watching the dead at least very close at hand, and they brew and drink unspeakable tea, and snooze, and knit knit knit, through the long and weary hours when everything in the mortuary is dark, and silent, and still.

Armed with their knitting they always made me regard them as cousins to those repulsive old women who used to squat at the foot of the guillotine during the Terror. These old Jewesses are our contemporary *tricoteuses*. I always found them rather fascinating, simply because they were so horrible. There was one at Poplar who would dart from her lair with all the unexpected agility of a toad, her big spectacles perched crookedly on her nose and her teapot in her hand. In Yiddish she would shriek at the mortuary keeper, or the undertakers, or the mortuary keeper's dog — just for the sake of shrieking. I would have liked to have asked her if she did not find the mortuary at night rather creepy, but I could not summon the courage to question her. She was not an inviting personality.

The watchers are well provided for at Poplar, however, with a little room exactly opposite the viewing-room, across a narrow passage, and a window of their own to peek through exactly facing the viewing-room window. So the watcher has only to raise her eyes from her knitting to be able to cast a vigilant glance at the corpse under her care.

The assistant mortuary keeper at Poplar in those days was a long-faced, lugubrious man who meandered vaguely about, dropping things and losing things and saying "Righty-o" to everything. As he bent over the

289

bodies, sewing them up, he always crooned, "You Are My Sunshine . . ."

Once, when C. K. S. was in a great hurry, I rushed into the p.m. room, snatched up what I thought was my white p.m. gown and began putting it on. But the strange, sour-sweet odour of the dead made me stop and take a second look at the garment; it was a shroud. I gave a shriek and tore it off. It was a horrid experience for me, but it gave "You Are My Sunshine" a rare and hearty laugh.

He thought I was very mimsy and choosy. When he stripped the bodies he would drop their clothes in piles on the floor and when these unsavoury garments were scattered around my feet I used to sniff and give him looks. Once when I had a very low chair and asked if he could find me a cushion or anything similar to sit on he picked up a bundle of clothes he had just taken off a very dirty-looking army deserter and trotted up to me with them, rolling them together into a cushion-shaped bundle as he advanced. I refused point-blank to sit on them. "You Are My Sunshine" was definitely miffed. He considered me a spoilt type, I could see.

The Coroner's officers, P.C. West and the late P.C. Hyde, presided over this Tudor and twentieth-century outfit. They had a Tudor office next to the front entry and here they maintained a gorgeously cosy, never-failing fug. They had a nice little fire in the Tudor fireplace, two tables, two phones, a map of Europe with Hitler's intended conquests marked in black, another map which West studded with flags showing the Allied advances against the enemy, a collection of framed family snapshots, a huge Victorian pin-cushion in which Hyde kept his pins, a kettle on the hob, tea things, and a cupboard crammed with stacks and stacks of Spilsbury p.m. reports, all written in the Great Man's illegible and inimitable hand.

In this office cups of strong, sweet tea were dispensed to a host of callers ranging from Scotland Yard chiefs to police constables, Home Office pathologists, local newspaper reporters, lawyers, undertakers, seamen, mission workers, oriental interpreters, firemen, clergymen, and a small child who used to pop in two or three times a day for "weeties".

P.C. Hyde was a big, quiet, gentle, charming man with a deceptively languid smile and quick, perceptive eyes. He and I were *sympathique*. One day when I charged in, grabbed a history sheet with a brief "Thank you" and charged for the door again, Hyde's slow, slyly humorous voice came after me, "Ah, Miss Molly, and just to think that Nature really intended you and me for the coach-and-wagon days."

Hyde had been born in Bedford and came to London as a shy, simple country boy, as he put it. He had joined the Metropolitan Police and spent thirty years in East London, becoming an expert on the district. Despite this he had retained his round, ruddy country face and a certain deliberation and simplicity of manner. He was kind, helpful, and when he died he had friends who missed him everywhere.

His partner, West, was as truly a Londoner as Hyde was not. Nervous energy exuded from him in all directions, his face was pale, quick and witty, his humour cynical and on the dot, his comments caustic. When the bombs fell he was very resigned. "Hitler'll get me. Of course he'll get me. I'm one of his targets. Know where I ought to be, don't you, Miss Molly? Marked up there on that map, in black."

Dr Simpson didn't believe in cups of tea during working hours, but on slack afternoons he would make an exception in favour of Hyde and West and together we would all settle down in their office to a good strong brew and conversation. Being policemen they of course adored chatting and their chat was most interesting. They knew the district inside out, and could talk knowledgeably about everyone from Clement Attlee to Comrade Phil Piratin, from these two political gentlemen to the local night-blooms of the district, past and present, and of the local "fences", missionaries, doctors, and murderers. But best of all C. K. S. liked Hyde to reminisce about the East End of thirty years back; an East End abounding in thieves' kitchens, notorious doss-houses, opium-dens and the like. Hyde would tell, a trifle nostalgically, of a Chinatown that really had been Chinese, of "Old Charley Brown's", that celebrated Limehouse tavern which in the good (bad) old days had been a jamboree of foreign sailors, strange tongues, loud-mouthed brawls, knivings and beatings-up, stuffed alligators, little live black bears on chains, cursing parrots, wonderful oriental carpets, joss-sticks, *Samurai* swords, Japanese lanterns, brass gongs, sharks' teeth, and a profusion of other marvels. "And he ruled over it all like a dictator," said Hyde. "He didn't stand for no nonsense, old Charley Brown.

He was famous throughout all Limehouse, and it really was Limehouse then. We hadn't cleaned it up. The police didn't walk about singly in those days, you had to go about at least in pairs, and then you wasn't really safe."

And Hyde would sigh. "Ah, but it's all altered now. Old Charley Brown wouldn't recognise the place now."

Old Charley Brown, of course, has become one of Chinatown's legends. Hyde really had known the legend when Charley was king of the West India Dock Road, accepting astonishing gifts from seamen from all parts of the world and piling these gifts in his bar, so that it was a museum-cum-zoo-cum-bazaar.

Old Charley Brown had been dead for many years when Hyde was recounting to us these nostalgic tales, but Young Charley Brown, Hyde explained, had moved the business to fine new premises in the eastern suburbs and had decorated this new "Charley Brown's" with part of his father's astonishing seamen's collection.

"They say it's quite worth going in to see," said Hyde. "But of course he gets an altogether different class of customers from what his father had to deal with," he added, with a twinkle.

The old pub was still standing on a corner of the West India Dock Road and we passed near it every time we drove to the mortuary. It had been knocked about a bit in the Blitz and looked weary and dilapidated. It was, however, still open to the denizens of Limehouse and although it had passed out of the hands of the Charley Brown clan it was still invariably referred to as "Charley Brown's".

One blustery March morning, several months after dear old Hyde had gone to join Charley Brown in a last long rest, P.C. West phoned us with a message that had an old-time ring about it. "There's been a murder at 'Charley Brown's'."

Dr Simpson said he would go down right away, and within twenty minutes or so we were scurrying up the steps into the little Tudor office of the Coroner's Court.

Hyde's place in this snuggery had been taken by P.C. Marshall. (It was a trifle confusing that we had a P.C. Marshall, and, of course, a West, at Southwark as well.) Poplar's Marshall was a cheerful man, a great one for Keeping Fit. P.C. West assured me wryly that Marshall did physical jerks in the mortuary yard.

On this particular morning West and Marshall were busy in their office serving tea to several C.I.D. men, and West smuggled me a quick cup while Dr Simpson went to the p.m. room to take a brief glance at the murdered man, who had already been brought in. While the tea was being finished a small car drew up outside the mortuary and from it stepped a very tall, broad-shouldered man with thick wavy hair, a face thoughtful and authoritative, and heavy horn-rimmed spectacles. This was Area Superintendent George Hatherill, and at sight of him everybody put down their tea and snapped to attention.

Mr Hatherill is famous at the Yard for, among many things, his great command of modern languages. He is a much travelled police officer of international repute. I had heard much about Mr Hatherill but had never met him before. Dr Simpson introduced me to him and we shook hands. The eyes behind the horn-rimmed spectacles had the usual penetrating Scotland Yard quality.

The murder at "Charley Brown's" was in the classical Limehouse tradition. The murderer was a carousing seaman and the victim was a customer of the pub. He had been stabbed in a brawl which had taken place at "Charley Brown's" the previous night. "Always was a dangerous job, keeping order at 'Charley Brown's'," murmured West. The tale had an up-to-date twist, however, for the brawling seamen this time were U.S. naval ratings.

Mr Hatherill went to the p.m. room to take a quick look at the dead man and I went too. The victim was well-built, in his mid-thirties. He wore grey flannel trousers and a bloodstained shirt. He lay stiff and toes-up on the p.m. table. "Before the autopsy we'll take a look at the scene of the trouble," said Mr Hatherill. He had already been to the dockyard to interview the ratings concerned. "They're only kids. But they were certainly armed to the teeth when they went out for a drink last night! Knives, knuckle-dusters, everything. Astonishing."

We got into our respective cars and drove, a rather grim little procession, through Chinatown to the grey, dismal, dusty tavern. All the windows of the establishment, like all the other windows in that bomb-rocked district, had been blown in and their glass was replaced by thin boarding. The place, therefore, wore that blank, blind expression so common amongst London buildings during the war.

Coroner's officer West knocked at the door of this moribund place; a pale, scared, red-eyed woman opened it. We were shown into the big public bar. It was dark and in considerable disorder; no attempt had been made to clear up since the night before — which had obviously been some night. The air was acrid with the smell of stale beer and cigarette smoke. Laden ash-trays were scattered around, dirty glasses, emptied bottles. Chairs and tables huddled in perturbed groups. Tatty oriental hangings on the walls and big Japanese lanterns dangling like dispirited mobiles from the ceiling added to the littered atmosphere of the place. At the further end of the bar, however, was a clearing in the disorder. Here, starkly, stood a plain wooden chair beside a large pool of blood.

The publican now hurried in to tell us about the happenings of the previous night. He too was pale and shaken in appearance, and his shirt was ripped in several places by the rating's knife — for there had nearly been two murders.

Apparently, the previous evening, a party of young U.S. naval ratings had come in to "Charley Brown's" and, as the evening had worn on, had become very difficult. Finally they had started a brawl, so the publican had called upon a customer to perform the difficult duties of chucker-out — which he did with consequences that were to prove only too tragic for himself a moment later. Together both publican and customer routed the U.S. Navy and they were bolting the door and breathing "Good riddance" when the ratings, who had lurched away up the street, returned.

One thrust his arm through the thin emergency panelling of the blitzed door (it had been a door with glass panels originally), and in his hand this sailor held a knife with which he stabbed at random, ripping the publican's shirt and fatally wounding the other.

The stabbed man was assisted to the chair already described . . . the pool of blood on the floor told the rest of the story.

The publican and his daughter answered Mr Hatherill's questions and watched Dr Simpson as he produced his tape-measure and took measurements of the doorway in which the stabbing occurred. But there was not very much to examine, really, in this dark, dank old bar, haunted by other days and other sailors and flickering now, by this blind and swaggering stabbing, into a last flame of its former fire. We said good-morning to Charley Brown's shirt-slashed successor and went back to the mortuary.

The stab wound of the dead man was deep and had been quickly fatal. The U.S. sailor may have been little more than a kid, as Mr Hatherill had said, but he hadn't brandished his knife in the air merely playfully.

So the evening at "Charley Brown's" culminated in a U.S. naval court martial in offices overlooking Regent Street. There were assembled U.S. naval officers bulky in gold braid, and A.B.s bristling with revolvers, and there was a general atmosphere of bustle and efficiency which seemed very impressive until I got involved in it and found myself, on C. K. S.'s behalf, having to fill in umpteen forms in triplicate, when I decided there was an unnecessary quantity of red tape.

The court-room itself was guarded by a gentleman heavily swagged with immense holsters, who took a very dim view of me. He didn't see why I needed to go into the court-room at all and eyed me suspiciously whilst I, with equal suspicion, eyed his holsters. Finally he allowed me in. But having got me in there he didn't know where to seat me. *Not* with C. K. S. and the other professional witnesses because I wasn't a professional witness. *Not* with the court shorthand-writers. *Not* with the legal gentlemen. Where did one seat a pathologist's secretary? He looked around, humming and hemming, and finally decided on the Press Bench. Next minute I was squeezing in beside my old acquaintance, *News of the World* chief crime reporter, Norman Rae.

He gave me a terrific wink. "Sit down and behave yourself or you'll get us all shot."

I had never been in a court-room like it before. The naval high-ups glittered in a row one side of the room, the professional witnesses, lawyers, Press and the rest sat on the other, while on a chair in the centre lolled the prisoner, a boy of nineteen, absorbed in reading a pile of "funnies" and paying no attention to the trial whatsoever.

Norman Rae drew my attention to the shorthand machines the Americans were using; something between typewriters and tape-machines combined. "Your boss is all a one for speed and efficiency. Next thing you know he'll be getting you one of those."

"Next thing you know you'll be using one yourself."

"I shall hand in my resignation before you catch me with a contraption like that. Life is complicated enough as it is."

Dr Simpson was now called upon to give evidence. There was no witness-box, he was permitted to stride up and down — if he chose — before the braided gentlemen while two lawyers, Prosecution and Defence, each in turn roved round him in cagey circles, peppering him with Humphrey Bogartish questions. C. K. S., endowed with a great sense of humour, and at the same time nourished in the Englishman's tradition of formality and respect for ceremony on serious occasions, was seized, I perceived, with both amusement and amazement. Nevertheless, he maintained an admirably dead-pan countenance, even when they handed him the fatal weapon and said, "Now, Doc, just show the court how *you* think the stabbing was done."

He took the knife, considered, then struck a realistic pose and made several stabbing gestures.

"Is this a dagger that I see before me, the handle toward my hand? Come, let me clutch thee . . ."

We all watched this dramatic performance with keen interest, excepting the prisoner, who chewed gum and selected another "funny".

The verdict was one of Guilty, and the prisoner was sentenced to the electric chair. But because of his youth President Roosevelt intervened and a long term of imprisonment at Sing Sing was substituted.

Thus ended the stabbing at "Charley Brown's". Not the first stabbing there, by any means, but perhaps the last. For Limehouse has become decorous and quiet; a respectable neighbourhood, cleaned up and polished and law-abiding. The undesirables of the capital have moved to other parts, further west, with excursions into the south and north. If you want to live in a really well-behaved part of the world these days, where you can rely on having neighbours who never break the law and respect the steady, bourgeois virtues, you should move eastwards to take up residence in Limehouse.

CHAPTER
TWENTY-FIVE

Coming Through the Rye

Dr Simpson, in between post-mortems, managed to do a great deal of lecturing and teaching, and as time went by more and more examining. Some of the students suspected I knew the questions he proposed setting them (actually I didn't), and a few bolder spirits used to waylay me in the Guy's quadrangle and make nervous attempts to wangle information out of me.

Their answers to the written section of the forensic medicine examination gave C. K. S. considerable entertainment, for medical students, like women novelists, never seem to be able to spell. There was one youth who gave particular delight, I remember, for, during an account of the effects of carbon-monoxide poisoning, he observed that, "Many a night-watchman has come to an untimely end whilst sitting in his hut gazing pensively at a red-hot brassière."

I enjoyed the examination periods because I found myself with spare time on my hands and was able to go shopping, or swimming, or poking around London or the second-hand book-shops. On one free afternoon I climbed the Monument, taking with me a girl friend from Dr Ryffel's department. She plodded doggedly up the three-hundred-odd steps, while I panted up in front of her, gaspingly giving her details about the Plague, for she was a German and ignorant of London's history. The ascent was a dark, dank and airless one, and we were thankful to emerge at the top, on a narrow parapet well enclosed with railings. I remarked, "It'd be very difficult to commit suicide from up here," and my friend paled a little and said yes, she supposed it would. Then she peeked between the railings over the edge of the parapet and went a little paler. I was enraptured and intoxicated by the feeling of height and space and exclaimed repeatedly, "Isn't it heavenly? Oh, wouldn't you just adore to be a pigeon, able to *launch* yourself into the air?" With appropriate launching gestures. She sank back from the dizzy view and shook her head. "Shall we eat our sandwiches up here?" says Lefebure, eagerly. "No, no. I think we should eat them on London Bridge."

I was very sorry to have to tear myself finally from the wonderful view and make the descent of those horrible, dank stairs. It was an excellent threepenny-worth of exercise and panorama, I must say. It would have been cheap at nine-pence.

On some of the slack examination days I used to "catch up with the filing", to use a Simpson expression. I had a small numbering mechanism with which I used to imprint the filing cards, and as I was dealing with figures running in odd thousands, and as thousands get me quite flummoxed, so that I quickly forget even how to count, I always emerged from these filing sessions feeling like a cow-puncher who has been trying to brand a herd of stampeding steers. Indeed, the nervous strain of those periods spent "catching up with the filing" did more damage to my nervous system than any gruesome mortuary scene.

These filing sessions, too, always left me deeply depressed, for they made me realise what a mug I really was, and how far, far removed from being a Perfect Secretary. "A secretary," they had taught us at secretarial college, "is made or marred by her files."

That last summer I spent with C. K. S. brought us a remarkable crop of murders. They were all in the country and entailed trips to places as far apart as Plymouth and the Isle of Ely.

The Plymouth job, I must admit, C. K. S. went to without me. It was a very long journey and he decided to make it alone. I was sorry because just before the war I had worked on a paper at Plymouth and had had very happy times there, so I felt disappointed not to be able to revisit the scene of my first experiences as a junior reporter. But C. K. S. went off by the late afternoon train from Waterloo and was back by midday next day, looking a trifle worn.

The case, to use his own words, was a sordid one. A girl of fourteen years, not inexperienced with men, had been found lying strangled by the side of the military road leading from Bloom Hill to Egg Buckland. (I had done a lot of horse-riding round there with one John Dingle, a fellow reporter, whose main ambition seemed to be to break every bone he possessed.)

The murdered girl, young as she was, had already become known locally as a sort of unprofessional prostitute. Her murderer was a little sailor, but although the police knew his identity they were never able to get enough of the right kind of evidence to arrest him. So the little sailor went on his way, no doubt rejoicing.

C. K. S. was rather disappointed at the non-arrest of this sailor. But in war-time murders have a habit of ending inconclusively. We had one case that summer which could never actually be proved a case of murder, although it seemed suspiciously like it.

The case concerned a W.A.A.F. who was found drowned in the River Nene on the Isle of Ely. Chief Inspector Thorp and the local police struggled with this baffling case for five weeks and in the end were obliged to leave it as unsolved.

The dead W.A.A.F. was a young married woman of twenty-eight. She was found in the River Nene, described as a dangerous river, by a local constable. The body, when found, had been in the water for about a fortnight. Dr Simpson thought that death was due to drowning, but it was difficult for him to say so categorically because the body was so badly decomposed. He found nothing to suggest foul play, but again the state of decomposition made any definite conclusion very difficult.

It was believed that the girl, who had disappeared on her way back to camp after a leave, had been hitch-hiking. The Isle of Ely was miles out of her course back to camp, there was no explanation as to why, or how, she had got there, and the police nursed a strong suspicion that she had been attacked by somebody giving her a lift and afterwards her body had been conveyed and dumped there. When found, her shoes, stockings and knickers were missing, but these clothes might have been washed from off the body by the river; indeed the shoes most certainly would have been.

The police were their usual thorough, dogged selves, but without success. Excerpts from two police statements will reveal some extent of their enquiries. The first, from P.C. Cox, reads:

"I have made numerous enquiries of persons living in the vicinity of the river, and also of roadmen, postal workers, farm labourers, lorry drivers, haulage contractors, and of tradesmen delivering goods, in an endeavour to obtain information, but without success."

And here is one of the detective officers in the case, Det Sergt J. Davis, reporting:

"Every possible and conceivable enquiry has been made to obtain information as to the movements of deceased on May 4th, 1945" (the day she finished her leave and departed from home for her camp), "and since, prior to the finding of her body, but to date without success. Special and detailed enquiries have been carried out by all police forces throughout Central Midlands, the whole of the Eastern Counties and Greater London."

What more could be asked? Everything had been done that could be done, but with no result. So an inquest was held in order that the case might be officially wound up and to this inquest C. K. S. went, taking me with him.

The inquest was held at Thorney, on a rather dull June day. The fen country, which so fascinates some people, holds no attraction for me. Like the psalmist, my help comes from the hills. The Isle of Ely and its surrounding countryside depress me.

The inquest was held in a small dance hall at the back of the Rose and Crown. A few idle locals had turned up in a mood of curiosity, and there were several police officials, all very spit-and-polish.

The dead girl's husband was there, a young man in R.A.F. uniform, together with his mother. We all sat in rows in the hall, watching the jury assemble and waiting for the Coroner to arrive. I found myself sitting next to Chief Inspector Thorp. I had met him on several previous occasions, and now we chatted amicably. Mr Thorp, witty, energetic and sartorially distinguished, reminisced nostalgically about the boat he owned and the happy pre-war voyages he had made in her. His memories had reached the Côte d'Azur and he was brooding aloud over Cannes harbour and Saint Tropez while the twelve good men and true clumped into the hall and took their places on the chairs reserved for the jury. Farmers, local tradesmen, retired white-whiskered old gentlemen and the like, they all had big red faces, obstinate English jowls and slow, deliberate glances. They stared around the court-room at us all, clearly saying, "Now we're the jury and we're the people who finally count, you know, and we're here to unearth the truth of this matter and give a just verdict, so you needn't try to take us in, even though you are policemen and pathologists and what not."

At last the Coroner arrived and the hearing began. It was certainly a problem case. The young widower told us his wife had been happy, healthy and contented, he could think of no reason why she might have wished to take her life, and he could give no explanation as to how she might have come to drown in the River Nene, which was so far from the camp to which she had been returning. His mother then described how the girl had spent her leave with her, had been cheerful and fit and had left to return to camp in the best of spirits. She recalled that the girl had said something about hitch-hiking back to the camp.

Dr Simpson explained to the jury that, so far as he could ascertain, the girl had been drowned and had not sustained any injuries suggestive of foul play. However, he had to point out that the advanced decomposition of the body made it difficult to draw any definite conclusions.

Chief Inspector Thorp described his enquiries and explained they had yielded absolutely no information and there was no point therefore in continuing them. Detective Sergeant Davis and P.C. Cox said their pieces to the same effect. The Coroner then summed up. He pointed out that the dead woman might have fallen in the river by accident, although there was absolutely no known reason why she should have wandered so far from her route back to camp as the River Nene. She might have committed suicide, although there was no reason why she should have done so. On the other hand she might have been the victim of foul play. There was no way of telling how she had come to be in the river, there was only the plain fact that her body had been found in the Nene and, so far as could be judged, she had died from drowning.

The jury listened with wary, earnest attention, consulted amongst themselves for a little and then returned a verdict that death was from drowning.

There was no other verdict possible. The mystery of this young woman's death remains a mystery to this day.

After the inquest we all went out into the yard of the Rose and Crown, where the sun was now belatedly shining. Our train back to London did not leave for an hour, and while we were debating what to do during that hour Mr Thorp came smilingly up to us to say we had been invited to a birthday tea-party and led us, despite our polite protests, into the Rose and Crown.

Now the Rose and Crown was where Mr Thorp had been staying the past five weeks, and during this stay he had clearly grown to be on the happiest terms with the publican and his family. It was their little daughter who was having the birthday — and the tea-party — and she had invited Mr Thorp, and as we were his friends what was more natural than that we should be invited too?

Consequently we found ourselves in a large dining-room, staring at the most marvellous spread any of us had seen for years. It was difficult to believe war-time England could produce such a tea. There were all kinds of sandwiches and scones and cakes, tarts and jellies and blancmanges, trifles and biscuits and bon-bons.

There were wonderful, luscious, strawberries-and-cream. And there was a heavenly pink birthday cake, with cherries on it, and candles.

The children had not yet been brought in to the table; we could hear them playing party games in another room, creating a joyous bedlam. We felt we simply could not desecrate such a miraculous tea-table, so we each had a cup of tea, a sandwich, a little cake and then, with a chorus of "Happy Birthdays" and "Thank yous" we departed. Mr Thorp remained behind at the Rose and Crown, looking very happy and obviously about to make a second, much heavier, attack on the party tea, in the company of the little guests.

While we sat admiring the party tea-table the young widower and his mother sat on a bench in the yard under a chestnut tree, drinking tea that was brought them there. What a strange thing life is, I thought. A drowning that was perhaps a murder, an inquest, a birthday tea-party, children playing "Oranges and Lemons", a Yard inspector and a Home Office pathologist admiring the *glacé* cherries on a cake, June sunshine, strawberries-and-cream, two mourning people sitting sadly on a bench, sipping tea and staring drearily at nothing. To what does it all add up?

In that same month of June C. K. S. went down to Leigh-on-Sea on a double murder at a bungalow. I missed this trip, to my intense annoyance, because it fell on one of my rare afternoons off. Not that I minded missing Leigh-on-Sea and its celebrated ozone. At the beginning of the Blitz I had been dispatched once a week by my editor, who owned a paper at Southend as

309

one of his side concerns, to rustle round Southend and environs collecting, or trying to collect, wedding and funeral notices from an almost entirely non-existent population. Everybody had been evacuated from Southend and its neighbouring resorts. German and British planes were fighting it out overhead as I pattered round those hot and deserted streets, where nine houses out of ten were empty and boarded up and where, needless to say, absolutely nobody was getting married and only a few aged people were dying, a few aged people who had refused to be evacuated and had remained to perish of heart failure in the citadel. These one or two funerals were to me nuggets of gold in the arid desert. Otherwise there was nothing, nothing. At least, nothing in the way of local parish-pump news. Plenty was happening, but not for me to write about. The sky was peppered with barrage balloons, floating lazily and tranquilly, the planes fought above them, parachutists could be seen if you were lucky — or if you weren't lying face down on the pavement at the time, praying — baling out from shot-up planes which were screeching down ground-wards. Shrapnel fell in little showers, more cruelly than the summer rain. Yes, Southend was hot that year, both with the sun and the Battle of Britain. I never saw the sea. I am told one frequently doesn't see the sea at Southend for ages, because the tide goes out so far, but even if the tide had been up I wouldn't have noticed it. I was too anxious to care about the sea. All I wanted to do was to get back to dear old London intact. So round and round I ran, clutching my little notebook, visiting the only citizens left in Southend: the undertakers and the clergy. The undertakers all complained because business was so terrible, there was nobody left in Southend to die, and how on earth was one expected to make a living under the circumstances? I uttered sympathetic tuck-tuck noises. The clergy were as unemployed as the undertakers, but most of them seemed pretty cheerful and were seizing this period of enforced leisure to catch up on their gardening, while one vicar told me he was writing all his sermons for the next twelve months.

So, you see, I knew Southend — and Leigh — quite well, in a rather original sort of way. Let me add that these original experiences had left me with a horror of these two celebrated resorts. I believe that in normal times they are quite nice places. But, to parody Sarah Bernhardt: for me, between air-raids, not.

So I wasn't exactly sorry to miss Leigh-on-Sea, but I was sorry to miss the murder. Also I was sorry I missed the drive down, with C. K. S. and Chief Inspector A. G. Philpot; a big, pithy man who later found fame in the Chalk Pit murder case.

The murder was an interesting one because of a unique clue. The victims were a Mr and Mrs Lucas, an elderly couple who had retired to Leigh to a bungalow and ozone. The newspapers described them as "wealthy", but in reality they were not. The husband was a former pawnbroker. They were found battered to death in their home and the motive of the crime seemed to have been robbery in the first place, for the bungalow was ransacked.

The detectives, searching round the bungalow, found a partly emptied milk bottle on the back doorstep and this milk bottle immediately became the darling of Supt Cherrill's heart, for on it were some splendid bloodstained fingerprints. The thief-cum-murderer had apparently hurried from the bungalow with still gory hands and, suffering from an acute thirst, he had spotted the milk bottle and immediately had picked it up and enjoyed a zesty swig. He had then put it down on the step and gone his way.

"See what happens, Dr Simpson, when you're not a beer-drinking man," observed Mr Philpot.

It seemed incredible that anybody could be so careless. The murderer might just as well have left a card with his name and address on it. Mr Cherrill took the bottle back to his laboratory and in no time the murderer was arrested.

But our most interesting murder case that summer was one which occurred in July, a horrible case, with a little girl as its pathetic victim. It was an all-night job, in the depths of remotest Suffolk.

We received the call to do the post-mortem one hot July afternoon. Scotland Yard phoned to say that Chief Inspector Greeno had been put in charge of the case and would take us down to Suffolk with him. I was at Dr Simpson's flat, typing manuscript, when the call came through and we waited there until six o'clock, when Mr Greeno arrived. He had with him Detective Sergeant F. Hodge, his invariable partner in crime, and downstairs waited a big sleek police car, in the back of which was stowed Mr Greeno's "murder bag" and an attaché-case full of cigarettes "for when we interview people", as Mr Greeno explained.

We all piled into the car and off we went. Mr Greeno told us what he knew of the murder, and I tried to take it down in shorthand and wondered, not for the first time, at that story of Bernard Shaw who wrote his plays, in impeccable shorthand, on the tops of buses. However did he do it?

Mr Greeno said that the murder victim, a little girl of fourteen called Daphne Bacon, had been to Sunday-school the previous day with her twin sister, across the fields from her home at Aldringham, a sleepy village where nothing ever seemed to happen. Life at Aldringham was so tranquil, indeed, that the appearance of a soldier in a black beret who hung around the village for several days — and who was said to have accosted one or two women in the locality — was regarded as a violent sensation. But Daphne was too young to worry about soldiers and the fields round her village were too familiar for her to think twice about walking in them alone. When she came out of Sunday-school she hurried home ahead of her sister and her friends. On the way back she encountered the soldier, sitting on a stile . . .

Shortly after five o'clock some picnickers heard moans and feeble cries for help coming from a rye-field. They found the little girl, terribly battered about the head and in a semi-conscious condition. One ran for help, the others did what they could for the child, who managed to gasp out an account of how she had been attacked by the soldier. Then she collapsed into total unconsciousness. She was rushed to Ipswich Hospital and operated on, but it was hopeless and an hour or so later she died.

The soldier had meantime disappeared.

This was the story of the case which Mr Greeno gave us. Then, as the drive was a long one, conversation in the car turned to other things, the car purred steadily on along the Essex roads, between dusty summer hedges and through quiet little towns, while the fine summer evening pleasantly waned. As we approached Colchester Mr Greeno suggested we should stop there for dinner at The George. Dr Simpson agreed; it seemed that on a previous murder job together they had made an excellent dinner at The George. So to The George we went.

That was my first visit to The George and Colchester. After the war I got to know the place well, for my sister Elizabeth spent several years scenic-designing for Robert Digby's repertory company at Colchester, and many an evening have I sat in The George talking with members of the rep. company and drinking cherry brandy. But I never went to The George without thinking of my first visit there with Chief Inspector Greeno, C. K. S. and Sergeant Hodge. We sat in the lounge, sipped sherry and talked not about Michael Redgrave's "Macbeth" and Olivier's "Mr Puff" and how ridiculous so-and-so had looked in those bishop's gaiters in last week's production of "Robert's Wife", but about murder. Murders past and murders present. And then we all went into the dining-room and ate a very large dinner and talked about food, and holidays in Cornwall, and The Three Pilchards at Polperro, and had a very merry time. Rather difficult to believe we were on a murder investigation!

After The George came the road again. Essex gave way to Suffolk and sunset to twilight. The motion of the car made me feel sleepy, and the gentlemen were talking cricket, which was not a subject liable to keep me on tenterhooks, anyway. But at length we arrived at Ipswich, which naturally brought my thoughts round to Mr Pickwick and the Lady in Curlpapers, and while I was reflecting cosily on these things the car stopped at the hospital and our party was joined by the County Pathologist, Dr Eric Biddle, formerly at Guy's and a great personal friend of Dr Simpson's. He climbed gaily into the car, cheerful and charming. Conversation, which had flagged, received a new impetus from Dr Biddle and he was soon talking, very delightfully, about the forthcoming election, the ancient Vikings and Beethoven's piano sonatas.

So on and on we went. Now we were gradually drawing towards the coast, and the sky, darkening as it was, assumed a translucent quality which betrayed that the sea was not so very far away. Presently we slackened in speed, the car was approaching Aldringham, at last we scrunched slowly along a rough and narrow lane and stopped outside a farm. Here two or three members of the Suffolk police awaited us. We got stiffly from the car and walked towards them.

It was now after ten at night; the light was the palest, dimmest grey and everything was silent as water, excepting for the crickets whirring in the grass. There was just enough light left for us to view the field where the murder had taken place. However, before we went to the field, Mr Greeno (as always very definitely the man in command), asked if accommodation had been fixed for himself and Sergeant Hodge. The hapless officer who had arranged these things replied that accommodation had been fixed at a temperance hotel. Mr Greeno quivered in the dusk.

"A temperance hotel?"

"Yes, sir. It was the most convenient place I could find for you."

"Temperance hotels," replied Mr Greeno, witheringly, "are never convenient. Find another hotel. Get on the telephone and book me rooms at The Dolphin."

"I'll try, sir."

The rest of the party gurgled delightedly. Obviously all shared Mr Greeno's views on temperance hotels.

For my part I have never stayed at a temperance hotel and would literally have to be dragged into one, because a dictum instilled into me by my father went, "Never go to a temperance hotel, my dear child. People who don't drink don't know how to eat, either. The result is they get all bunged up with wind and water, and a bloke who is all bunged up with wind and water's no good to anyone. Just one big belly-ache. Keep off temperance hotels."

Therefore I perfectly understood Mr Greeno on temperance hotels.

The officer went off to telephone The Dolphin as instructed and the rest of us walked a short distance further up the lane to the stile; the stile on which the soldier in the black beret had loitered. "And nothing's been seen of the fellow since the murder?" observed Mr Greeno.

"No, sir. He's made himself scarce. But we've had a man here all the time keeping a watch, in case."

"Yes, he may come back. Anything more known about him?"

"Two or three attacks on women and girls by a soldier have been reported in the neighbourhood recently, prior to the murder. It sounds as if they might be the work of the same chap."

We came to a gate in the hedge and went into a rough meadow which led into the rye-field. The rye was tall, ripe and ready for cutting, growing thick and sere, the long-bearded heads hanging heavily and smelling bitter and dusty. We skirted round the field by the hedge, a local officer leading the way. "This is where she was first attacked, sir. There's a bloodstain here, a pretty large one." Somebody produced a torch and C. K. S. and Mr Greeno bent over the dark ground. After examining this place we followed a track beaten through the rye, obviously made by the soldier trampling through the rye dragging the girl along the ground after him. Blood was sprinkled on the stalks of rye along this track, and these the detectives collected. "He pulled her by the feet, her head trailing," commented C. K. S. We spent some time examining this track, collecting bloodstained pieces of rye and grass.

Then we came to the place where the dying girl had been left lying and had finally been found by the picnickers. Here there were more heavy bloodstains and we spent some time there while the two pathologists and the detectives peered minutely at everything. I was kept busy putting stalks of rye into the little buff envelopes and labelling these and jotting notes. The night was falling fast and a hungry throng of mosquitoes had come out to feast on our legs. It was sheer torture, and to add to it I couldn't slap or scratch myself or exclaim, but had to stand coolly taking notes and gumming down envelopes, as if there were no such things as mosquitoes. Furtively I rubbed my legs one against the other, swearing to myself. The rest of the party were protected somewhat by their trousers; undoubtedly my legs were the main target. But at last somebody did remark upon the insects. But Mr Greeno and C. K. S. were so engrossed they wouldn't have turned a hair, I do believe, had they been attacked by a swarm of vampire bats.

It seemed a very long time to me before we left that rye-field. It was now quite dark. We stumbled back into the lane and halted once more by the stile. Instructions were issued that a watch should be kept there all night and that if anybody came along they were to be closely questioned. I am glad I did not have to take part in this eerie vigil.

Then back our original party drove to Ipswich for the post-mortem. The journey nearly sent me to sleep; it was after eleven and I always find travel by night a sleepy business. At Ipswich we went for a few moments into Dr Biddle's house, where we had hasty coffee and sandwiches. I made a quick attempt to tidy myself up, my hair was literally on end, but I was past the quick tidy-up stage, and had to resign myself to spending the rest of the night looking like a head-hunter from Borneo. I made a pass at myself with a lipstick and scurried off to join the gentlemen, who were all agog to get to the mortuary. Thence we repaired, just after midnight, and at 12.15 a.m. the two pathologists started the p.m.

This was in the p.m. room of the Suffolk County Hospital, but to be perfectly honest I do not remember the occasion very clearly, for the autopsy was a lengthy one and before long I was engaged in an awful struggle to keep awake. Not only to keep awake, but somehow or other to appear alert and bright-eyed and to take Dr Simpson's dictation.

The two pathologists of course were wide awake and intently bending over the body. Behind them Messrs Greeno and Hodge, both also wide awake, peered intently too. The surgeons who had operated on the girl, the anaesthetist and two house officers stood around the table, in white surgery coats and heavy mufflers — it was very cold in the p.m. room — and tried to appear as lively as Dr Biddle and C. K. S. The several police officers present allowed themselves occasional semi-stifled yawns — which was a relief to me — while the mortuary attendant blinked and swabbed, swabbed and blinked, and looked as if he took a very dim view of murders. But the most touching sight were three little students, Guy's students, who happened to be at that time (under some emergency training scheme or the other) working at

Suffolk County Hospital and who had turned gallantly out to watch C. K. S. do this p.m. Poor creatures! Muffled in coats and scarves they stood there, like Winkin, Blinkin and Nod, and I kept jerking myself awake by watching them jerking themselves awake.

The autopsy showed that the girl had been attacked with a stick or some similar heavy weapon. She had warded off the first blows with her hands, but had ultimately fallen to the ground and while lying there had received two further very savage blows to the head. After this she had been dragged along the ground, head trailing, through the rye. The cause of her death was shock from multiple fractures of the skull with contusion of the brain.

As a matter of fact that midnight autopsy was a tragic occasion for other reasons than those we knew at the time. The little body on the p.m. table aroused everyone's pity, but we could not know that within a few weeks Dr Biddle himself would die of violent head injuries, an emergency brain operation being performed in that same hospital in a desperate attempt to save him. He was an enthusiastic motorcyclist, and while driving a sidecar he had himself constructed, and of which he was very proud, he crashed head-on into a concrete road obstacle. Therefore the p.m. report which he and C. K. S. constructed together was finally put before a jury by C. K. S. alone.

But luckily that night — or rather morning — the two pathologists, who were also such great friends, did not know that this was the last murder case they were going to work on together. When the p.m. was over we said good-bye to the members of the hospital staff who had attended the post-mortem, and to Winkin, Blinkin and Nod and returned to Dr Biddle's house. He wanted us to have something more to eat before the journey back to London, but C. K. S. had discovered there was a train at two-forty-something-or-the-other, and so he and I made one of our famous whirlwind departures. Mr Greeno put his car at our disposal and we vanished into the night, leaving Mr Greeno and Dr Biddle joking together in the roadway . . .

The two-forty-something-or-the-other was late, and distinguished pathologist and secretary waited for it, perched disconsolately side by side on an empty luggage-truck on the windy deserted platform, and shuddered. Presently along came a goods train, the longest I've ever seen, an infinite line of trucks rocking along like a procession of elephants linked trunk-by-tail, I thought, all wearing heavy metal anklets and clanking and mumbling and clinking and grumbling their way to the next town and the next circus. And then they had gone, and their metallic bumps and jostlings had dwindled into the darkness and after what felt like an age our train arrived. We seemed to be the only passengers on it. We fell into a carriage and dozed dismally and uncomfortably, like two wretched strays, all the way to London.

"Well, if this is what being a detective means, you can keep it," I thought at one point, and then fell into a bitty doze again.

At Liverpool Street we were met by a Flying Squad car — oh blessed vehicle! sleek and shiny and driven by

321

a detective who was well known to us, for he had accompanied us on several country jobs himself. He looked spruce and natty and lively as a lark, so that you would have thought it four in the afternoon instead of four in the morning. We made a last, brave attempt to appear frisky ourselves. Nevertheless, we sank rather limply into the seats of the car as we were whisked away through the City by our friend, who was chuckling over a drunk he had just trodden on in a doorway. "A Canadian. Just mumbled 'Um-um' and went on sleeping, peacefully as they come. They certainly breed 'em tough."

"You're on a spell of night duty?"

"Yes. Sometimes we hit lively spots, but it's all very quiet tonight."

We drove down the empty, silent streets, glistening and cold as steel in the earliest early light. Outside Mansion House a constable stood on point-duty, even though there wasn't any traffic. "Keep a constable on duty outside the Mansion House all night every night," explained our driver. "Always somebody on duty there." In that deserted roadway the man looked weird and fantastic, standing motionless, gestureless, controlling traffic that never came in a London that appeared completely dead.

About ten past four I had the exquisite, glorious, miraculous delight of laying me down in my bed. And then it was morning, an alarm clock was ringing and Poplar mortuary was waiting with three p.m.s to be done at nine sharp . . .

The soldier in the black beret was finally arrested for little Daphne's murder and on the last day of October

C. K. S. and I drove to Bury St Edmunds for the trial. It was a very sunny, golden day, and we drove through Epping Forest, where the trees too were golden with autumn leaves. We passed through Bishops Stortford and from thence to Newmarket, where races were being held. Crowds of people were going to the races, including several gaunt old gypsy women in long black cloth coats trimmed with the famous "mog". I thought secretly I would have liked to have spent the day at Newmarket while C. K. S. tootled on to the trial alone (not the thoughts of a Perfect Secretary by any means), but when we reached Bury it had a sound and scent of Assizes, lawyers and judges which was positively nineteenth-century and Dickensian. Sergeant Buzfuz might have appeared at any moment, I felt, along with Messrs Snubbin, Skimpin and Phunky, and we had lunch in an hotel thronged with red-faced English legal types who could all have sat as models to Cruikshank or Phiz.

After lunch we strolled round the ruins of the old castle and then it was time to go into court. The court-room was dark, sombre, crowded and very stuffy. While we were waiting for the trial to begin we were told some anecdotes about the prisoner, the soldier in the black beret, and the reign of terror he had imposed upon the women of the villages near Aldringham in the weeks preceding the murder.

During the war often the strangest things happened so that even the sleepiest little country villages felt the impact of the violent world around them.

323

When the prisoner appeared in the dock he was smiling broadly and seemed as proud and pleased as pie. He continued to beam all the way through the trial, and it was no surprise when he was found guilty but insane. He was sentenced to Broadmoor.

We left Bury in late afternoon sunlight and drove past broad fields of sugar-beet where cheerful parties of Italian prisoners-of-war, in shabby old uniforms, were taking up the beet crops to load on to lorries. The sun sank, the light dwindled and a thick fog arrived. We also became involved in a fierce stream of traffic returning to London from Newmarket, so our journey home was highly unpleasant, driving virtually blind in the fog, only able to distinguish with difficulty the rear-light of the car ahead of us, and the fog slowly freezing us. And it had been such a lovely day, almost like summer. But now, with a vengeance, we were driving into darkness, fog, London and winter. October was gone, it was November. The last country murder of that summer season was finished, ahead of us lay fog-bound London and all its sooty crime. So we drove back into The Smoke.

CHAPTER
TWENTY-SIX

The Black in The Smoke

Time: the early hours of an autumn morning. Place: Lambeth Bridge. Character on stage: a police constable. He is walking slowly across the bridge and approaches a small brick N.F.S. pump-house, disused now that the war is over. The constable flashes his torch methodically at the pump-house and then flashes it hastily again, going close to look. There is a narrow aperture in the wall of the pump-house and through this aperture somebody has stuffed the body of a rather large man. The constable looks again, just to make certain, and then hurries off to a call-box.

Later in the morning: a number of detectives arrive, headed by square-set, rosy-faced Chief Inspector Chapman. With him is Dr Keith Simpson. They spend a considerable time poking round the pump-house. Then they drive away and an undertaker's van comes up and the body of the large man is with difficulty removed from the pump-house and taken to Southwark mortuary . . .

Mr Chapman was present at the p.m. The dead man had been shot through the back of the head with a small-calibre revolver at very close range. Mr

Chapman, at that early stage, could only tell us that the Yard thought the deceased was probably a taxi-driver named Everitt, and it was suspected he had been mixed up with the Black Market.

After the p.m. Mr Chapman returned to the Yard for a conference on the case, while C. K. S. and I went round to Guy's to write a detailed report. We finished it just before lunch and Dr Simpson said, "I'd like to re-check Everitt's sitting measurements, Miss L. After you've had a bite could you stroll round to the mortuary and get West to help you take them? Measure him in a sitting position, sitting upright. Can you manage that, do you think?"

I replied I certainly could and borrowed C. K. S.'s tape-measure for the job. After a quick lunch I scurried round to my fellow conspirator, Harry West. He was sitting in his little office, drinking a cup of tea and eating Spam sandwiches. I explained my mission and West said of course he'd help, anything any time you ask, Miss Molly. So into the refrigerator room we went.

The premises were deserted at that hour, we had the entire mortuary to ourselves. This gave us a gay and lively feeling. West opened the big refrigerator and drew out a long metal tray on which lay the murdered man. With considerable skill West slid the tray on to a trestle table. The dead taxi-driver was, as I have said, a very large and heavy man, and moreover he was stark stiff with rigor mortis. West suggested he should raise the man to the required sitting posture and that I should measure him. I agreed and West, with difficulty, propped up the body. But then came a snag. I wasn't tall enough to reach from the tray on which the body sat to the top of deceased's head. West said we'd better swap. I would have to prop up the body while he measured it.

No sooner said than done. He took the tape-measure and I put my shoulder to the dead man's brawny back. But there is nothing in the world so unresponsive and difficult to manage as a stiff. There was a sudden heart-rending shriek from me . . . and a yell of horror from West as I collapsed backwards with the naked and dead taxi-man clutched in my arms. I fell flat backwards under his weight and West, whose horror had turned to laughter, had a lot of trouble rescuing me. It was a ghastly moment and I became convulsed with, let me admit it, hysterical giggles. The dead man looked as if he must have been a pretty obstinate person in life, he was certainly so in death. Somehow we got him sitting upright again, with West holding him, and somehow I managed to reach and take the measurements. It was the most remarkable lunch-hour I have ever spent.

The dead man, Dr Simpson decided, had been shot from behind, at very close range, unexpectedly, while he was seated at the wheel of his taxi.

A week or two now passed, with the police busy over their investigations.

London's Black Market was, by the end of the war, a vast racket system attracting an array of crooks and criminals of all sorts. The "regular" London underworld was at that time swollen by hundreds of deserters from the Services of the Allied nations; men in hiding who turned to the Black Market as their only possible source of income.

The dead man was soon identified for certain as one Frank Everitt, a fifty-six-year-old driver employed by a Brixton taxi-pool which specialised in conveying people home from West End night-clubs in the small hours. Everitt, however, had not been precisely what one might term a crystal-clear character. He was an ex-police sergeant, an ex-Home Guard corporal, and he was reputed to have been a "copper's nark" (otherwise, a police informer). This wasn't true, but the Yard did think it worth while probing other allegations that Everitt had been a "tea-leaf carrier", i.e., a taxi-driver who conveys crooks around in the darkness.

Whether this was so or not never really emerged, although it was presently pretty plain that he had been carrying a couple of crooks at the time he met his death. It certainly was established that Everitt, for the past fifteen years, had been living a double life. He enjoyed the pseudonym "The Duke", because he had a weekend residence in Gloucestershire, which his associates considered very classy, indeed positively aristocratic. Hence the title of The Duke. To others he was known as "Honest Frank", a name which may or may not have had a satirical ring. Besides the *ménage* in Gloucestershire he rejoiced in two other addresses, one in Battersea, where he didn't live, and one in Streatham where, during the week, he did live.

He was a married man who had succeeded in living apart from his wife for the past fifteen years. He had a substantial banking account. He appeared, on the surface, to be making a success of this Jekyll and Hyde existence. However, police probing revealed that he had been a person of uneasy disposition; acquaintances hinted he had behaved like a man who carried a "secret fear". There was some evidence that The Duke had been planning to quit London for good; it had become a little too hot for him. But why?

Nobody would answer that one, although it was clear there were several who could. Mr Chapman received numerous anonymous phone calls about The Duke's associations with a Black Market gang headed by a foreigner, probably a Russian. Obviously many Londoners who preferred to remain nameless were taking a keen interest in the Yard's investigations. And reporters who began sleuthing around on their own investigations, anxious to get some exclusive inside stuff, were told to "lay-off" by similar anonymous phone callers. The underworld wasn't going to welcome front-page *exposés* of The Duke's private life — or lives.

The murdered man's taxi had meanwhile been found abandoned on a pile of rubble in a North Kensington cul-de-sac. It was plain that Everitt, as Dr Simpson had claimed, had been shot from behind while in his driving-seat. He had then been lifted on to the back seat of the taxi, driven to Lambeth Bridge and stowed away in the pump-house. His taxi-man's registration badge had been torn from his jacket. His pockets had been ransacked. Under the driver's seat was found the top of a propelling pencil. The pencil itself, however, was missing.

C. K. S. and Mr Chapman were both of the opinion that one man alone could not have lifted the bulky Everitt from the taxi, carried him to the pump-house and squeezed him through the aperture of that little building. The murder definitely looked like a two-man job. And presently a witness came forward to say he had seen Everitt pick up two well-dressed men at 12.15 a.m. October 18th (the morning of the murder), close by the Richard Cœur de Lion statue outside the House of Commons.

Tracing these two men, however, proved impossible, even though Mr Cherrill did discover what were thought to be the murderer's fingerprints on the steering-wheel of the taxi.

So the investigations into The Duke's death hung fire for a fortnight; then a second murder occurred. This second murder never actually led to the solving of the mystery of The Duke's death, officially, but after the second killing had been unravelled the Yard dropped investigations into the Everitt case. There really seems little doubt that the men who killed Everitt were the men who killed . . .

The man who was found lying in the back of a small saloon car parked near a Notting Hill bomb-site between five and six in the morning two weeks after the Everitt murder. He too was found by a constable on patrol. This constable shone his torch into the car and saw a man stretched out on the back seat, his hat over his face, apparently asleep. The constable tried to waken the man, and in so doing dislodged the hat, which fell aside to reveal the bloodstained face of a very obvious corpse.

Investigations into this case came under Chief Superintendent George Somerset (later to take charge of the Hendon Detectives' Training School). Mr Somerset was quickly able to identify the dead man as one Reuben Martirosoff, known generally as "Russian Robert"; no other, in fact, than the foreign Black Market gang leader Mr Chapman had anonymously been phoned about so often in connection with the Everitt murder.

The car in which Martirosoff was found lying was his own, and he had driven out in it, Mr Somerset ascertained, at 11p.m. the previous night, in a great hurry, in response to a phone caller who wanted Russian Robert to meet him at Edgware Road Underground station.

Dr Donald Teare did the p.m. on Russian Robert. He found that the deceased had been shot, as Everitt had been shot, with a small-calibre revolver, at very close range, through the back of the head. Russian Robert had clearly been killed in the early hours of the morning he was discovered in his car.

The police now began a detailed combing-out of London's Black Market.

This comb-out presently produced the information that Russian Robert had frequently been seen in the company of two Poles, one of whom was named Marian. These two Poles were working several rackets in the Black Market, including the "handbag game", deals in foreign currency and in looted jewellery and so on. Finally, Mr Somerset succeeded in arresting the man Marian, whose full name was Marian Grondkowski.

Grondkowski was a good-looking young man of thirty-three, a Polish Army deserter, who had started his adventurous career gun-running for the Spanish International Brigade, had fought with the Brigade, escaped to France after being taken prisoner in Spain, had fought with the French in World War II, had fought with the Foreign Legion after the fall of France, volunteered for the Polish Army and thus had come to England. After two years in a Special Sabotage Unit he had deserted and resorted to London's Black Market for a more profitable and less gallant livelihood than soldiering. He ran very successful rackets in foreign currency exchange and was not slow to threaten his clients with a revolver if intimidation were necessary to make them come across with currency or jewellery. He was not at all a salubrious character, and it was no surprise to the police that the bloodstained fingerprints Mr Cherrill discovered on Russian Robert's steering-wheel belonged to Grondkowski.

In Grondkowski's pocket was a small piece of paper bearing the name and address of a Henryk Malinowski.

The police went to Malinowski's lodgings and found Russian Robert's signet ring among Malinowski's things. He was therefore arrested and taken to the Yard.

Malinowski was also a Polish Army deserter, aged twenty-five. He had fought in the defence of Warsaw in 1939, had been taken prisoner by the Germans and put in a concentration camp, had escaped, joined the Foreign Legion, had come to England and enlisted in the Polish Armoured Division and had deserted from the Division in May 1944. He had been caught and sent to the International Glass House, from which, nothing daunted, he had escaped. He had then come to London, where he started working foreign currency rackets. Both he and Grondkowski had finally joined forces with Russian Robert, thirty-nine years old, Caucasian born; an international crook with convictions in Paris, Berlin, Vienna, Istanbul, Potsdam, London. Yes, Russian Robert had been around. He had, however, reached the stage where getting around was difficult, since he had been permanently banished from France, Germany, Austria, Czechoslovakia and South America. So he had settled down — for the time being at any rate — in London, where he led a lucrative existence as a "fence" and a Black Marketeer in currency.

Exactly why the trio reached the point where Grondkowski and Malinowski found it necessary to murder Russian Robert is not known. Which of the two Poles actually shot Russian Robert is not known either, although Grondkowski's fingerprints were on the steering-wheel. Both men habitually carried revolvers and neither of them could have entertained scruples about killing after the lives they had led.

Grondkowski, questioned at the Yard, accused Malinowski of doing the actual shooting. He said on the night of the murder they had met Russian Robert at an Underground station, had had drinks with him and had discussed future Black Market plans. Finally, they had come out of the pub and had all got into Russian Robert's car, which had refused to start. So the two Poles pushed the car while Russian Robert remained at the wheel. Malinowski then muttered to Grondkowski that he was going to finish Russian Robert off. Grondkowski told his companion he was crazy to think of such a thing. Soon they got the car to start, Grondkowski climbed into the seat next to the driver while Malinowski got into the back. They had only driven a short distance when Malinowski shot Russian Robert point-blank in the back of the head. Directly he had fired Malinowski leaned over, grabbed the steering-wheel and Grondkowski stopped the car, opened the door and got out. He had decided to have nothing further to do with the matter. But Malinowski threatened to shoot him too, so he was obliged to assist in lifting Russian Robert into the back seat. After Malinowski had ransacked the murdered man's pockets the two shared his money between them.

But there has never yet been a murder in which two killers have been involved without each accusing the other of doing the actual deed of destruction. Malinowski in his turn described how Grondkowski had done the shooting. "It was *I* who sat beside Robert. Marian was in the back. Then I heard a shot and Robert's head fell forward. Marian asked me to find the brake and I stopped the car. I got out of the car and did not do anything." In other words, a complete reversal of roles.

Marian insisted (according to this version) that Malinowski must help him move the body into the back seat. But Malinowski refused, so Grondkowski pulled the dead man into the rear seat single-handed. He then ransacked the deceased's pockets and the cash found therein was divided between the two Poles, Grondkowski getting the larger share.

At Grondkowski's lodgings the police found a .32 automatic which was undoubtedly the weapon used for the murder.

Which man actually fired the shot didn't really matter technically, for under the law both were chargeable with the murder. Both of them were tried, found guilty and executed.

Everything pointed to the fact that in all likelihood they had shot Everitt too. He had been killed in exactly the same fashion as Russian Robert and with a similar, although not identical, weapon. And articles belonging to Everitt, including the propelling pencil which had lost its cap, were found in Grondkowski's pockets. But at the time of his arrest for the killing of Russian Robert there was not enough hard evidence available to charge him with the murder of Everitt too.

It is said that Chief Inspector Chapman visited the two Poles in their condemned cells shortly before they were executed in an eleventh-hour attempt to discover whether they had shot Everitt. Mr Chapman never disclosed whether they talked or not.

So the public will never know whether Grondkowski and Malinowski shot taxi-driver Frank Everitt. The final verdict of the Coroner, Mr Harvey Wyatt, was one of "Murder against a person or persons unknown".

There was an interesting little tail-piece to this story. On the morning of November 12th, about a fortnight after Russian Robert had met his death, another Pole, a young soldier of twenty-six, was found dead on Westminster Bridge, kneeling in a huddled attitude at the side of the N.F.S. pump-house there, with close-range firearm wounds of the head. (He was, most conveniently, only a few hundred yards from Scotland Yard's main entrance.)

The police thought this might be yet a third Black Market murder, so they began making full investigations into his death, and Dr Simpson was asked to do a p.m.

Detective Superintendent W. Parker and D.D.I. Swain began searching for the revolver with which the dead man had been shot. They asked themselves if it might not be the weapon which had been used for killing Everitt. But this Pole, whose name was Tadeusz Rybczynski, had clearly committed suicide, Dr Simpson discovered.

The evidence at the inquest bore out his findings. Two British servicemen turned up to give phlegmatic British evidence. They had been on leave in London and had been crossing Westminster Bridge at 1 a.m. on November 12th when they had noticed a young Polish soldier leaning on the balustrade of the bridge beside the pump-house. He looked deeply depressed and self-occupied, and one of the witnesses, turning to the other, said briefly, "Come on, let's get out of this. There's going to be another suicide . . ."

So, being British, they left him to it. A chap can commit suicide if he wants to, dammit!

336

Nobody could discover why Rybczynski shot himself. He did not appear, however, to be in any way connected with the Black Market, and his death provided no clues to the Everitt killing. And certainly there were plenty of personal reasons why a lonely Pole, in England in 1945, should commit suicide. It has not been a happy thing, since 1939, to be Polish.

Not for honest Poles, anyway. For the Grondkowskis and Malinowskis life was simple; life always is simple for them. First of all, fighting kept them busy, and then they found crime more lucrative than fighting so they turned to crime. The Black Market provided them with a satisfying existence. Not for them home-sickness or despair; they forged ahead in a devil-may-care, hand-to-mouth, flourishing style, that went very well until they forgot themselves and adopted Foreign Legion tactics in real Hollywood manner. They blocked The Duke's light, they blocked Russian Robert's light. But you can't get away with things like that in The Smoke. To quote one of my more colourful acquaintances, "Block a light, and the horse's nightcap is a stone ginger".[1]

---

[1] Kill someone, and the hangman's noose is a sure thing.

CHAPTER
TWENTY-SEVEN

I Find a Successor

By the late autumn of 1945 I had been working for Keith Simpson nearly five years. Those five years had been so interesting they seemed like no time at all. I had seen between seven and eight thousand autopsies and the work fascinated me more even than when I had started it. But the time had come for me to change to another sphere.

The war had finally wound up and letters from India indicated that my future husband would be home some time at the end of November. We had decided to marry as soon as he arrived home. J. pointed out that I could either go on working after I was married or retire and devote myself wholeheartedly to domesticity. Being a determined careerist I decided to retire from my job the day before I married him and settle down to a profound bout of matrimony.

"You see, it is like this. I am not really at all a domesticated person," I explained. "But I've thought it out, and I reckon I can do about eight years hard domesticity, but I doubt if I'll be able to stick it much longer than that. So I'll do eight years and devote myself to having children and taking care of them while they are really little. Then you'll have to let me broaden my activities and have a serious attempt at the writing. O.K.?"

"O.K.," said J. "Fair enough."

It was with a sad heart, nevertheless, that I set about looking for a successor to my job with C. K. S. I knew quite well that marriage and mortuaries wouldn't mix, I also firmly believed that when a woman marries she should genuinely devote herself for several years at least to nothing but marriage (it's the only way to learn the business properly and make it work), but all the same it made me very dismal to think I would have to give up my mortuary existence with Dr Keith Simpson. The least I could do for Dr Simpson, I felt, was to bequeath to him a new secretary who was absolutely a hundred-per-cent Perfect. The sort of secretary people dream about. Then he would be able to say, "Well, it's true Miss L. married and left me, but if she hadn't done so I would never have found Miss X, and that would have been a calamity, for Miss X is . . ." And here my imagination soared into starry-eyed visions of what Miss X would be.

So I started looking for Miss X. She proved exceedingly difficult to find.

I let it be known among my good friends at Guy's that I was ultimately marrying, and that a successor would therefore be needed. The response was terrific. Apparently nearly every young woman in the place had a burning desire to work with Keith Simpson and learn the ins and outs of murder.

Because the stream of applicants was so heavy one of the other secretaries let me use her office during the lunch hour. So there I sat, behind an impressive desk, interviewing would-be successors.

Would-be . . . Would-be? Yes, aching to be, until they came to that question, "Oh, by the way, I wouldn't have to go into the actual mortuaries, would I?"

"You would work in the mortuaries, dear."

"But not along with the bodies, surely. Don't you have your office somewhere else?"

"You sit alongside the corpse and type. Dr Simpson dictates his p.m. report as he does the actual p.m. When he's dictating his findings in the heart he is cutting up the heart. The same with the brain, and so on. But don't you worry about that. You'll soon grow to love it. It's terribly interesting."

They made it very clear they wouldn't grow to love it, and returned to their own work with eager expressions.

I began to feel pretty desperate. Then one day while I was walking in the Guy's quadrangle there came up to me the secretary of one of the senior members of the hospital staff. She was fortyish, very smart, highly efficient, charming, an experienced and perfect secretary to her finger-tips. She smiled and began:

"Excuse me, Miss Lefebure, but I hear that you are soon getting married and that you are looking for somebody to take over your job."

I replied that was so.

"I think I might be interested. You see, I've been doing my present job for a very long time now and I really should adore a change. Besides, I have always envied you your work with Dr Simpson. I'm frightfully interested in crime."

"What about the bodies?" I had grown wary by this time. "You would find that you worked all day every day in public mortuaries, doing p.m.s. It's nothing but p.m.s, really, the job is one continuous round of post-mortems which you attend with Dr Simpson."

"Oh, but I wouldn't mind the mortuaries. Bodies don't worry me in the least, I'm perfectly used to seeing bits and pieces of people all the time. I've always wanted to see a post-mortem examination. But let's discuss it some other time, shall we? I really ought to fly now. Can you have lunch with me tomorrow?"

We arranged a luncheon date and she turned towards the car park and I began hurrying to the Medical School. As I was tripping up the front steps C. K. S. shot out of the entrance, greeting me with, "Come on, Miss L. I've arranged to do a quick one at Essex County Hospital before we go to Buckhurst Hill." He was running down the steps past me as he spoke, and I wheeled round in my tracks and scooted after him. We dashed across the quadrangle to the car and were in it and driving out into the Borough in a flash.

Next day I met the distinguished secretary who coveted my job. "Now, let's discuss things," I began. She shook her head.

"My dear, it wouldn't do for me at all."

"But you said you didn't mind bodies and mortuaries," I said.

"Oh, I'm not worried about the bodies. The trouble is I'm too old. I was watching you and your Dr Simpson yesterday, sprinting across the quad. My dear, I can't run like that, I haven't run like that for years. I'd never keep up with him. I've never done an awful lot of sprinting anyway, and I'm too old to start now."

So that was the end of that. She continued with her senior member of the staff. Moodily I re-compiled the list of qualifications required by applicants. It now read:

"Typing.
Good verbatim shorthand.
Tact.
Interested in crime.
No objection to mortuaries and corpses.
Reasonably fast runner."

After this the applications dwindled and finally dried up, even though I rustled round amongst all my friends who had so often declared they would give anything to have a job like mine. It was no use. The ones who didn't object to bodies couldn't run fast, or skip around, while the rare ones with athletic abilities had no inclination towards mortuaries.

"Women," I complained angrily to my sister, "don't seem to be able to run and they don't seem to be genuinely keen on dead bodies."

She thought it was terribly funny.

And then the clouds lifted. One day at Guy's a physiotherapist came up to me and said, "Oh, Miss

Lefebure, I do hope you haven't found anybody to take over your job yet."

I replied I hadn't.

She looked pleased and explained she had a cousin to whom she had mentioned my job and the cousin had expressed a very keen desire to know if it were still going vacant. "She's working with the Brighton police. She's a trained secretary, very efficient and reliable, and extremely interested in crime."

"Does she mind post-mortems? For it's all post-mortems. Close up," I said, hopelessly.

"Oh, she'd rather enjoy them, I think. Her father's a vet, so she's used to cuttings-up."

I became much more interested. "Is she a brisk, nippy type? I mean, can she move fast? Can she run?"

"She's very healthy and lively," said the physiotherapist, looking a trifle surprised. "I daresay she could run quite fast if she had to."

"That sounds marvellous." I tried not to become too optimistic.

C. K. S. was very charming and understanding about my leaving him and assured me, with a twinkle in his eye, that the first ten years of marriage were the worst.

On November 1st Miss X, whose real name was Jean Scott Dunn, came along to Harley Street for an interview. It all went swimmingly. At the end of November J. flew home from India, we got married, and Miss Dunn took over my job. Suffice to say she has proved to be a far more Perfect Secretary than I ever was, lightning-quick, highly efficient, everything I had planned Miss X to be.

Apart from being a perfect secretary she is very charming, and I am happy to say we are excellent friends.

As for me, I soon discovered I had exchanged the comparative peace and quiet of the mortuaries for a life of nerve-racking hurly-burly.

From time to time I go back to Guy's to visit my old friends and occasionally then I get a peek into a mortuary. I have heard retired reporters remark upon the nostalgia which fills them when they return to their old office, see the familiar old typewriter standing on the familiar old desk. The same nostalgia grips me when I see a body lying on a p.m. table.

Yes, I still miss the job sadly. I miss the mortuaries, the murders, above all I miss all those very good friends I made. The Coroners' officers and mortuary keepers, the police officers and detectives I met, the eminent personalities I knew, and the more humble yet equally individual and interesting people who kept me so happy in their company . . . I miss them all. Those five years I spent as Dr Keith Simpson's secretary were five of the happiest and most absorbing years of my life.

This is not to say that I am not happily married, because, thank Heaven, I am. But sometimes, at tea-time, seated amidst the din and turmoil of nursery tea, I long suddenly for those afternoons in the Gordon Museum, eating anchovy-toast and tranquilly describing carcinomas of the bowel and tumours of the breast. Or I think how nice and *quiet* the corpses were. How altogether better balanced my nerves were, in those days when I devoted myself to crime, to autopsies and violent deaths and gruesome murders. Motherhood and domesticity have undoubtedly undermined me. Nowadays I jump when doors slam, and wake up imagining burglars are moving round my kitchen in the small hours. The dear old public mortuaries, without exaggeration, were sanctuaries compared with my present existence; which is a cross between living in the monkey-house and a reserve for Red Indians. Murders are infinitely less exhausting than motherhood.

Which is not something I am saying merely for effect. Like everything else in this book it's the truth, the whole truth and nothing but the truth . . .

Also available in ISIS Large Print:

Murder at Wrotham Hill

Diana Souhami

Murder at Wrotham Hill takes the killing of Dagmar Petrzywalski in October 1946 as the catalyst for a compelling and unique story of murder and fate.

Dagmar, a gentle, eccentric spinster, was the embodiment of Austerity Britain's prudence and thrift. Her murderer Harold Hagger, with his litany of petty crimes, abandoned wives, sloughed-off identities and army desertions, was its opposite. With their characters so indelibly marked, their tragic meeting seemed in some way destined. Featuring England's first celebrity policeman, Fabian of the Yard, the celebrated forensic scientist, Keith Simpson, and history's most famous and dedicated hangman, Albert Pierrepoint, this is a gripping and deeply moving account of true crime by one of our most acclaimed writers.

ISBN 978-0-7531-5332-1 (hb)
ISBN 978-0-7531-5333-8 (pb)

A Spoonful of Sugar

Brenda Ashford

"They say you can never truly love a child that is not your own, but that goes against every instinct that runs through me . . ."

Brenda Ashford is 91 years old and spent 62 years working as a Norland Nanny. Brenda began training at the Norland Institute in 1939 at the age of 18, shortly before war was declared. Even as a nervous young trainee, Brenda was determined to give the children in her care a wonderful childhood. She worked with evacuees from the East End, as well as in the nurseries of smart Kensington homes. She frequently put her life at risk, dashing to air raid shelters with her charges clutched to her chest. But the war was also a time when people pulled together like never before or since, and it called upon Brenda to make sacrifices she'd never imagined having to make . . .

ISBN 978-0-7531-5324-6 (hb)
ISBN 978-0-7531-5325-3 (pb)

All's Fair in Love and Law

Alan Hammond

Dufty Dufty Popple & Dunn is a traditional solicitors' firm in the small Midlands town of Hockam (pronounced "Hokum", as the local residents are at pains to point out). This heart-warming collection of stories revolves around the lives, relationships, triumphs and failures of the people of Hockam and of the lawyers to whom they look for help.

We meet the lonely dentist and his noisy neighbours, the TV celebrity chef and his complex family, the policeman and his beloved budgies. These and many others bring their problems to Dufty Dufty Popple & Dunn, to the well-meaning members of the firm, all of whom have their own lives to live — from Bernard, the hapless trainee, to Hugo Dufty, the nominal senior partner. And then, of course, there are the rumours concerning Robert Popple, the former partner who departed from the firm in mysterious circumstances.

ISBN 978-0-7531-5310-9 (hb)
ISBN 978-0-7531-5311-6 (pb)

Young Elizabeth

Kate Williams

Williams is acclaimed for her sharp writing and scholarly depth . . . intense, intelligent and hugely entertaining read **Guardian**

This is the story of how Elizabeth became Queen. It seems to be the job she was born for. And yet, for much of her early life, the young princess did not know the role that her future would hold. Kate Williams explores the sheltered upbringing of the young princess, with a gentle father and domineering mother, her complicated relationship with her sister, Princess Margaret, and her dependence on her nanny. She details the profound impact of the abdication crisis, when, at the impressionable age of eleven, Elizabeth found her position changed overnight: no longer a minor princess she was now heiress to the throne. Elizabeth's determination to share in the struggles of her people marked her out from a young age. Kate Williams reveals how the 25-year-old Queen carved out a lasting role for herself amid the changes of the 20th century.

ISBN 978-0-7531-5318-5 (hb)
ISBN 978-0-7531-5319-2 (pb)